To the men and women of the
Los Angeles County Sheriff's Department
…and for Grant and Tristan.

CONTENTS

CONTENTS

ACKNOWLEDGMENTS

No work like this could be completed without the assistance of many thoughtful and caring people. A very special thank you to Sheriff Leroy D. Baca for his support and guidance, and authors William B. Secrest and John Boessenecker for taking the time to review and comment on the manuscript. In my opinion their knowledge of historical California lawmen and desperados is without equal.

Thanks to Mike Bailey from badgehistory.com, James Casey from policeguide.com, and Edward Godfrey, Andrew Thompson, and Bob Zaricor for their help with badges; Jon Orantes, Joseph Krivda, and Paul Fielding for their insight on black powder weapons; and retired Chief Marvin Dixon for sharing his abundant knowledge of department history. I would also like thank Elaine Goodness and the entire staff at the Sheriff's Museum in Whittier, as well as Lieutenant Michael Parker for his support, and Mary Kludy from the Virginia Military Institute for her research on Sheriff Henry Milnor Mitchell.

The following libraries and their staff were of invaluable assistance: the Huntington Library in San Marino California, the City of Los Angeles Public Library, the Natural History Museum's Seaver Center, the University Of California, Los Angeles, California State University Northridge, California State University Long Beach, and Loyola Marymount University. Many thanks to the following historians, who helped to give me deeper insight into the subject material: William Deverell from the University of Southern California History Department, John Boston from the *Santa Clarita Signal*, J.J. Leonard and Richard Kalk from the Los Angeles Police Historical Society, and Dr. Eric Monkkonen from the University of California, Los Angeles.

FOREWORD

As a longtime California history enthusiast, particularly for its law enforcement and Wild West aspects, I was delighted when Sven Crongeyer asked me to read his history of the Los Angeles Sheriff's Office in manuscript form. I was also glad to learn that a book on southern California peace officers was in the works, since so little published work has been done in this area.

This project is unique, since the author is a Los Angeles deputy sheriff and has a unique insight into his subject. Published histories of California police and sheriff's departments tend to be brief, of limited scope, and are seldom written by law enforcement officers themselves. They are often found within early county histories, but are necessarily sketchy, as they compete for space with many other subjects.

An additional reason for this dearth of peace officer history is a lack of information. As county departments, sheriff's offices have undergone constant reorganization and regular weeding of old records and documents. This has often been done by clerks or deputies possessing scant appreciation of historical material. Unless sheriffs took a personal interest in history, they cared little for the past, since they had their hands full with the present. Consequently, much early information on California law enforcement has been lost.

Today, any history of a sheriff's office is necessarily gathered from newspapers and court records, a job that few other than serious, dedicated researchers care to tackle. John Boessnecker's recent biography of Alameda County's famous lawman, Harry Morse, is an expertly-done example of this kind. Few such thorough insights into our early peace officers are possible, however, since Morse was among the few who kept journals and wrote up his colorful experiences.

There are further signs that this disregarding of peace officer history is changing. Increasingly, modern sheriff's offices are recognizing the value of their heroic and neglected pasts, and capitalizing on the public relations value they contain. It is history well worth knowing.

In assembling the story of the Los Angeles Sheriff's Office, Crongeyer records a powder-smoked time in a colorful area that was extremely difficult to police. The sparse settlement of the 1850-1900 period, and the vast desert areas that had to be patrolled, made the pursuit of horse thieves, fugitives and outlaws dangerous, exhausting and time-consuming. Reciting the exploits of the early sheriffs and their deputies pays tribute to the courage and dedication of these brave, resolute officers.

Crongeyer's tale is fascinating and told well. He has dug deeply into the remaining, available materials to give us an entertaining, informative and picturesque account of a time we can hardly imagine today. This is a welcome and long-overdue addition to the saga of pioneer California law enforcement and, indeed, to California history as a whole.

William B. Secrest
Fresno, California

INTRODUCTION

In the middle of the 19th Century, the need for law and order in Los Angeles County was perhaps greater than at any other time in its history. The City of Los Angeles was a dusty, lawless pueblo whose anxious residents demanded both safety and justice from its fledgling government. Sheriff George Burrill was the first man to begin what is now the department's motto, the *Tradition of Service*, and the Los Angeles County Sheriff's Department has been proudly serving its residents ever since. *Six Gun Sound* portrays the colorful history of the sheriff's department, from a small rented office in the Bella Union Hotel in 1850, to the year 1900, when a whole new era of modern law enforcement was ushered in, and the pioneer days of horse and rider began to fade away. Today the Los Angeles County Sheriff's Department is one of the largest and most well-respected law enforcement agencies in the world, but it all started with one sheriff, one jailer and one deputy. Chronicled in this work are the daring exploits of the first nineteen men to serve as Los Angeles County Sheriffs, some of whom paid the ultimate price for stepping into the line of fire.

We see that diversity in Los Angeles was present from the very beginning, and we also see how law enforcement efforts were both enhanced and hampered by the influx of ranchers, cowboys, farmers, miners, gunfighters and gamblers. For more than one and a half centuries, the sheriff's department has met the challenge of public safety head on. Deputies are sometimes placed in life and death situations where decisions that are made in a fraction of a second affect the lives of hundreds, if not thousands, of people for years afterward. History shows us that the battles of yesteryear resonate deeply with us today, and though we have made much progress, there is still much work to be done. This study offers a fascinating insight into the legacy of the department's past accomplishments and failures. It demonstrates how the sheriff and his deputies maintained law and order through the use of aggressive law enforcement, courts, jails, courage, bravery and guts.

Through the years this department has seen many changes, but one thing has always remained constant: the hard work and dedication of the men and women who serve this county and defend it from crime twenty-four hours a day, three hundred and sixty-five days a year. Our history is of the utmost importance to us. It defines us. It tells us how we got to this point in time and it gives us clues as to the paths we might take in the future. The incredible accomplishments of those that have gone before us give us the strength and courage to continue our struggle to do right and fight wrongs. *Six Gun Sound* shows us a window through which we can view our past, and therefore it is a tool which allows us to renew our hope for the future. I am proud to lead the finest men and women in law enforcement today. This book is dedicated to them. Together, we will continue the *Tradition of Service* into a new millennia.

Leroy D. Baca, Sheriff
Los Angeles County

Chapter *1*

FROM INDIAN VILLAGE TO STATEHOOD: THE BACKGROUND OF LAW ENFORCEMENT IN LOS ANGELES

Early Los Angeles was a fascinating and combustible mix of Native Americans, Californios, Mexicans, Afro-Mexicans, Chinese, Spanish, Basque, English, Irish, Dutch, Germans, and a host of other peoples from nations all over the globe. The end of the Mexican war in 1847 left many armed men unemployed and desperate for money. For years past, officials in Mexico had sent their criminals northward in an effort to be rid of them. Men who had hoped to strike it rich in the gold fields abandoned their mines and wandered southern California, looking for an easy way to "make a quick buck." Almost everyone carried firearms.

It is no wonder, then, that early Los Angeles was considered by many to be the most dangerous town in the West. Criminals, vagabonds, and scalawags roamed the streets and freely patronized the many bordellos, bars, and saloons. There were only about 12 streets in 1850s Los Angeles; the most infamous was Calle de los Negros, which was jammed to overflowing with saloons, bars, and bordellos. Everyone back then knew where to go if they wanted to find a poker game, a shot of whiskey, and some trouble.

In 1926, many years after his famous gunfight adjacent to the O.K. Corral, Wyatt Earp was deposed in Los Angeles for a Massachusetts lawsuit:

Q: I would like to ask you to state your observation of those times and tell us what the condition of this community (Tombstone) was for law and order?
A: It was not half as bad as Los Angeles.
Q: Tell us whether it was good or bad or whether it was a lawless outpost?
A: I called it good.[1]

Los Angeles, on the other hand, was not "good."

While there is a plethora of media and print about famous lawmen of the Wild West, literature that thoroughly explains who the law enforcement officers of early southern California were and how they operated is scarce. The stories of Dodge City, Tombstone, Kansas City, and Abilene are exciting, but they pale in comparison to the gunfights, shootouts, and mayhem that occurred daily on the dusty, grimy streets of Los Angeles.

It was in this most dangerous of places that the Los Angeles County Sheriff's Office was established in 1850. This book explores the first 50 years of this organization, from its small beginnings of one sheriff and one deputy through its evolution to a much larger agency at the turn of the century, when law and order was the norm and no longer the exception.

The earliest reference to the word "sheriff" comes from England where the person responsible for policing the town or shire was known as the "shire reeve." Over the years the term "shire reeve" developed into the word sheriff. In the 1850s, as is the case today, the sheriff's office was responsible for maintaining the county jail and policing those parts of the county that were not incorporated into cities. Cities typically hired their own police force or town constable, which gave them more direct control over the law enforcement functions within their jurisdiction.

The early history of the Los Angeles County Sheriff's Department is filled with colorful characters, heroic deeds, and despicable acts of crime and debauchery. This period, from 1850 to 1900, was a time when judges slung shotguns over their shoulders and hung Bowie knives from their belts. Small groups of lawmen would travel hundreds of miles on horseback to bring their man to

The Bella Union Hotel was the scene of many bar room brawls and gunfights. It was also the location of the first sheriff's office, which was in a rented room. – SECURITY PACIFIC COLLECTION / LOS ANGELES PUBLIC LIBRARY

justice, only to find that vigilantes had hanged the suspected criminal before any semblance of a trial could be held.

From its meager beginnings in a small rented office at the Bella Union Hotel to its transformation into one of the largest law enforcement agencies in the world, with over 16,000 employees, the Los Angeles County Sheriff's Department has seen many changes in the past 150 years. Yet some old traditions die hard. Other California agencies that work closely with the department still refer to it as the "S.O." (Sheriff's Office). This sometimes causes rookie deputies to wonder, "Why do they call us the S.O., when we always call it a sheriff's department?"

Native Americans in Los Angeles

Early pueblo documents speak of rangers, vigilantes, constables, marshals, sheriff's deputies, and, of course, bandidos. But who was who? Who did what? How were they all tied together, if at all? It is true that Los Angeles was built with the muscles, sweat, and ingenuity of pioneering settlers; but, more often than not, the hardest, most backbreaking labor came from the indigenous peoples who were there first. To understand early Los Angeles, one must first understand them.

The first peoples to inhabit the area in and around present Los Angeles County were Native Americans of the Tongva tribe. The Tongva, who were related to the Shoshone, had lived on this land for thousands of years prior to the arrival of the white man, and numbered from 1,000 to 10,000 by the time the Spanish arrived in the mid-18th century.[2] They lived a simple hunting and gathering lifestyle in the mostly mild southern California climate. The men went naked and the women wore deerskin or sea otter skins around their waists. The staple of their diet was the acorn, which was ground into a bitter paste and eaten cold. They were excellent hunters and fishers. Tribesmen manufactured fishhooks from abalone shells and used them to fish in the waters off the coast. The oceans at that time were abundant with marine life and provided the Indians with plenty of food.

Archaeologists and anthropologists have found substantial evidence leading them to believe that the Tongvans constructed plank canoes and sailed to the Channel Islands off the coast of California. Some of these brave explorers even ventured as far as San Nicolas Island, 60 miles from San Pedro.[3]

The women were known to have woven intricate baskets, using eelgrass found on the islands. On the mainland, baskets were made of stouter materials such as splints from the three-leaf sumac, deer grass stems, and a type of rush called the *juncus*.[4] The Tongvans were a peaceful people, and there is no evidence to show that they organized a resistance against the Spanish settlers. The Spaniards named the local tribes after the missions that they founded in southern California. Therefore, the Indians living near the San Gabriel Mission were called Gabrielenos and those living near the San Fernando Mission were called Fernandenos. Early California historians also called them by this name. However, more recent historical texts refer to them by their original tribal name of Tongva.

Almost 80 years after the Spaniards arrived, the Tongvan tribes were near extinction. This unfortunate occurrence was primarily due to disease, alcohol, and abuse from European settlers. There was a small Tongvan Indian village named Yang Na near what is today downtown Los Angeles.[5] This village came to a sad and bitter end, as witnessed by Horace Bell in 1852:

> They would be sold for a week and bought up by the vineyard, men and others from prices ranging from one to three dollars, one third of which was to be paid to the peon at the end of the week, which debt, due for well performed labor, would invariably be paid in *aguardiente* (a type of strong brandy), and the Indian would be made happy until the following Monday morning, having passed through another Saturday night and Sunday's saturnalia of debauchery and bestiality. Those thousands of honest useful people were absolutely destroyed in this way.[6]

The Calle de los Negros was named after the Tongvans. Historian John Weaver wrote: "One morning in 1832, so the story goes, Don Jose Antonio Carillo posted a sign, *Calle de Los Negros*

The Calle de los Negros was known as the "wickedest street in America" and its reputation was rightly deserved. – SECURITY PACIFIC COLLECTION / LOS ANGELES PUBLIC LIBRARY

(Negro Street), at each end of the narrow block long alley southeast of the Plaza occupied by Los Negros, as all dark-skinned Angelenos were called at that time."[7] This notorious alley would come to be known as the "wickedest street in America," and murder statistics from that era prove this statement to be true. The 166-yard-long street was located in what is now in the 400 block of North Los Angeles Street. It was jammed with wall-to-wall saloons, gambling houses, and bordellos.

Long before the Calle de los Negros was built, the Tongvans led their quiet and peaceful lives, completely unaware of their impending doom. They had experienced infrequent contact with white men for many years, but the Spanish explorers who visited never stayed. In 1781, however, all of that was to change when a small group of settlers from Mexico arrived to establish a pueblo. It would change the Tongvans' lives forever.

The Spaniards

Christopher Columbus opened the way for colonization of the new world with his famous voyage in 1492. Following in his wake were numerous explorers from Spain, including Hernan Cortes, who landed on the eastern coast of Mexico on April 21, 1519. Cortes laid the foundation for a vast Spanish colony that was to become the country of Mexico. It would include Texas, Wyoming, most of Arizona, New Mexico, Utah, Nevada, California, and parts of Colorado. On September 28, 1542, Juan Rodriguez Cabrillo sailed from Mexico into the San Diego Bay. He and his crew were the first Europeans to set foot in the state of California. In 1769, another Spanish explorer, Gaspar de Portola, led a land expedition from Baja (lower) California to Alta (upper) California. Accompanying him was Father Junipero Serra, who was charged with establishing a system of missions in the new territory.

Another valued member of the Portola expedition was Father Juan Crespi. He kept a journal, in which is noted the first written documentation of Los Angeles. On Tuesday, August 1, 1769, Father Crespi noted:

This day was one of rest, for the purpose of exploring and especially to celebrate the jubilee of our Lady of Los Angeles de Porciuncula.

The following day he continued:

This plain where the (Los Angeles) river runs is very extensive. It has good land for planting all kinds of grain and seeds, and is the most suitable site for all that we have seen for a mission, for it has all the requisites for a large settlement. As soon as we arrived, about eight heathen from a good village came to visit us; they live in this delightful place among the trees on the river. They presented us with some baskets of pinole made from sage and other grasses. Their chief brought some strings of beads made of shells, and they threw us three handfuls of them. Some of the old men were smoking pipes well made of baked clay and they puffed at us three mouthfuls of smoke. We gave them a little tobacco and glass beads, and they went away well pleased.[8]

A mission was not established at Los Angeles, however, but rather nine miles away in San Gabriel, in 1771, by Fathers Pedro Cambon and Angel Somera. This was the fourth mission to be established in California, and it was to become one of the largest and wealthiest in the 21-mission system chain.

Ten years later the governor of the province, Felipe de Neve, ordered a second California town to be established adjacent to the Los Angeles River (the first town was San Jose near the Santa Clara Mission).[9] Spain's reasoning for establishing these towns was to make California self-reliant. Officials concluded that, if the California province could produce its own food and supplies, goods would not have to be shipped to them from Mexico. This would prevent large sums of money being spent from the Spanish royal treasury.[10]

On September 4, 1781, 44 men, women, and children left the San Gabriel Mission to found the pueblo of Nuestra Senora de Los Angeles de Porciuncula. The name was too long for them, so they

The San Gabriel Mission, founded in 1771, was nine miles from Los Angeles and built 10 years before the pueblo. — AUTHOR'S COLLECTION

just called it El Pueblo. It later came to be known simply as Los Angeles.[11]

The first settlers were country folk who were recruited from Mexico. Among the men, two were Spanish, two were black (Afro-Mexican), two were *mestizo* (part Spanish, part Indian), and four were Indian. All of them brought Indian or mulatto wives. There were 22 children in the group.[12] It is interesting to note that, in 1742, there were 15,980 blacks (Afro-Mexicans) in Mexico. The Spaniards bought them from slave traders and had them transported to Spain. They were then loaded onto ships bound for New Spain (Mexico) to help build the empire. Once in the new world, Spanish law made it relatively easy for them to purchase their freedom. Blacks outnumbered Spaniards in Mexico until 1810.[13] Diversity in Los Angeles began at its inception, and it continues to have a dramatic impact regarding the enforcement of laws in Los Angeles County to this day.

Mexican Rule

Spanish rule of California lasted 280 years, until 1822, when Mexico broke away from Spain and became a sovereign state. This had little effect on the small pueblo, as it merely switched flags and swore its allegiance to Mexico. At that time, the estimated population of Los Angeles had grown to 650.[14]

As the little pueblo developed, several large *ranchos* were granted to Spanish citizens in the surrounding countryside. These ranchos, established according to Spanish property law, encompassed many thousands of acres, upon which grazed cattle, sheep, and other livestock. Rancho names such as Los Cerritos, La Cienega, La Brea and La Tijera are easily recognized by Angelenos today. The names of ranch owners can also be seen in almost every part of Los Angeles, especially on street signs. Bandini, Sepulveda, Pico, and Olvera are just a few examples. Many of these powerful families owned large, comfortable adobe houses in town, while simultaneously maintaining country estates on their ranches. The walls of an adobe house were up to three feet thick, and were extremely efficient at keeping the house cool in summer and retaining fireplace warmth in the winter.

The owner of a rancho held the title of Don and his wife was called Dona. According to custom, parts of the rancho would be given away as dowry and it would also be subdivided among the heirs. Early *gringo* or white settlers such as Abel Stearns and John Temple received the title of Don by marrying into wealthy Mexican families and becoming naturalized citizens.[15] These enterprising men had a distinct business advantage over other Dons because they

An early view of the Plaza. – Security Pacific Collection / Los Angeles Public Library

understood U.S. law and the basic principles of American commerce. They were also aided by the fact that they embraced the Californio culture and language, which endeared them to the locals and enabled them to operate efficiently in both worlds.

During the early 1800s, trade with American ships began to increase dramatically, as well as overland trade via pack mules from Santa Fe. The little Los Angeles pueblo grew. Ranchos began to expand and herds with several thousand head of cattle and sheep were openly grazing the land. Along with the herds came a need for highly skilled *vaqueros* or cowboys. The word "buckaroo" claims its origin from the word *vaquero*, which is often pronounced "bah-care-oh". These highly skilled, rugged horsemen were handy with lassos and firearms; they would come to play a major role in the future of Los Angeles law enforcement, both on the side of the law and against it.

The responsibility for law enforcement in the pueblo was given to the *alcalde*. The alcalde was both mayor and judge, as well as a member of the *ayuntamiento* or town council. He was elected annually and reported only to the *comisionado* (governor's military representative). His authority was derived from Governor Felipe de Neve's *Regalmento de 1779*.[16]

Early pueblo dwellers were expected to follow both the laws of the church and those of the ayuntamiento. Depending on the severity of the violation, law breakers could have their heads shaved and be made to stand in public. They could be whipped, beaten, or exiled from the town. The military had the responsibility for tracking down violators and punishing them. Legal execution could occur only when the alcalde received permission from the high court in Mexico. By 1791, Los Angeles already had a *calabazo* or jail.[17]

In 1828, two Americans, John Temple and George Rice, opened the town's first general merchandise store on what is now the corner of Temple and Main. Americans were starting to trickle into California. There were visits by famous trappers and scouts such as Jedediah Smith and Kit Carson. On one of his visits, Kit Carson remarked that drinking the local grape brandy distilled at Mission San Gabriel was "as deadly as taking two dueling pistols fired into your gizzard."[18] The Americans who stayed began to

Pio Pico was governor of California and actively involved in politics and business. – SECURITY PACIFIC COLLECTION / LOS ANGELES PUBLIC LIBRARY

open businesses and culti-vate farms and vineyards. They built sawmills and grazed cattle.

Los Angeles was changing, and so was its reputation. By 1844, the little pueblo had become the capital of Alta California under Governor Pio Pico. Succeeding California gover-nors preferred to stay in Monterey, however, and refused to live in Los Angeles. They rightfully claimed that the town was filling up with saloons, bordellos, and gambling houses. Northern officials reasoned that a governor could not reside in a town in which there were no public buildings to accom-modate his needs.

An 1836 census showed the town as having a population of 1,978 men and 250 women, 15 of whom were listed by profession by the initials M.V. for *Mala Vida,* meaning "bad life" or, essentially, prosti-tute. There were 50 foreigners in this population, 29 of whom were Americans.[19] American expansion was pushing steadily from the East, and it was not long before the United States government would make its own move against Mexico.

The Mexican War

In 1836, Texans declared their independence from Mexico. This act lit the fuse that led to open war between Mexico and the United States in 1846. As part of this war, the U.S. Army sent Colonel Stephen W. Kearny with his ragtag Army of the West to take California by land, traveling west along the Gila river to San Diego.

Meanwhile, Major John C. Fremont was supposed to be on a "surveying expedition" in Oregon, but most historians believe that he was given secret orders to start a revolt in California. He went south into northern California and urged the American settlers there to revolt against the Mexican government, which was weak and fractionalized.

In June 1846, the settlers agreed with Fremont and revolted, taking power in what is known as the Bear Flag revolt. The rebels raised the flag in Sonoma, and Fremont declared himself governor of California. A short time later, Commodore John D. Sloat landed troops at Monterey, the Mexican capital of California. Sloat also claimed the territory as part of the United States. When Sloat became ill, Commodore Robert F. Stockton replaced him and continued to advocate that California was U.S. territory.

Realizing a threat to their power base, the Californios put aside their differences and organized in an effort to resist the Americans. Commodore Stockton continued down the coast and arrived by sea at the port of San Pedro, near Los Angeles. Major Fremont arrived by land on August 13, 1846. Together, the marines, sailors, and soldiers commandeered governor Pio Pico's office and declared that Los Angeles was now a U.S. territory. The stars and stripes went up over the city without the rest of the world even noticing. The American military encountered no resistance, so the troops stayed on for two weeks. Stockton then made a poor tactical decision by leaving newly promoted Marine Captain Archibald Gillespie with an undersized garrison of 50 men to occupy the town.

Unfortunately for the United States and the townspeople of Los Angeles, Gillespie may have been the wrong person to be put in charge of this or any garrison. He was known to be vindictive and to have little tact. One soldier wrote that Gillespie was "an overbearing bully, a martinet, and so blown up with his own importance, that he turned the people against the Americans."[20] Thomas Larkin wrote: "It appears even from the Americans that Captain AHG punished, fined and imprisoned who and when he pleased without any hearing."[21] Townspeople charged that Gillespie had his troops search homes at random. He outlawed public meetings and put local inhabitants into jail for no good reason.

It was not long before General M. Flores, Andres Pico, and Jose Carillo plotted a revolt against the *Yanquis*. They took back the city by raising a militia of townspeople that eventually outnumbered and overpowered the Captain and his tiny garrison. On September 29, 1846, the Americans were offered terms of surrender and then forced to leave town. The Mexicans celebrated, but their victory would be short lived.

Colonel Kearny's troops joined forces with Gillespie's men in San Diego County. The total combined force, which consisted of 160 men included 100 dragoons and two howitzers. They clashed with Andres Pico's lancers near the Indian village of San Pascual. Kearny lost eighteen men and was forced to regroup. Realizing that the Californios were not going to give in easily, the Army reorganized and made new battle plans for defeating the Mexicans. Kearny made for San Diego, where he joined up with Commodore Stockton. Sailors, soldiers, marines, and volunteers combined to make a new battalion of 607 men.

The small army marched north to Los Angeles, where two battles were fought: one at the Paso de Bartolo on the San Gabriel River on January 8, and the other at La Mesa (what is now Pasadena). The Americans were victorious in both battles, and they marched back into Los Angeles on January 10, 1847. Three days later, Major Fremont and Andres Pico signed the Treaty of Cahuenga at a ranch house called the Campo de Cahuenga. This treaty officially ended the war in California. A replica of the house is now a museum, located on Lankershim Boulevard in North Hollywood, adjacent to Universal City. Captain Gillespie, who was wounded at the battle of San Pascual, was promoted to Major and helped organize the military reoccupation of Los Angeles.

Desiring to both protect the pueblo from attack and maintain a strong U.S. presence, the federal government ordered the Army to establish an outpost in the frontier town. In the spring of 1847, a Mormon army battalion began construction of a fort on a hill overlooking the Pueblo of Los Angeles. The fort was dedicated on July 4, and named Fort Moore, after Army Captain Benjamin D. Moore, who was killed at the battle of San Pascual. The Los Angeles Unified School District Headquarters now rests on this site.[22] The fort was

The old flagpole and some leftover cannons at the top of Fort Moore. The Fort was abandoned in 1853. – Security Pacific Collection / Los Angeles Public Library

designed to hold a garrison of at least 200 soldiers. The flag that flew over the outpost was raised on a pole that came from the San Bernardino Forest. The flagpole, or part of it, was said to have been moved to the main entrance at the Sheriff's Hall of Justice building, located on the corner of Temple Street and Grand Street.[23] Fort Moore did not have a long life as an army outpost, however, for it was decommissioned in 1853, six years after it was dedicated. Although the war had formally ended, there was lingering animosity between the Californios and the Americans.

The Mexican War veterans who found their way to Los Angeles were a strange lot. Experienced with firearms and fighting, many of them eventually faced off against each other in the pueblo's saloons and gambling dens. They seemed either to enforce the law or to disregard it altogether. Regardless of their feelings for the Americans, the patriarchs of the great Californio families started to become familiar with Anglo culture and tried to assimilate what parts of it they could tolerate.

As if the strife and pains of war did not cause enough turmoil for the inhabitants of the pueblo, whispers had begun to spread across the countryside, and like a wildfire they blazed to the far ends of the earth: "*There's gold in California!*" The rush to "see the elephant" would have an impact on the infant state that few could imagine.[24]

The California Gold Rush

Sutter's Mill was not the only place that gold was found in California. It was discovered in southern California first, six years before it was found in northern California. On March 9, 1842, while looking for stray horses in San Francisquito Canyon (now called Placerita Canyon in the Santa Clarita Valley), a rancher named Francisco Lopez dug up some wild onions and discovered several flakes of gold.[25] When word of the discovery spread, miners from Sonora, Mexico, came north to get rich. They worked the mines until 1848, when a much larger gold strike was discovered near Sutter's Mill, 40 miles east of Sacramento.

Placerita Canyon was abandoned until 1854, when miners in the north realized that their sluice box and panning methods were yielding less and less gold. They either had to switch to more organized, complex gold hunting methods such as hydraulic mining and tunneling, or they had to prospect elsewhere. Some of them returned to Placerita Canyon to try their luck at the old digs. More than $145,000 worth of gold was taken from the canyon between 1842 and 1855 ($3,000,000 in today's money). Prospectors can still be seen panning for gold at Placerita Canyon but, as in the past, their efforts are greatly hampered by the scarcity of water in the area.[26]

The discovery of gold in California had a tremendous impact on southern Californians, not all of which was negative. Ranchers benefited greatly from the sale of their beef, lamb, tallow, and hides to residents in the north. Cattle drives were organized, and many thousands of "dogies" (cattle) were herded up the El Camino Real to be sold for huge profits. Prospectors in San Francisco and the surrounding towns were buying all available food and mining supplies.

Men with "gold fever" were streaming in from all over the world at an incredible rate. Ex-Marine Officer Archibald Gillespie must have made at least one friend when he was in Los Angeles, for on October 14, 1848, he wrote to Don Abel Stearns from New York:

> The public in general are mad about California and the late news about El Placer has made many adventurers look towards that region. But there are very many solid people about to emigrate to California. . . . The emigration next spring overland will be very large, many families have already rendezvoused upon the frontier.[27]

After working for years, spending long hours in the sun, wind, and rain, thousands of men came to the difficult realization that they were not going to get rich. In fact, many of them were destitute. Daniel Woods wrote in January 1850, "Cheerful words are seldom heard, more seldom the boisterous shout and laugh which indicates success, and which, when heard, sink to a lower ebb the spirits of the unsuccessful. We have made 50 cents each."[28] J. S. Holliday, in his book *Rush for Riches* wrote:

> Left embittered and desperate, not a few washed up miners turned to robbery and murder. The ill concealed bulges of pistols tucked into every belt and waistband brought heightened tension to even minor disagreements. And many succumbed to the comfort of the bottle to ease their aches and hardships. Criminals and "dregs" from cities around the world added to the social degeneracy.[29]

Many of these former gold seekers decided to stay in California. Some refused to go home out of shame; others stayed because they had come to enjoy the warm California climate and saw opportunities to make their fortunes by trying their hands at something else.

In 1848, many Angelenos abandoned their rancho lifestyles to try their luck in the gold fields. They had a distinct advantage over their Anglo competition. First, they were already in California, so they did not have to spend their life savings to travel half way around the world to reach San Francisco. Second, they made quick friends with the local Indians in gold country, many of whom spoke Spanish. The Indians led them to some of the best sites in the area in exchange for mere trinkets. In some cases, they could even get the Indians to help them dig.

While not all of the Angelenos "struck it rich," some of them did quite well. Historian Leonard Pitt wrote:

> In one day Antonio Coronel himself ended up with 45 ounces of gold; Dolores Sepulveda found a 12 ounce nugget; and Senor Valdez discovered a boulder buried only three feet down which had once blocked the flow of an ancient alluvial stream and produced a towel full of nuggets in a short time. He sold his claim to Lorenzo Soto, who took out a whopping 52 pounds of gold in eight days and then sold it to Senor Machado, who also became rich.[30]

The Californios brought their riches back to Los Angeles and lived in grand style. However, they had to be extra careful not to be too ostentatious with their newfound wealth; if word got out to the wrong people, desperadoes would soon be knocking on the door. Desperate prospectors and disgruntled miners who had given up on the gold fields were working their way down to the little pueblo. Their arrival merely added to the crime and debauchery that were so prevalent in 1850s Los Angeles.

The Most Violent Town in America

It is shocking to see how truly out-of-control and dangerous 1850s Los Angeles really was. Comparing the population with the crime statistics of the time helps to give an accurate picture of the level of violence. Author John Boessenecker wrote:

> Between September 1850 and September 1851, 31 homicides were committed in the pueblo and its suburbs which had a population of about 2,500. The resulting rate adjusting for population was 1,240 (homicides) per 100,000. This

is far and away the highest reported homicide rate in American history.[31]

In contrast, the American homicide rate average in the 1990s was 9 per 100,000. It should be noted that the statistics used include only the homicides that the pueblo reported; they do not include the many other killings that no doubt took place and were never officially recorded. The killings of Indians in particular were often not documented.

A young man named Horace Bell arrived in Los Angeles in 1852 with plans to make his fortune in law as a real estate attorney. Many historians agree that Mr. Bell had a tendency to embellish his stories and that his facts were not always accurate. Nevertheless, Bell's extensive memoirs are some of the few remaining eyewitness accounts from this era. He spoke with authority in the area of law enforcement, since he was one of the founding members of the Los Angeles Rangers, an early law enforcement group that assisted the sheriffs during the 1850s and 1860s.

Horace described Calle de los Negros, or what the white man called, in the vernacular of the day, Nigger Alley:

> Every few minutes a rush would be made, and maybe a pistol shot would be heard, and when the confusion incident to the rush would have somewhat subsided, and inquiry made, you would learn that it was only a knife fight between two Mexicans, or a gambler had caught somebody cheating and had perforated him with a bullet. Some things were a matter of course, and no complaints or arrests were ever made. An officer would not have had the temerity to attempt an arrest in Nigger Alley at that time.[32]

Mr. Bell speculated about why the crime in early Los Angeles was so bad:

> It was a fact that all of the bad characters who had been driven from the mines had taken refuge in Los Angeles and for the reason that if forced to move further on, it was only a

The stagecoach for the Lafayette Hotel waits in the Calle de los Negros. – SECURITY PACIFIC
COLLECTION / LOS ANGELES PUBLIC LIBRARY

short ride to Mexican soil, while on the other hand all of the
outlaws of the Mexican frontier made for the California gold
mines, and the cut-throats of California and Mexico natural-
ly met at Los Angeles, and at Los Angeles they fought. Knives
and revolvers settled all differences, either real or imaginary.
The slightest misunderstandings were settled on the spot
with knife or bullet, the Mexican preferring the former at
close quarters and the American the latter.[33]

On September 27, 1851, the town's only English newspaper, the
Los Angeles Star, wrote, "Who can name one instance in which a murderer has been punished? Homicides averaged one for each day of
the year".[34] Historian John Weaver concurred: "At one time, it was
averaging a homicide a day, not counting Indians."[35] J. S. Holliday

wrote, "Despite an array of law enforcement officers and sixteen judges with the power to hang without a jury, murderers and desperadoes virtually ruled the town from their brothels, gambling halls and saloons."[36] On March 5, 1855, *The Southern Californian* newspaper wrote: "Last night was a brisk night for killing. Four men were shot and several more were wounded in shooting frays."[37]

Stephen Longstreet wrote about Los Angeles nightlife:

The most notorious place was "La Aguila de Ora" (The Golden Eagle), where the play was for gold and the gambling tables ran at all hours, guarded by musclemen. They took care to drub any clients who claimed they were cheated. A few blows, and men were tossed out into the ally. There, Indians, demoralized by their craving for drink, stripped the victims and went hunting a bottle of rotgut whiskey in exchange for whatever hat, coat or boots they had taken from their prey.[38]

Another eyewitness of the times wrote:

Human life in that period was about the cheapest thing in Los Angeles, and killings were frequent. Nigger Alley was as tough a neighborhood, in fact, as could be found anywhere, and a large proportion of the twenty or thirty murders a month was committed there.[39]

Even the courtroom was not a safe haven. There are tales of inkpots being thrown by lawyers, jeering spectators, and mobs breaking up furniture in the most sacred place of law. Harris Newmark, who lived in Los Angeles at the time, wrote:

On one occasion for instance, after the angry disputants had arrived at a state of agitation which made the further use of canes, chairs, and similar objects tame and uninteresting, revolvers were drawn, notwithstanding the marshal's repeated attempts to restore order. Judge Dryden in the midst of the melee hid behind the platform on which his judgeship's bench rested; and being well out of the range of the threatening irons, yelled at the rioters: "Shoot away damn you! And to hell with all of you!"[40]

Another perspective of the seriousness of the crime problem can be found by examining the fate of the pueblo's practicing ministers. Renegades, who do not live their lives in accordance with biblical law, are not likely to listen to preachers, especially when they talk of "loving your neighbor." From 1853 to 1857, at least three enterprising men of the cloth attempted to save the souls of gamblers, miners, and desperadoes.[41] Rev. Adam Bland tried first, working out of a small adobe on Commercial Street. Then Rev. James Woods tried preaching out of a carpenter shop near the Plaza. Reverend Woods had a hard time adjusting to the dangerous and callous lifestyle. In his diary he wrote:

> Thus while I have been here in Los Angeles only two weeks, there have been it is said eleven deaths, and only one of them a natural death—all the rest by violence—some killed in quarrels—some in being taken for crimes—some assassinated. . . . Last week a Mexican called upon an Irish woman who kept a drinking establishment and as she was opening the door he shot her in the breast; he then rode around to the Bella Union (hotel) and snapt his pistol at a man who immediately pursued him on horseback to take him prisoner, but refusing to surrender the man shot him in the groin and took him. He died the next day in the jail yard, the woman whom he had shot died also.[42]

Rev. Elias Birdsall worshipped God and read the gospel aloud from a church building at the corner of New High and Temple. Unfortunately for the reverend, his church failed also, and the building was used for other enterprises. All three men abandoned the ministry in search of other ways to make a living.

The Spanish missions, which previously offered religion to the masses, had been secularized by the newly independent Mexican government in 1833. Accordingly, the San Gabriel Mission lost much of its land and power. The Tongvan Indians who had for generations looked to the mission for guidance and support now had nowhere to go. The Indians were trapped between cultures and lost in a violent town that was rapidly changing before their eyes.

Things did not get much better during the first 30 years of American rule. In the 1870s the population had risen to 5,614; of the 285 businesses in Los Angeles, 110 were saloons. In those days it was common for hotels, theaters, drug stores and boarding houses to have bars inside their establishments. Although prostitution was outlawed in the central business district in 1870, laws were not being enforced. Even though the murder rate had dropped significantly, Los Angeles was still one of the wildest towns in the West.

The American Government Sets Up Shop

The U.S. government ended its military rule of California in 1849. A new government structure was created that included a state supreme court, district courts, county courts, and justices of the peace. A temporary governing body called the Court of Sessions was created in each of the counties throughout California. This "court" consisted of a panel of three judges who presided over cases involving lesser crimes and handled the day-to-day business of the county. The first Los Angeles County Court of Sessions members were Augustin Olvera, Louis Robidoux from Missouri, and Jonathan R. Scott. Later, in 1852, a county board of supervisors was elected which absorbed most of their duties.

The first criminal court judge of Los Angeles was former *alcalde*

Judge Agustin Olvera, first jurist of Los Angeles, presided over the Lugo Brothers trial.
— Huntington Library

22

Augustin Olvera. His home doubled as the courthouse and, although he did not speak English very well, he thoroughly understood the basics of law and justice. The well-known tourist attraction and cultural center, Olvera Street, is named in his honor. The first District Attorney was William C. Ferrell, who was elected to office on April 1, 1850. His jurisdiction was the unwieldy First Judicial District, which ran from San Diego County to Ventura County.

The *Juez del Campo* (Judge of the Plains) was one of the few legal traditions held over from Mexican-ruled California. *El Juez* presided over rodeos and settled disputes regarding the ownership of cattle and horses. The authority allowing for this prestigious position remained on the county's law book for many years, however it was eventually phased out due to the breakup of the large *ranchos* and the growing power of local courts.

Early Los Angeles Courts were informal and often humorous. Judge William Dryden, in particular, was a colorful character who was not unaccustomed to the use of profanity in his courtroom. On one occasion, Attorney Cameron Thom was searching for an ordinance in a large legal volume. He took up so much time that the judge became frustrated and asked the lawyer to give him the book. When the good judge could not find the ordinance, he shouted: "I'll be God Damned Mr. Thom, if I can find that law!"[43]

The early courts were so informal that they could be "understanding" when unique occasions arose. There was a particular man who, in the 1850s, decided that he wanted to run for the office of sheriff. He figured that the best way to win the popular vote was to marry a Californio woman from a respectable family. A deal between the family and the man was made, and the young suitor was elected to office.

Not long after he was sworn in, a band of horse rustlers began to terrorize the countryside. The sheriff rounded up his posse, hunted down the gang, and brought them back to Los Angeles, where they were promptly locked up in the *calaboose*. During the trial, the greenhorn sheriff was politely informed that one of the horse thieves was his brother-in-law, whom he had never seen. The sheriff was dumbfounded. He immediately asked for a side bar and, quietly spoke to the judge, begging for leniency. Nevertheless, the bandit was tried and found guilty. Judge Dryden then proceeded to lecture the

Cameron Thom was one of a handful of rugged pioneer lawyers in the pueblo. He was the county's fifth district attorney and later became mayor of Los Angeles.
— SECURITY PACIFIC COLLECTION / LOS ANGELES PUBLIC LIBRARY

young horse thief about the evils of his ways and told him that stealing would only lead to more trouble. After one of the longest scoldings ever handed down by a jurist, the judge told the thief: "But the jury recommends clemency. Accordingly, I declare you a free man and you may go about your business." A heckler in the courtroom asked, "What is his business?", and Judge Dryden shouted back, "Horse stealing sir! Horse stealing!"[44]

Another incident that occurred in Judge Dryden's courtroom involved the investigation into the cause of death of an Indian. The citizens sitting on these investigations were called the "coroner's jury." After a long discussion and heated argument, the jury was deadlocked and not sure exactly how the Indian had died. The judge and jury decided that they could not ponder the case forever, so they came up with their best answer. The *Los Angeles Star* reported: "Justice Dryden and the jury sat on the body. The verdict was: 'Death by intoxication, or by the visitation of God!'"[45]

The first person to be elected Sheriff of Los Angeles County was George T. Burrill, on April 1, 1850, in an election in which 377 votes were cast. At that time, the county sheriff was responsible for the collection of taxes as well as criminal matters. The sheriff's office would continue to act as ex-officio tax collector until 1875, when the tax collector's office was established. The sheriff's office paid the exceptionally high salary of $10,000 a year, equating to $230,000 in today's dollars. The sheriff was also allowed to keep a small percentage of the taxes collected as a "fee."

At least part of the reason for this large salary was the round-the-clock work hours and the thousands of square miles of jurisdiction, not to mention the extreme danger inherent in the job. Sheriff Burrill was also paid $50 a month to act as court interpreter for Judge Olvera, who was still learning English. Although Sheriff Burrill was the chief executive responsible for law enforcement in the county, he did not work alone in this capacity. The board of supervisors allowed sheriffs to select at least one paid deputy to assist him with his duties. The sheriff was also given the power to deputize citizens to assist him during emergency situations.

When gunfire erupted in the courtroom, Judge Dryden would duck under his desk and wait until the sheriff intervened. – SECURITY PACIFIC COLLECTION / LOS ANGELES PUBLIC LIBRARY

In the 1850s, sheriffs were assisted by the City Marshal, the Town Constables, the U.S. Army, and an armed cavalry group called the Los Angeles Rangers. Indeed, there was so much crime that these pioneering forces of law and order frequently banded together for their safety. Benjamin D. Wilson, mayor of Los Angeles, appointed the first City Marshal, Samuel Whiting, in 1851. Whiting was responsible for keeping law and order within the city limits. He could hire deputy marshals when the budget allowed. Mr. Whiting started out his career in law enforcement working for the sheriff as the county's first jailer.

Duty as a marshal was just as risky as that of a sheriff. On December 7, 1853, Jack Whalen (sometimes cited as Whaling or Wheelan), the pueblo's second Marshal, was fatally stabbed while attempting to arrest a murder suspect. In 1870, Marshal Warren was shot to death in a dispute with one of his own officers. Juan C. Carillo was the last man to serve as City Marshal, in 1875. In that year the city formed the Los Angeles Police Department (LAPD), and the title of City Marshal was changed to Chief of Police.[46]

The city marshal's office is not to be confused with two other marshal's offices. The first was the Los Angeles County Marshal's Office. This office, which did not exist in the early days of the city, was created in 1952. The County Marshal's Office faithfully served the superior courts of Los Angeles until 1994, when they merged with the sheriff's department to save costs. The last County Marshal, Robert F. Mann, was appointed by Sheriff Leroy D. Baca to manage the department's Court Services Division. This division was much larger than the marshal's department because it included the transportation of inmates and conducting the day-to-day transactions of both the superior and municipal courts.

The second marshal's office was in existence during the frontier days but did not become very active until Los Angeles had its population boom. This office was the federal government's United States Marshal's Service. The U.S. marshal's office has been in existence since 1789 and is still in service today. The mission of the U.S. Marshal's Service is to protect the federal courts and ensure the effective operation of the judicial system. The Marshal's Service is responsible for providing security for the federal judiciary, transporting federal prisoners, protecting endangered federal witnesses, and managing assets seized from criminal enterprises. In addition, the men and women of the Marshal's Service pursue and arrest 55% of all federal fugitives, more than all other federal agencies combined.[47]

From 1850 to 1912, township constables were elected by local community members to serve as law enforcement officers and to assist the Justice of the Peace. The constables purchased their own badges, which identified them simply as "constable" or "township constable." The constables served in a similar capacity as the U.S. marshals, except in support of the justice courts. Their tasks included collecting fines, serving warrants, and assisting the sheriff as needed. Township constables were crucial to insuring everyday law and order in the community. The small sheriff's office and the immense county made it all but impossible to police the jurisdiction in an effective and timely manner. The constables helped to close this gap and make it possible to enforce laws and carry out court business at the local level. The Sheriff's Department absorbed the Los Angeles Township Constables in 1912 in a concerted effort to coordinate criminal investigations and standardize policing in the unincorporated county areas.

As part of an Army experiment, camels were brought to Camp Drum in Wilmington. The experiment was a failure, but during the Civil War Camp Drum succeeded in keeping Confederate sympathizers at bay, including Sheriff Tomas Sanchez and his deputies.
— CALIFORNIA CENTER FOR MILITARY HISTORY

Another important and desperately needed resource for the beleaguered sheriff was the United States military. The U.S. Army garrisoned troops at Wilmington Drum Barracks from 1861 to 1871. This important army base served to ensure that California would remain part of the Union during the Civil War. The barracks was the main staging, training, and supply base for military operations in the Southwest. It also housed one of the most modern medical facilities west of the Mississippi River.

Fort Tejon in the Tehachapi Mountains was another important army base during the frontier era. Established on August 10, 1854, the outpost was built in a strategic location called the Grapevine Canyon, which is a route connecting southern California with the central plains of the state.

> Its mission was to protect and control the Indians who were living on the Sebastian Indians Reservation, and to protect both the Indians and white settlers from raids by the wide-ranging and warlike Paiutes, Chemeheui, Mojave, and other Indian groups of the desert regions to the southeast.[48]

Occasionally, the Army would assist local law enforcement with searching for and detaining outlaws.

In response to the violent crime, the Los Angeles City Council authorized the establishment of a "police force" on July 12, 1851. This force became the forerunners of the Los Angeles Rangers. Dr. Alexander W. Hope volunteered to be their "Chief." The all-volunteer rangers were issued Spanish lances and "badges" made out of white ribbon with the words both in English and Spanish: "City

Police organized by the Common Council of Los Angeles July 12, 1851," and *"Policia Organizado por el Consejo Comun de Los Angeles."*[49]

The rangers took their orders from both the mayor and the sheriff. They were not paid for their services, and they were responsible for purchasing most of their own firearms and equipment. Many of their members would become county law enforcement officers. Future Sheriff Billy Getman was a Lieutenant in the rangers. Out of the 100 Los Angeles Rangers on record, only about twenty-five of them were active. By 1854, the group was authorized and paid for in part by the state government. They were not compensated monetarily for their dangerous work. In that respect, they are the forefathers of today's reserve deputy sheriffs.

Tools of the Trade: Badges

The sheriff's badge was made famous by stories of the Old West, in print as well as on the silver screen. People around the world instantly recognize the western lawman, confidently striding down the street, spurs jingling and badge glimmering in the sun. The sheriff always had one hand near his gun, while clear, piercing eyes scanned the street for trouble from beneath a dusty cowboy hat. This image was not always historically accurate, however, and movie directors in recent years have tried with increasing frequency to make films that reflect a truer image of frontier life (e.g., *Lonesome Dove*, *The Jackbull*, and *Unforgiven*).

Since early sheriffs did not wear uniforms, their only form of identification was the badge. For this reason alone, wearing a badge was an essential part of being a lawman in the Wild West. Most of the time, badges were worn on the inside of the lapel.[50] This was done for two reasons: First, the population of frontier towns was so small

Shield badges like this were worn in the latter half of the 19th Century. – JIM CASEY AT POLICEGUIDE.COM

28

that everyone knew who the sheriff was anyway. Second, when strangers came into town, the sheriff could continue sipping his whiskey at the bar while keeping an eye on the newcomer. This allowed him to size up the stranger in case of trouble. The anonymity also allowed him to go about his business without being bothered by drunks and interlopers. Of course, wearing the badge was a personal decision, and every sheriff had his own opinion about the best way to operate.

The badge was, and still is, a symbol of authority and order. When groups of lawmen gathered, as in a posse, they would pin on badges to identify themselves so as not to shoot each other in a gunfight. It was true that badges were handed out to posse members as the sheriff saw fit. If a man was willing to help and looked trustworthy, the sheriff would give him a badge and deputize him on the spot. This carefree hiring system often ended up enabling "gentlemen" of less-than-desirable qualities to take advantage of the meek and less fortunate. In 1899, Sheriff Billy Hammel fired Deputy Edward Virgin for extorting $5.00 from an Italian woman. Virgin said he was drunk and had no distinct recollection of the incident.[51]

It is interesting to note that, in times of trouble, a deputy can still invoke the law of *posse comitatus* using his badge. The law, which was enacted in 1872, is still listed in the California penal code, section 150:

> Every able bodied person above 18 years of age who neglects or refuses to join the posse comitatus or power of the county by neglecting or refusing to aid and assist in taking or arresting any person against whom there may be issued any process . . . being thereto required by any peace officer who identifies himself or herself with a badge . . . is punishable by a fine of not less than fifty ($50) dollars, nor more than one thousand dollars ($1,000).[52]

The power of the badge is taken very seriously by modern law enforcement agencies. Sheriffs and chiefs of police understand all too well that when this power is egregiously abused disastrous consequences are often the result.

Today, applicants for the position of peace officer in the State of California must go through a thorough background check, which can take up to a year or more. If they successfully complete this process, they still will not wear a badge until completion of a 5-month sheriff's or police academy. On graduation day, the rookie deputies and officers are finally presented with their badges and live "duty" ammunition for their sidearm.

Original badges worn by Los Angeles County law enforcement officials in the 19th century are extremely rare finds today. There were several different types of badges worn between 1850 and 1900. These early badges would probably have been made of sheet silver, and hand-engraved with the words L.A. COUNTY DEPUTY SHERIFF or DEPUTY L.A. CO. SHERIFF. The badges may have been either star- shaped or shaped as a shield. The badge worn by the first Sheriff of Los Angeles County in 1850 was very likely much the same as his deputies' except that it would have been engraved L.A. (or Los Angeles) COUNTY SHERIFF. There is a high likelihood that his badge may have been made of gold, while his deputies wore silver. There is only one badge per sheriff worded in this manner. All other sheriff's badges are stamped with the words DEPUTY SHERIFF, as is the tradition to this day. Ranks such as Sergeant, Lieutenant, etc., were not stamped on badges until the 1930s.

Between 1850 and 1900, local jewelers made badges for lawmen; the more money the officer spent, the better looking the badge. Some of the most elegant badges from the early days were made for town constables. Sheriff's badges made subsequent to the 1850's-style badge were lettered in a variety of ways. They displayed anything from DEPUTY L.A. CO. SHERIFF to just plain DEPUTY

This badge dates from the early 1900s.
— J.R. Sanders Collection and Mike Bailey at Badgehistory.com

*The Los Angeles County
Sheriff's Department's
Millennium Badge.* – MIKE BAILEY
AT BADGEHISTORY.COM

SHERIFF. The badges from the 1870s and possibly even the 1860s were shaped as shields as evidenced by the few surviving examples we have today.

In 1880, the Board of Supervisors authorized Sheriff William Rowland to purchase new badges for his deputies at a cost of $5 each ($87 in today's dollars). These high-quality sterling silver badges read "DEPUTY L.A. CO. SHERIFF."

After the turn of the century, ball-tipped stars were being made for the sheriff's office. The points of the star were ball-tipped so as not to injure the wearer during physical activity. The wording on these badges was identical to earlier badges. The Los Angeles County Sheriff's badge would go through many more changes until the department arrived at its current style, which was designed by Deputy Bob Brown in 1947 and approved by the Board of Supervisors in 1948.

In 1999, the Los Angeles County Board of Supervisors and Sheriff Leroy D. Baca authorized sterling silver badges to be manufactured by the Ed Jones Company of Berkeley, California, as part of a special sesquicentennial year 2000 celebration. These badges were larger than the originals but they emulated much of the style of the early badges. Deputies were allowed the opportunity to purchase their own "millennium" badges, which could be worn during the year 2000. Their original badges were held for safekeeping by the department because, per statute, a deputy is not allowed to have two badges at the same time. Once the deputy was finished wearing his or her millennium badge, it was exchanged for the original badge. The millennium badge was then encased in Lucite and returned to the deputy as a permanent keepsake.

Tools of the Trade: Guns

Early lawmen required sturdy and reliable firearms in order to protect themselves while taking outlaws into custody. The Mexican War introduced new gun technology to the West. Almost without exception, every settler, pioneer, hunter, trapper, gambler, buckaroo, and prospector carried some type of firearm. The years between 1850 and 1900 saw unprecedented advances in the development of these weapons.

The first major breakthrough was the invention of the copper percussion cap in the early 1800s. The percussion cap replaced flint-and-steel ignition systems for firearms, and was much more reliable and quicker on the reload. It allowed inventors such as Samuel Colt to patent his 1835 revolver. Researcher Joseph Rosa wrote, "Along trails, in the western gold fields, gambling dens and elsewhere there were other types of handguns, but none was ever as popular as the Colt."[53] As cartridge revolvers were not yet available, the first sheriffs of Los Angeles County exclusively used cap and ball black powder revolvers, such as Sam Colt's early models.

Historical records from the mid-1850s frequently mention the 1851 Colt "Navy" revolver. It was designed as a practical holster handgun and not specifically for the Navy's use. The Navy was extremely popular among law enforcement officers because it was not as heavy as the .44 and not too small, like some of the .31 caliber "pocket" models. The Colt Navy pistol was easily recognizable by its namesake, the engraved naval battle scene on the barrel. This .36 caliber pistol, along with the 1848 Colt Pocket Pistol and the much heavier Colt .44 caliber Walker and Dragoon models, were among the most commonly used handguns in Los Angeles.

Toward the end of 1860, geologist William Brewer wrote to his brother:

> This Southern California is unsettled. We all continually wear arms—each wears both Bowie knife and pistol (navy revolver), while we have always for game or otherwise, a Sharp's rifle, Sharp's carbine, and two double barrel shotguns. Fifty to sixty murders per year have been common here in Los Angeles, and some think it odd that there has

The preferred sidearms for sheriffs and villains alike, the 1861 Colt Navy Pistol (top) and 1851 Colt Navy Pistol (bottom). These highly popular .36 caliber weapons were deadly at close range. – KEN MESSENGER COLLECTION

been no violent death during the two weeks that we have been here . . . as I write this there are at least six heavily loaded revolvers in the tent, besides Bowie knifes and other arms.[54]

By the late 1850s, cartridge-style rim-fire ammunition became available. This type of round was ideal for derringers and, accordingly, their popularity skyrocketed. The derringer was a small, lightweight, and easily concealable handgun, making it a perfect weapon for gamblers who did not want to "tip their hand" in a gunfight, or for ladies of the evening whose clients got a little too aggressive. Although there is documented use of derringers by Los Angeles lawmen, it was considered to be more of a backup weapon than a primary duty pistol.

In the 1870s, the introduction of the reliable center-fire cartridge and "bored-through" cylinder technology completely changed the way in which pistols were made and used. The cartridge, also called a round, consisted of a shell casing that housed the gunpowder and the bullet. The bullet, usually made of lead, is the part of the round that leaves the gun once it has been fired. The gunpowder ignites when the primer in the center of the butt end of the cartridge was struck. This round, in conjunction with the bored cylinder, enabled the shooter to reload much more quickly. It also offered greater protection from the elements as well as ease of storage.

Pistols made using cartridge ammunition are what moviegoers usually see in westerns. The single-action .45 caliber Colt Army model 1873, also known as the "Peacemaker," is recognized by millions as being the standard Western sidearm for sheriffs, cowboys, and desperadoes on the silver screen. This tremendously popular weapon was sold throughout the West to many a lawman in the latter half of the 19th Century and early 20th Century.[55]

Los Angeles gunfighters also used shotguns and rifles. Many of the rifles used in the mid-1800s were percussion-style weapons which had been upgraded from old flintlocks. Some of these had been in use prior to the Revolutionary War. Converting older flintlock rifles was relatively easy: The "lock" mechanism was removed and a more reliable and easier-to-use percussion hammer and strike plate were installed. As with the pistol, the invention of the cartridge revolutionized the design of the rifle.

Rifles with names like Sharps, Spencer, Henry, and Winchester were widely manufactured throughout the 1800s. These reliable and highly popular weapons gave gunfighters the advantage of accurately striking a foe from great distances—something that handguns are generally incapable of doing.

Shotguns, such as the ones made by Remington, were also popular because they are easy to use. Since the buckshot fired from a shotgun scatters when it is dispersed, it allows even the worst shooter a good chance of hitting his target. At close range, being struck with buckshot from a shotgun almost certainly resulted in death.

Proper care and maintenance of an officer's pistols, rifles, and shotguns was not a trivial pursuit but rather a matter of life and death. A gunfighter's worst nightmare was hearing the fateful "click" of a misfire instead of the expected "boom" that he was counting on.

Armed with a good rifle, a couple of Colt pistols, a Bowie knife, and a trusted horse, men such as George Burrill were ready to ride out West and take their chances at whatever obstacles the fates might toss in their direction. When they arrived in the dusty little pueblo called Los Angeles, they found a bubbling cauldron full of trouble, as if witches were throwing in every possible volatile ingredient to make this place like a hell broth. So begins the exciting story of the LASD.

Chapter *2*

A DEADLY BEGINNING: EARLY SHERIFFS LOSE THEIR LIVES FIGHTING CRIME IN THE FRONTIER TOWN

Sheriff George T. Burrill, April 1850–September 1851

George Thompson Burrill was born in Rhode Island in 1810, a descendant from the Burrill family of Lynn, Massachusetts. Records from his early life are scarce and not much is known about his formative years. He moved to Mexico, where he spent time in Sonora and Chihuahua. While working as an official in some unknown capacity, he met a young woman named Doña Concha (nickname). The two became lovers, but they did not marry. Since the Mexican War had increased anti-American sentiment, Burrill decided to avoid hostilities and moved north to Los Angeles. The pioneer lawman took his paramour and her little dog, a Chihuahua named Santa Ana, with him.

Not long after arriving in Los Angeles, Burrill went on a business trip to San Pedro. Upon his return, he was discreetly informed that Doña Concha had run off and married a gambler named Henry Lewis. Instead of flying into a rage or falling into a depression, Burrill anxiously inquired as to the whereabouts and well-being of Santa Ana. It seems that the diminutive dog was more important to him than Doña Concha ever was. Sheriff's department historian Dr. Frank Emerson claimed that the good-looking frontiersman soon

*Artist's conception of the county's first
Sheriff, George Burrill.*
— LOS ANGELES COUNTY SHERIFF'S
DEPARTMENT ARCHIVES

found another companion. The Los Angeles widow Refugia Cassanova attracted Burrill's attention and the two were soon married.[1] (It should be noted that Emerson's protégé, Eunice Crittenden, contended that Cassanova and Doña Concha were the same person.)[2]

George Thompson Burrill was elected the first Sheriff of Los Angeles on April 1, 1850, mostly due to the fact that he made a strong and lasting impression on everyone he met. Burrill's demeanor and appearance were exceptionally well-polished, especially for a rough-and-tumble frontier town like Los Angeles. He was a fastidious man and meticulous in his ways. The 40-year-old sheriff preferred to be called by his middle name, Thompson—he did not like to be called Tom or Tommy, simply Thompson. Burrill was tall and clean-shaven with a long handlebar mustache. The sheriff was never seen in public without his infantry dress sword, which he wore religiously on his side. The blade was not just a prop for display to the public; it was a symbol of authority—and a deadly weapon. It could also be used as backup when guns misfired or had spent their ammunition. On at least one occasion he used it to prod a prisoner on the way to court who was moving along at a snail's pace.

Sheriff Burrill appointed Elijah T. Moulton as his first deputy. The deputy directly subordinate to the sheriff is sometimes referred to as undersheriff. Moulton was a Canadian who had immigrated to California with one of the Jim Bridger expeditions, and had fought in the Mexican war under Major Fremont. Elijah served with Burrill during the entire time that the sheriff held office. After finishing his stint as deputy, Moulton started a small dairy business in East Los Angeles. He reached the zenith of his political career when he was elected to the City Council in 1860.[3] Moulton Avenue in East Los Angeles is named after him.[4]

As sheriff, Burrill was obligated to carry out the orders of the recently formed District Court and the local Court of Sessions as well. The former was presided over by Judge Oliver S. Wetherby and the latter by Judge Augustin Olvera. Sheriff Burrill's collateral job of county tax collector kept him extremely busy. This added responsibility compounded the difficulty of managing day-to-day law enforcement and jailing duties. Burrill traveled throughout the massive county to levy taxes and bring them back to Los Angeles. This was no small feat, considering that in 1850 Los Angeles County was eight times the size it is now. It consisted of what are now Ventura, Riverside, San Bernardino, and Orange Counties.

Jailer Samuel Whiting, who was paid $7.50 a day, assisted the sheriff with prisoner care and feeding. When Mr. Whiting required a relief jailer, he had to pay the guard out of his own pocket. The going rate for assistants was $3.00 a night. Jailer Whiting was directed to feed each prisoner at the cost of 50 cents a day (Indians 25 cents). The meal was to include 12 cents worth of bread or its equivalent in rice and beans. The remaining 38 cents was to be spent on "good meat."[5]

The first county jail was located on a hill west of Main Street and south of Arcadia Street above the Lafayette Hotel. It was a one-room adobe building with a heavy log in the middle of it. Anchored in the log were thick iron staples, into which chains were fastened. The chains were shackled to the inmate's wrists to prevent his escape. If a prisoner wanted to attempt a jailbreak, he would have to figure out a way to drag the log with him.

The door was a simple rawhide curtain. Because they were considered inferior to other prisoners, Indian inmates were chained to a log outside of the jail. It was said that, for the right amount of money, the guards would look the other way during an "escape." In October 1850, the grand jury released the following report:

The county's first jail was located on a hill above the Lafayette Hotel. – Security Pacific Collection / Los Angeles Public Library

Upon a personal examination of the jail, we find it entirely unfit for the purpose for which it is used, the walls are constructed of adobes which are of so frail a nature, that they may be easily pierced in any part with a knife or sharp stick, the roof is composed of pitch and earth, supported by reeds which can easily be cut with a knife, no other resistance being offered to the exit of prisoners at the top; it seems it is entirely unventilated, all the prisoners for whatever cause imprisoned are crowded together in a vitiated atmosphere destructive of health, more suitable to the dark ages.[6]

In 1851, Sam Whiting took a job as city marshal and George Robinson was offered the position of county jailer. Unfortunately, the $7.50-a-day salary was not enough to satisfy Mr. Robinson. After only a short while on the job, he was indicted by the grand jury:

> The mayor, city marshal and jailer of Los Angeles were indicted by the grand jury for selling out the services of Indians arrested for minor offenses and dividing the funds thus received. The jailer (George Robinson) was also charged with such negligence that it was altogether a matter of their own choice whether prisoners remained in jail or not. In one case he furnished meals to the prisoner to effect his escape.[7]

The case went no further than the grand jury. Toward the end of his term in office, Burrill accepted an appointment as Justice of the Peace for the pueblo of Los Angeles. To his dismay, he discovered that the infant state's constitution called for elections to be held in September. This meant that Sheriff, now Judge, Burrill had to serve double-duty for five months until the next sheriff could take office. Burrill took on this challenge without much complaint, however, as he was being paid handsomely.

After leaving office, Judge Burrill sat on the bench and dispensed justice for a few years, until he became ill. At the age of forty-six he was no longer able to work. Thompson Burrill died in Los Angeles on February 7, 1856. Among his personal effects was an autographed picture of the famous "Swedish Nightingale" singer Jenny Lind.[8] Miss Lind toured the United States during 1850-1851. She performed in ninety-two cities during her record-breaking tour, and the public simply could not get enough of her.[9] Lind must have made a lasting impression on the sheriff, too, for he surely attended one of those memorable concerts. How he maneuvered backstage in order to obtain her autograph is another mystery altogether.

The Lugo/Irving Party Incident

Hundreds of crimes occurred during Sheriff Burrill's year and a half tenure in office, including at least thirty-one murders. Of these crimes, one double homicide case in particular, the Lugo/Irving Party incident, proved to be the most challenging and controversial.

*Don Antonio Lugo owned the massive
Rancho San Bernardino. He defended
his grandsons who were put on trial
for murder.* — HUNTINGTON LIBRARY

It is also the most interesting and well-documented crime of his term, and serves as an excellent example of the extreme prejudice, racism, and violence of the times.

In January 1851, a band of thirty Ute Indians raided the immense Rancho San Bernardino and made off with several hundred horses. The owner, Don Antonio Maria Lugo, responded by hiring a band of friendly Cahuilla Indians to pursue the rustlers. The band, which was led by Chief Juan Antonio, joined forces with Antonio's son, Jose Maria, and several vaqueros and local ranchers. Antonio's grandchildren—Francisco, known as "Chico," age 18, and Benito, age 16—also accompanied the posse.

The vaqueros trailed the bandits into the Cajon pass, where they ran across two teamsters who were headed toward Los Angeles.[10] The teamsters were camped out for the night. Patrick McSwiggin and "Sam," a Creek Indian, told the posse that they had seen the Indians heading north. They mistakenly told the Lugos that the Indians were only lightly armed with bows and arrows. The Lugos spent the night in an area near present-day Victorville and caught up to the Utes the following day. To their surprise, the posse discovered that the Utes were not just carrying bows and arrows—they were heavily armed with rifles. The Indians defeated the Californios in a deadly shootout in which one of Lugo's men was killed. The Utes escaped with all of the stolen horses in tow.

41

On January 26, the vaqueros retreated to the mouth of the Cajon Pass, where they camped out. Exhausted and demoralized, they went their separate ways and returned to their ranchos. In one account of the story Mariano Elisalde, Ysidro Higuera, Chico, Benito, and an unknown vaquero lagged behind the rest of the party. Benito and Chico were angry at what they believed was a deliberate attempt by the teamsters to get them killed.[11]

On the trail back home, the Lugo boys again came across McSwiggin on a mule and the Indian Sam driving the wagon. They engaged the pair in conversation and Chico asked Sam if he could see his rifle. The Indian refused, and then Chico asked whether the native wanted to swap rifles. When Sam made a sign that he did not understand, Chico drew his revolver. Ysidro Higuera later testified:

He fired the pistol at him and the other two fired. The Indian fell dead in the wagon. The white man then dismounted and ran behind the wagon to keep them from killing him. Then they took the white man out into the road. [Chico] Lugo shot the white man with his other pistol. Lugo shot first, then the others, including a man whose name Higuera did not know who had two pistols. Elisalde had a rifle. [Chico] Lugo tied the Indians feet and ordered Higuera to tie a rope around the white man's feet and drag him out of the road, which he did. Higuera dragged him some distance off the right side of the road. [Benito] Lugo fastened a rope to the Indian's legs, hauled him out of the wagon and hauled him some distance to the left of the road. [Chico] Lugo told me not to say anything about the matter. The murder was committed between 8 and 9 of morning. [Chico] Lugo brought away the Indian rifle.[12]

Three days after the murder, a troop of U.S. soldiers from Company A, 2nd Infantry, were traveling through the Cajon Pass and discovered the bodies of the victims.

In the Californio account of the story, Ysidro Higuera was a renegade and a thief from Sonora. Twenty witnesses backed the Lugo brothers' side of the story, testifying that the brothers had not committed the crime. The boys themselves denied any wrongdoing.[13]

A coroner's jury presided over by Justice of the Peace Jonathon R. Scott indicted the Lugos for murder. The Californios became outraged for several reasons. First, Judge Scott had taken the word of a thief over that of a respected Californio family. Second, prior to the murders, Jailer George Robinson's wife had been a guest at the Lugo residence. During a visit, Robinson had become involved in a physical altercation with his wife. Don Lugo and Chico had broken up the fight by separating the couple. The jailer had been humiliated, and he developed a deep-seated hatred for the Lugo family. He had filed charges, and Chico and Don Lugo had been fined $2.50 each for their "crime" of assault against him. The Lugos believed that Robinson had persuaded Higuera to lie about the murders in order to get revenge.

Jose Lugo admitted that he and his men had seen the teamsters but asserted that they had not murdered them. A coroner's jury indicted the Lugo brothers, along with Mariano Elisalde and Ysidro Higuera. The first three were arrested and brought to jail. Higuera was later arrested for horse stealing and brought to the Los Angeles County Jail. Higuera turned state's evidence and explained his story, as noted earlier. Jose Lugo hired Joseph Lancaster Brent, the best lawyer in town, for $21,000, or $450,000 in today's money, to get his sons acquitted. Brent believed that the boys were innocent and began to prepare their defense.[14]

Brent's plan was to prove that since the county jailer was an enemy of the Lugos and had convinced Higuera to lie about the incident, Higuera's testimony should be dismissed. The whole community was in an uproar, divided along racial lines. At this point, another twist was thrown into the plot that further complicated an already complex and explosive situation.

In April, ex-Texas Ranger John "Red" Irving was leading a band of 25 desperadoes down to Mexico on a robbery and plundering expedition. Irving was described as "tall and spare, with steely blue eyes and a red beard."[15] When the Irving party rode into town, they gave the locals the weak excuse that they were on their way to Sonora to fight Indians at the request of the Mexican government.

Joseph Brent defended the Lugo boys in court. During the civil war he joined the Confederate Army and was given the rank of Brigadier General. — HUNTINGTON LIBRARY

Rumors of an attack began to spread when the band made camp on the outskirts of town. The *Los Angeles Star* reported that the outlaws "excited the terror of the citizens and many offenses were charged upon them."[16] When Irving learned about Jose Lugo's situation, he offered to manage the escape of the Don's sons from jail for $10,000. Don Lugo refused and went to his lawyer for help.[17]

Brent persuaded the judge to release both boys on $20,000 bail. When the attorney returned to his office, George Evans, John Irving's lieutenant, greeted him. Evans told the lawyer that his gang had been promised $10,000 by the Lugos to "break the boys out of the calaboose." He warned Brent that, if the brothers left the jail without Irving getting his money, they would be killed. Brent went to Jose Lugo for clarification. Lugo explained that he had made no such deal with the outlaw. As the two men were concluding their business, Irving's gang rode up to the jail compound.

Townspeople began to crowd around the area, expecting to witness a gun battle. Someone ran and called for the sheriff. Thompson Burrill realized that he was in dire straits, severely outnumbered and outgunned. Brent told the sheriff that, if he tried to transport the boys now, they would be slaughtered. Thinking quickly, the attorney asked for and received permission to continue the bail release procedures on the following day. He then advised the Californios to gather a posse to oppose the Irving gang. Vicente Elisondo, Mariano's brother, rapidly went about the business of sounding the alarm. Throughout the night, ranch hands began to gather by the jail. By morning, seventy-five armed vaqueros had taken up a strategic position in ravines near the compound.[18]

As luck would have it, a troop of fifty U.S. soldiers from San Diego was on routine patrol near the area. Elated by his good fortune, Burrill immediately asked their commanding officer, Major Edward H. Fitzgerald, for assistance.[19] The major was more than happy to oblige, and dispatched his men to the jail forthwith. The soldiers formed a protective circle around Elisalde, the Lugo boys, and the sheriff. The dragoons escorted them safely into the courtroom, where the tension inside was at a boiling point. Red Irving's men took up most of the seats inside, while friends of the Lugo's waited outside. The peacekeeping soldiers were situated between the groups. All three factions were armed to the teeth, and the court was jammed to maximum occupancy.

Irving was furious when he realized that his scheme had failed. He turned on his heel and bolted from the room. The judge ordered the boys freed on bail, and they were escorted home by a contingent of fifty vaqueros. In celebration of the day's events, Brent went to the Bella Union Hotel to dine in style. As he was preparing to eat, an intoxicated Irving walked up to the table and told the attorney that he had no hard feelings against him. However, he blamed Major Fitzgerald, and he threatened to "pay him back." He told Brent that he was going to get even with the Lugos or "see himself in hell."[20] On May 23, the outlaw rode out of town.

The gangsters galloped into Rancho Chino, stealing cattle and horses as they went. From there, the party split up, half of them riding toward the Colorado River and the others toward Rancho Lugo. Word of the gang's whereabouts spread rapidly throughout the Southland. A posse of fifty men was formed in Los Angeles under the command of General Joshua Bean, and a messenger was sent to Rancho Lugo to warn of an impending attack. Upon hearing the news, the entire Lugo clan abandoned the ranch, taking with them their most valuable possessions.

The three servants who had been left behind told Irving that the family had gone to a rodeo. Irving and his men ransacked what remained in the house, pilfering $2,000 in valuables. Soon after departing the rancho, the outlaws were greeted by Chief Juan

Antonio and twenty of his Cahuilla warriors. The chief, who had been hired by the Lugos, gave chase but did not engage in direct combat. Chief Juan used his superior knowledge of the terrain to his advantage. Although his warriors were armed only with bows and arrows, the Indians now outnumbered Irving's gang by two to one and they subsequently maneuvered the bandits into the foothills.[21]

When the Cahuilla posse pressed harder, Irving began to panic. He fled into a box canyon near Yucaipa where one hundred Cahuilla warriors were patiently lying in ambush at the top of the steep canyon walls. They showered the outlaws with a fusillade of arrows and stones, killing Irving and all but one member of his gang, who escaped to tell the story.[22]

After news of the incident broke, many white men were outraged that Indians had killed the Irving party only because of some stolen property. Californios, on the other hand, felt that the bandits had got what they deserved. A coroner's jury proclaimed that Lugo and the Indians had overstepped their authority. Jose Lugo defended his position, stating that he was *Juez del Campo*, and that by law he was authorized to use force against cattle thieves. He said that the Indians were merely acting on his authority as "policemen." County Attorney Benjamin Hayes calmed the Anglos by convincing the jury that the killings were justifiable.[23]

The Lugo boys remained free on bail, but their story does not end here. They would soon join forces with a notorious bandit named Salomon Pico.

The Los Angeles Rangers

During those early lawless days some community leaders stepped forward to assist the beleaguered sheriff and marshal. A Mexican War veteran and physician named Alexander W. Hope was one of these men. Hope opened a drug store in Los Angeles in 1848 and was one of the first Anglo physicians to settle in the pueblo. He began to lead posses when General Joshua Bean's state militia required troop augmentation to cover the vast southern California frontier. The militia was searching for Indian raiders from Utah who were stealing cattle and horses from wealthy Californio ranchos. On June 4, 1851, this appeared in the *Los Angeles Star*:

A scouting party commanded by Dr. Hope left Gen. Bean's camp about three weeks ago, intending to be absent five days. They returned yesterday and reported having had an engagement with the Pah-Utah's (Paiutes) in which thirteen Indians were killed. Dr. Hope and his men, only five in number, were in a natural fort when they were attacked by the Indians who gathered in great numbers.[24]

Dr. Hope's success as a leader made him a natural choice to command the county's first organized posse. In response to the city's spiraling crime problem, Mayor Benjamin Wilson appointed Hope to serve as "Chief of Police" to head a 100-man, all-volunteer force. The company-sized group was somewhat effective in deterring crime but they were slow to mobilize. Often, by the time the posse rode out of town, their suspects were long gone. City leaders recognized that a militarized, highly mobile, and rapidly deployable force was required to track down the elusive desperadoes. On August 1, 1853, the Los Angeles Rangers were formed, with Dr. Alexander Hope as their Commanding Officer.

The Rangers enlisted 100 men during their first meeting at Billy Getman's saloon. Of this group, twenty-five were selected to be full-time posse members, ready to respond at a moment's notice. The men lived together in a military-style barracks. They did not receive pay but all of their supplies, including horses,

Mayor Benjamin (Don Benito) Wilson asked Dr. Alexander Hope to help him solve the crime problem in Los Angeles by forming the Los Angeles Rangers. – SECURITY PACIFIC COLLECTION / LOS ANGELES PUBLIC LIBRARY

were donated. The only item that the rangers had to purchase was their own firearms. The Spanish lances that the town issued were mostly useless in a gun battle, so the relics were usually left behind at the barracks.

The Rangers were extremely effective in tracking down criminals, as reported in the *Southern Californian* newspaper in November, 1854:

> Los Angeles Rangers—In our last week's issue we regret to say that we neglected the active and prompt assistance rendered by the Los Angeles Rangers in assisting in the arrest of some of the most dangerous desperadoes in this country, and who are, no doubt, in some way connected with the brutal murder of Mr. Ellington, of the Monte. . . . Our only excuse to offer to the Rangers is that the actions of this company are so prompt, active and secret, that in almost all cases the company is out on scout, returned, and the prisoner arraigned , before our citizens are aware of an outrage being committed.[25]

These brave men put many in long hours in the saddle hunting down outlaws in all types of terrain and in all kinds of weather. The citizens of Los Angeles became defensive when aspersions were cast against their volunteers. The *Southern Californian* reported:

> We regret to see any unkind reflections upon the Rangers. They have always evinced a commendable willingness to do their duty in bringing violators of the law to merited justice. Public good and public protection are all they have brought, which to say the least of it, should command our thanks.[26]

To show their appreciation, the townsfolk threw a Rangers anniversary party on August 6, 1854. A toast was offered to Captain Hope at the Bella Union Hotel: "The peaceful citizen, the fearless and energetic soldier and firm friend—may his shadow never be less!"[27]

Dr. Alexander Hope passed away on January 17, 1856, from a sudden illness. On January 19, the *Los Angeles Star* commented:

> Dr. Hope was a useful and respected citizen—energetic, prompt and always willing to render a service to his fellow citizens at a moments notice. As a private man, he was hospitable, generous and kind. He leaves many warm friends to regret his unexpected death.[28]

Sheriff James R. Barton, September 1851–October 1855

James R. Barton hailed from Howard County, Missouri. The future sheriff immigrated to Mexico in 1841, and moved on to Los Angeles in 1843. Barton was a carpenter by trade and a veteran of the Mexican War. His partner in the construction business was a rugged 49er named William Nordholt, who continued the business on his own after Barton was elected sheriff. Barton was the first treasurer of Masonic Lodge #42 F. and A.M., one of Los Angeles' earliest fraternal organizations. The hard-working carpenter married Lucinda Rowland, daughter of John Rowland, leader of the renowned Rowland-Workman party that migrated to California in 1841. Lucinda died childless shortly after their marriage, and Barton did not remarry. Lucinda's younger brother, William, eventually became the 11th Sheriff of Los Angeles County.

James Barton was elected sheriff in September, 1851. He selected William B. Osburn to be undersheriff. Osburn, who came to Los Angeles in 1847, was an energetic man with a wide array of business interests and skills, including physician, postmaster, photographer, drugstore owner, florist, auctioneer, and school superintendent. Barton was re-elected six times during his career, which sadly ended with his murder on January 23, 1857. Besides City Marshal Jack Whalen, who was killed on December 7, 1853, Sheriff Barton and three members of his posse were the first United States lawmen in Los Angeles County to lose their lives in the line of duty.[29]

One of the sheriff's earliest challenges came on November 12, 1851. A new judge had just revoked the Lugo brothers' bail, and a warrant had been issued for their arrest. Upon hearing that they were wanted men, the siblings decided to steer clear of the nascent American legal system. The pair surmised that their chances of surviving as fugitives were better than waiting to be lynched by vigilantes, so without hesitation they joined up with the notorious outlaw Salomon Pico. At the time, Pico was one of the most famous desperadoes in California.

Pico had been born to a respectable Californio family near San Juan Bautista on September 5, 1821. His cousin was the former California governor and Los Angeles resident Pio Pico. His other cousin was General Andres Pico, who successfully fought the Americans at the battle of San Pascual. Salomon had lost his land to the *Yanquis* when he was younger, and he vowed that he would "kill every American" falling into his hands.[30] Pico once bragged that he had killed thirty-nine Americans, so one would assume that the last person with whom he would become a partner would be a white man. Oddly enough, his *compadre* in crime was just that—a desperado named William Hall. Pico was not bashful about showing off his trophies. He was known to cut off his victim's ears and place them on a necklace, which he displayed around his horse's neck.

In late summer 1851, Pico was wanted for horse theft. He jumped bail and left his partner, who was captured and hanged by Monterey vigilantes on August 10. Pico worked his way south from San Jose to Los Angeles, where he joined forces with Chico and Benito Lugo. The boys complained to Pico that white lawyers in Los Angeles were "railroading" them. They told him that they wanted to do something about their predicament but they did not know what. Pico sympathized with the brothers and assisted them by devising a bold plot. The trio galloped off, heading directly to Los Angeles— and the judge's office.[31]

County Attorney Benjamin Hayes was helping to prosecute the case against the Lugo brothers.[32] He was working alone in the judge's office when he heard riders dismounting outside. The lawyer went out to see who it was, and was met by the three bandits. Salomon Pico fired a round that blew Benjamin's hat off his head. The quick-thinking lawyer shouted "You scoundrel!" and slammed the door closed. He took cover and waited for the bandits' reaction. When he heard no more shots, he moved back to the door and pushed hard on the portal, hoping to knock the assassins to the ground. The door gave way with a crash, which panicked the desperados and caused them to flee.

Barton formed a posse and chased after Pico and the Lugos. He caught up with them ten miles from the pueblo, and a nasty gun battle ensued. The Sheriff and his deputies fired at least twelve rounds each, and one of Barton's bullets struck Pico in the arm. However, the posse abandoned their hopes of making an arrest because the outlaws were more heavily-armed. Barton realized that staying in the fight meant certain death, so he ordered his posse to return to Los Angeles at full speed.[33]

Realizing that he now had the advantage, Salomon pressed the sheriff for half a mile, continually firing at him from a distance of at least 150 yards. As the posse neared the pueblo, the three outlaws broke off their pursuit, allowing the lawmen to reach town safely.

Sheriff Barton: Fearless or Reckless?

On July 4, 1852, Barton was called to the "Higuerra House" saloon in the Calle de Los Negros regarding a disturbance. Soon after the sheriff arrived, he got into an altercation with gambler Joseph Caddick and several others. Instead of backing off and going for help, he provoked the troublemakers by asking them to step out into the street. Caddick told the sheriff that he had better "defend himself," as he simultaneously fired his pistol. Barton returned fire, and at least three or four shots were exchanged. One of Barton's rounds punched a hole in Caddick's right lung, causing the gambler to lose the gunfight and nearly die. Judge Mallard acquitted Barton, saying that the sheriff had acted in self-defense.

It was actions like this that caused some Angelenos to be concerned about Barton's behavior. Harris Newmark said that Barton was "brave but reckless."[34] There is plenty of evidence to demonstrate that the sheriff pressed his luck on more than one occasion. Today, the sheriff's straightforward but heavy-handed approach to law enforcement seems a paradox to many. In frontier times however, his actions were not uncommon. Historian Ronald Woolsey commented, "Barton was a confusing symbol, inextricably linked to controversy, reflecting the excesses of police power associated with frontier lawlessness, and yet the best hope of stability and order on the frontier, despite Hispanic resentment."[35] Early sheriffs were often "caught between a rock and a hard place." Enforcing laws and easing racial tension was a complex job, made even more difficult by the lack of resources and the primitive nature of pioneer life.

Emboldened by his victory against Barton's posse, Pico initiated with renewed confidence a crime spree that continued through the fall of 1852. His band of desperados ravaged southern California ranches, stealing horses and cattle at will. These comments appeared in the *San Francisco Daily Alta California* newspaper:

> Already the laws cannot be enforced against any Californians of influence. Although the Sheriff, with several posses, has endeavored to arrest some of the Lugos under a bench warrant, he is unable to do it, for the fact that they range from ranch to ranch, over an immense area, secreted by their "parientes" and "compadres." To arrest those who secrete them, as accessories after the fact, would fill our jail with the most venerable old men, women, and young men, and produce at once war to the knife, and from the knife to the hilt, between Californian and American. . . . It is said that Salomon Pico ranges with impunity in our county, secreted by the rancheros; and if his own countrymen are to be believed, he is an "incarnate devil." That he was concerned with the Lugos in the attempt to assassinate Benjamin Hayes, is generally conceded by Californians.[36]

The Lugos were never brought to trial for the murders of Patrick McSwiggin and Sam the Indian. Judge Augustin Olvera dismissed the charges against them for "lack of evidence."[37] The same held true for their attempted murder of Benjamin Hayes and the shootout with the sheriff. These incidents greatly inflamed the tempers of the Anglo community. They felt that the legal system was wholly inadequate and an insult to their sense of justice. The Lugo case, in particular, was the catalyst for the formation of the Rangers, thereby putting Los Angeles vigilantism on the map.

Salomon Pico fled to Mexico where, several years later, a pioneer named Alfred Green picked up his story:

> In 1856 I was at the port of Mazatlan, when word was sent to the English Consul at that place that an Englishman had been killed at La Paz, and they wanted a war vessel sent there. It seems that Salomon Pico, who had found his way to La Paz, on entering a restaurant there, saw a man sitting at a table eating his meal, and supposing that he was an American, drew his knife and killed him on the spot.[38]

The governor of Baja California ordered Pico and several other desperadoes to be arrested. Upon their capture, they were executed by firing squad on May 1, 1860.[39]

In 1853, Sheriff Barton lost 20,000 square miles of his jurisdiction due to the formation of San Bernardino County. The county was sparsely populated and mostly desert, so its loss was of no great concern to the Sheriff or the Board of Supervisors.

Although it got off to a slow and shaky start, the wheels of the Los Angeles County legal system began to turn. The justice system received a major boost with the construction of a new jail in 1853. The new brick county jail was described as follows:

> The jail is a two-story brick building. The first floor is occupied as city prison or lock-up, and is divided into two apartments, for males and females. The upper story is the county prison. The joists which support this floor are traversed with strong iron bars throughout, about six inches apart. Over these is laid down thick planking, then a covering of sheet iron, and over all planks again, forming a floor which it would be impossible to cut through without detection. The prison comprises a large room, well ventilated, and six cells, deficient in that respect. The partitions are made of heavy timber, well secured by iron clamps. The doors are massive iron gratings.[40]

Although there were attempts to escape from this jail, there is no documentation that anyone ever actually succeeded. On February 13, 1854, Los Angeles County had its first legal execution at the jail. Ignacio Herrera killed a young Californio man in a love triangle dispute. Ignacio was "freed from this worldly existence" as hundreds of Angelenos watched.

Judge Roy Bean and Joaquin Murrieta

There are times in history when the lives of famous and infamous men brush up against each other, and only from a historical perspective can one see how close the two men came to making contact. On the night of November 7, 1852, an incident occurred a few miles northeast of the pueblo in which this very scenario took place. One of the most written-about and notorious outlaws in California history was Joaquin Murrieta, and one of the most famous frontier jurists ever to sit on the bench was Judge Roy Bean.

Joaquin Murrieta was a Sonoran miner who came to the California gold fields with his family in 1848. Legend has it that Joaquin's claim was jumped and that he was tied to a tree and beaten while his wife was raped before his eyes and his half-brother Jesus was murdered. Jealous white miners, who were working the same gold diggings as Joaquin, supposedly committed all of these crimes.

While the legend makes for a tragic, heart-wrenching story, it is most likely not historically accurate.[41] Historian Remi Nadeau concurred, "The evidence of Joaquin's grievances is nothing more than hearsay."[42] There is no documentation of Jesus being murdered, and Murrieta family history claims that he was actually alive and living in Mexico in 1860. There really is no way to know whether Joaquin's wife was raped, as documentation from that time is lacking. However, the claim that Anglos mistreated Joaquin is not only believable but likely, as racism in the gold fields was widely prevalent at the time.

The first family member to turn to crime was Joaquin's brother-in-law, Claudio Feliz. Claudio started his criminal career in 1849 at age sixteen by stealing gold nuggets. Feliz quickly stepped up the ladder to armed robbery. His thirst for riches motivated him to gather a group of bandits to assist him with his endeavors. Joaquin is rumored to have joined Claudio's band, which terrorized settlers by committing brazen acts of robbery in the east San Francisco Bay area and Yuba and Sonora Counties. In late 1852, Claudio was gunned down by a sheriff's posse near the Rancho El Tucho on the Salinas River.[43]

The reins of leadership passed to Murrieta, who headed south and temporarily partnered with Salomon Pico. On November 7, Joaquin and his girlfriend, Ana Benitez, went to San Gabriel to see a Mexican acrobatic show called the *maroma*. After the show, they visited a friend, Juan Rico. The couple was spending the night at Juan's adobe when Joaquin's peaceful evening was suddenly interrupted. Through the door, Murrieta heard the sounds of a drunken man arguing with an Indian woman. He took his pistol and went outside to investigate.

The drunken man was Joshua Bean, Major General of the State Militia. He was a Mexican War veteran and Indian fighter who operated a nearby saloon. The major wanted to take his thirteen year old girlfriend, Cristovala, to bed, but she had her infant child with her and refused.[44] The two commenced arguing; Bean was pulling Cristovala's hair when he heard footsteps in the dark. Gunshots rang out and a bullet slammed into his chest. The general reeled from the blow. After firing three wild shots in return, he staggered toward Juan Rico's adobe calling, "Rico, Rico, Rico!"[45] Cristovala screamed when a bullet struck her in the foot; her baby began to cry. She watched Bean stagger off toward Rico's house; soon thereafter, she was taken to Senor Pena's abode, where she received medical attention. The scrappy Indian fighter, who also happened to be the first Anglo alcalde of San Diego, agonized through the night. He was taken to his saloon, where he died at 2:00 a.m. the following day. His Colt Navy six-shooter, serial number 1507, was never found.[46] Vigilantes arrested several members of Salomon Pico's gang and hanged three of them, but Joaquin had headed north with stolen horses.

Some researchers calculate that Murrieta shot Bean upon discovering that the general was trying to take advantage of a woman. However, this has never been proven, and others argue that the killer was possibly Cristovala herself.

After the shooting, Joaquin and his desperadoes met with the notorious Three-Fingered Jack Garcia. Together, they went on a 9-month bloody rampage in northern California. Captain Harry Love and his upstate Rangers tracked the band to Cantua Creek, south of

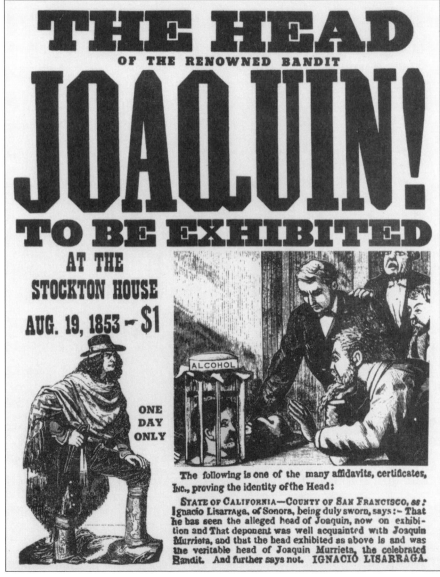

THE HEAD

OF THE RENOWNED BANDIT

JOAQUIN!

TO BE EXHIBITED

AT THE STOCKTON HOUSE

AUG. 19, 1853 — $1

ONE DAY ONLY

ALCOHOL

The following is one of the many affidavits, certificates, &c., proving the identity of the Head:

STATE OF CALIFORNIA—COUNTY OF SAN FRANCISCO, ss: Ignacio Lisarraga, of Sonora, being duly sworn, says:— That he has seen the alleged head of Joaquin, now on exhibition and That deponent was well acquainted with Joaquin Murrieta, and that the head exhibited as above is and was the veritable head of Joaquin Murrieta, the celebrated Bandit. And further says not. IGNACIO LISARRAGA.

Outlaw Joaquin Murrieta's head was put on display in northern California.
— SECURITY PACIFIC COLLECTION / LOS ANGELES PUBLIC LIBRARY

where Interstate 5 and Highway 33 intersect today. Rangers Billy Henderson and John White chased the desperado into the arroyo bottom, where they gunned him down. The outlaw's last words were *"No tire mas, Yo soy muerte* [Don't shoot anymore, I'm dead]."[47]

Fauntleroy "Roy" Bean had followed his brother, Joshua, to San Diego. Roy stayed behind, near Los Angeles, after Josh left to start up his saloon business in San Gabriel. Several months later, on February 24, 1852, Roy was involved in a duel where he shot a Scotsman named Collins in the leg. The *San Diego Herald* stated:

Shooting Affair — Mr. Roy Bean was held to bail on last Tuesday, for shooting a man, whose name we did not learn. The wound is in the leg, and he was shot while on his horse, and in the act of escaping from Bean, who had a moment previous snapped the pistol at his head. Private difficulty was the cause.[48]

San Diego Sheriff Haraszthy arrested both men, but Roy escaped within a few weeks. He then rode to San Gabriel, where he joined his brother, who was proprietor of the Headquarters Saloon. Seven months later, Josh was dead. Like his sibling, Roy was a hard-drinking, rough-and-ready frontiersman. He inherited his brother's business and during his travels he may well have bumped into Joaquin and his men. Roy eventually settled in Los Angeles and joined the Rangers. He became friends with Horace Bell, who wrote:

I rode up to Headquarters and was met by a very handsome black bearded young man by the name of Roy Bean, brother and successor of General Josh Bean. The General had been proprietor of the Headquarters, the first grog shop of the place. Roy was dressed in an elegant Mexican costume, with a pair of revolvers in his belt, while a Bowie knife was neatly sheathed in one of his red-topped boots.[49]

By 1855, the good times at the Headquarters Saloon were coming to an end. He may have left for bankruptcy reasons, but Bean gave his own more romantic reason for leaving. He claimed that after the smoke cleared from a nasty gunfight, he realized that he had killed a Mexican official. The fight was over a pretty *senorita*, and the official's friends decided to take justice into their own hands by hanging Bean from a tree. As luck would have it, the rope stretched and Roy managed to support himself by touching his toes to the ground. The woman that he was fighting over came to his rescue and cut him down. After thanking the *senorita*, Bean discreetly moved to New Mexico to work for his other brother, Sam, as a bartender. He carried an ugly scar on his neck for the rest of his life.[50]

When the Civil War broke out, Bean scouted for the Confederate Army. In 1863, he realized that he could make a profit by smuggling southern cotton overland to Matamoros, Mexico, where British ships would trade for money and European goods. In 1866, with his war business at an end, he settled in San Antonio, Texas, married eighteen year old Virginia Chavez, and had five children. Roy's drinking, wild lifestyle and failed business ventures did not suit married life very well, so, in 1882, he left his family and moved to Vinegaroon, Texas. He found work as a saloonkeeper and when the state offered him a position as Justice of the Peace, Roy jumped at the chance. He moved to the small tent city of Langtry, Texas, and set up shop.

The *Smithsonian* magazine commented:

By Gobs! There was nothing judicious about Judge Roy Bean. Doffing his saloon apron, the grizzled barkeep dons a dirty alpaca coat, sits himself down behind the bar, draws a pistol and bangs for silence using the butt as a gavel. "Order, by Gobs! This honorable court is now in session, and if any galoot wants a snort before we start, let him step up to the bar and name his pizen (poison)." The good judge had never seen the inside of a law school. His only book was the 1879 *Revised Statutes of Texas*. But the self-styled "Law West of the Pecos" knew how to hold court. There, in his Jersey Lilly saloon in the minuscule West Texas town of Langtry, Roy Bean doled out drinks and his own brand of justice for more than 20 years.[51]

Judge Roy Bean, the self-declared "Law West of the Pecos," holding court at his Jersey Lilly Saloon.
— NATIONAL ARCHIVES AND RECORDS ADMINISTRATION

Horace Bell stayed in touch with Bean even after the then-future judge moved to Texas. Bell disagreed with the *Smithsonian* when it came to which law book the judge used. He quoted Bean from a letter:

They send me the Texas statutes, codes and so forth every year, but I never read them. All the law I want I take from the compiled laws of the State of California. They are good enough for any state, they are good enough for anybody, they are good enough for me. I administer the law upon the authority of that book and don't need any other.[52]

Judge Bean is most famous for his courtroom witticisms, a few of which are listed below:

It is the judgment of this court that you are hereby tried and convicted of illegally and unlawfully committing certain grave offenses against the peace and dignity of the State of Texas, particularly in my bailiwick; I fine you two dollars; then get the hell out of here and never show yourself in this court again. That's my rulin.'[53]

Without making excuses for Judge Bean, this next quote is prefaced by the fact that several local residents apparently threatened to burn down his saloon if he found the Anglo suspect guilty: "Gentlemen, I find the law very explicit on murdering your fellow man, but there's nothing here about killing a Chinaman. Case dismissed."[54]

Another famous Bean quote, notable for its candor, was, "I know the law . . . I am its greatest transgressor."[55]

The following quote is attributed to Judge Bean, but the fact that a justice of the peace generally had no business trying a death penalty case raises the question of its genuineness.

> You have been tried by twelve good men and true, not of your peers but as high above you as heaven is of hell, and they have said you are guilty. Time will pass and seasons will come and go. Spring with its wavin' green grass and heaps of sweet-smellin' flowers on every hill and in every dale. Then sultry Summer, with her shimmerin' heat-waves on the baked horizon. And Fall, with her yeller harvest moon and the hills growin' brown and golden under a sinkin' sun. And finally Winter, with its bitin', whinin' wind, and all the land will be mantled with snow. But you won't be here to see any of 'em; not by a damn sight, because it's the order of this court that you be took to the nearest tree and hanged by the neck til you're dead, dead, dead, you olive-colored son of a billy goat.[56]

Judge Roy Bean is without question one of the most famous frontier jurists that this country has ever known, but few people know that he was also a Los Angeles Ranger, and one of the wildest and most colorful citizens in town. Most of Bean's tough brand of street justice was learned while living in southern California. He served as judge in Langtry until his death in 1903.

Crime and Vigilante Action

Late in 1854, Sheriff Barton unknowingly began to set in motion a series of events that would eventually lead to his untimely death. There are two basic accounts of this story. The first claims that Barton arrested Andres Fuentes (alias Fontes) for horse stealing. The second story adds an interesting twist, as narrated by Horace Bell:

Our angel sheriff was an unmarried man and lived in illicit intercourse with an Indian woman, who, for some alleged ill treatment, left him and went to a family residing on the east side of the river. Barton went for her and on her refusal to go with him violently seized and was dragging her away, when Andres happened to be riding along the road, interposed in favor of the woman, and Barton was constrained to desist. One or two days thereafter Andres, at the instance of the sheriff, was arrested on a charge of felony and was convicted and sent to San Quintin, and hence his desire to murder Sheriff Barton, and the cause that induced him to join the embryo revolution under Juan Flores.[57]

More than one historian has sought to make Barton out to be the "bad guy"; however, there is evidence to suggest that he was a man of moral character, as demonstrated by his behavior regarding his son. At the time, many frontiersmen had illegitimate children with Indian women, but few would have ever thought to make out a will testifying to this fact. Perhaps, Barton sensed his impending doom, for in an eerily prophetic will, drafted two-and-one-half years before his murder, he wrote:

Los Angeles August 24th, 1854. In the presence of the undersigned witnesses I hereby acknowledge Jose Santiago who was born on the 25th day of March A.D. 1854 of an Indian girl named Maria de la Espirita Santa to be my son and as such entitled to heir all property that may belong to me. J. R. Barton.[58]

The mere fact that Barton took the time to draft this document shows that, despite how he may have treated Maria, the sheriff cared for the welfare of his infant son. When an editor from the *Los Angeles Star* tried to blame Sheriff Barton for the county's crime problems, the *Southern Californian* responded: "We think his [editor's] remarks in reference to our officers are extremely unkind, for everyone who knows Sheriff Barton will award him the merit of being a very efficient officer."[59]

Horace Bell claims that while Fuentes was preparing for his prison departure, he threatened Barton, saying, "I am innocent. You put up this job on me. In two years, I will return and kill you."[60] Some claim that Fuentes was in love with the woman, and others say that he was her brother. Either way, the die was cast, and the sheriff's time on earth was running out.

Several months later, in 1855, Barton arrested a notorious and dangerous criminal named Juan Flores for stealing horses in Los Angeles. Flores was convicted and sentenced to three years at San Quentin. Juan and Andres met in prison and together they plotted revenge against the sheriff. Not long after Fuentes was released, Flores escaped with several of his compadres.

Meanwhile, Barton was too busy dealing with murderers and cutthroats to worry about horse thieves getting out of prison. On October 13, 1854, the sheriff and his deputies arrested Dave Brown for murdering Pink Clifford. Dave Brown was a notorious outlaw and member of the John Glanton gang in Mexico. An intoxicated Brown had gotten into a fight with Pinckney Clifford in one of the pueblo's livery stables, a fight which he won by stabbing Pinckney to death.

At the time of Brown's arrest, an angry crowd gathered outside the jail to lynch him. Ironically, Brown had been a member of the Los Angeles Rangers, but now his vigilante friends had turned against him. Mayor Stephen C. Foster appeased the crowd by promising that, if the courts did not find Brown guilty, he would resign and lead the lynching himself. A month later, Judge Hayes convicted Brown for murder and sentenced him to hang on January 12, 1855, along with another murderer, Felipe Alvitre, who had been convicted of murdering James Ellington in El Monte. Both men appealed to the California Supreme Court in Sacramento.

While the prisoners awaited their fate, other crimes were in progress. A Californio rode up to the front door of Mr. Cassin's abode and fired a round into the house. The bullet struck Mrs. Cassin in the left breast and killed her. The bandito was chased to the outskirts of town and gunned down. Murders like this only further inflamed hatred between Californios and Americans.

Alvitre and Brown both received stays of execution from the court. Unfortunately, for both prisoners, the mail was slow and inefficient. Sometimes it took as long as 52 days for mail to go from Sacramento to Los Angeles. Brown's reprieve arrived first, but there was none for Alvitre. Having no way of knowing that the second reprieve was on its way, the Californios became outraged. They believed that white men were being treated differently from them. They held a meeting and released the following statement:

> Whereas the time for the execution of Brown and Alvitre will have arrived by tomorrow . . . and as by some means Brown had received a respite and Alvitre none; and as they are both equally guilty—we the committee think they should both be executed at the same time and on the same day.[61]

Many Anglos felt the same way. The *Southern Californian* reported, "We believe that Brown and Alvitre inasmuch as they have alike been found guilty of a brutal murder—alike sentenced to undergo the penalty of death, their destinies should be united, and live or die together."[62]

On January 12, more than 2,000 armed men gathered around the gallows. All businesses were closed. Sheriff Barton asked the good citizens in town to help guard the jail. While most of them refused to assist, some actually stepped up to help.

At 3:00 p.m., Barton prepared to hang Alvitre before a huge crowd of angry spectators. The sheriff must have been a novice in the art of hanging, for he used a weak rope that broke when Alvitre's weight was placed on it. The murderer fell to the ground, grunting and writhing in pain. The crowd exploded in anger and began to stone the guards. Some shouted *"Arriba!, Arriba!"* for Alvitre to be put out of his misery.[63] In great haste, Barton and his men placed Alvitre back into the noose and hanged him. The crowd was stirred into a frenzy, and they shouted for Brown to be hanged immediately. All eyes turned towards the mayor.

Mayor Foster never actually believed that either one of the prisoners would receive a stay of execution. He was now trapped between two cultures and facing the decision of a lifetime.

Although a white man, Foster was married to Antonio Lugo's daughter, and was therefore Chico's and Benito's uncle. He did not have to think about his decision very long. The mayor resigned his position and agreed to lead the mob.[64] At 4:00 p.m., they "persuaded" Barton and his deputies to step aside.[65] The mob smashed in the jail doors and dragged Brown to the nearest corral gateway, where they strung up a rope. Before they hanged him, they asked whether he had any last words. The outlaw said that he wanted to be hanged by white men, not "a lot of greasers."[66] The *Los Angeles Southern Californian* told the story:

> There being no scaffold prepared, he was taken across to a large gateway opposite the courthouse, to the heavy cross-beam of which a rope was fastened, and a chair being placed beneath; Brown was elevated thereon, and the rope fixed about his neck, some time was allowed him during which he evinced the utmost coolness, recognizing and speaking to his acquaintances in the crowd, and reflecting in jocular terms upon the crowd who were engaged in his execution; he stated that he had been told that he killed Clifford, and supposed of course that he did, although he said that he had no recollection of it, or to that effect; perceiving that those about were ignorant of the method of preparing the rope, he called to an acquaintance and requested him to get some Americans who understood it, to hang him. Throughout the scene he manifested the most careless indifference and finally jumped off into eternity with the same coolness and hardihood as had characterized him through life.[67]

Newmark claimed that the above story was actually written several hours *before* Brown's hanging by newspaperman Billy Workman. Apparently, the steamer was leaving for San Francisco that same morning, so in order to get his story aboard ship in time, he took his best guess at how Brown would die! After Workman finished the article, he printed out a few extra copies for the locals. Some of the vigilantes witnessing Brown's execution read about it as they watched the event unfold. Newmark did not mention that there were any inconsistencies between Workman's article and the real event, so perhaps the newspaperman got the story right after all.

Two days later, Alvitre's stay of execution arrived. Mayor Foster did not really care, however, as he was soon re-elected in a landslide vote and there was not a thing the Sheriff could do about it. Barton was so angry that he refused to run for re-election, even though he loved the job and believed in the legal system. Instead, he ran for a position on the Board of Supervisors; he won.

While recovering on his peaceful ranch, the ex-sheriff had time to think about his future. He must have come to terms with the fact that Los Angeles was a rough-and-tumble frontier town. Barton learned that justice was different out on the frontier and, although it was not perfect, it was the only law that the pioneers had. After a year-long hiatus from law enforcement, James Barton would run for Sheriff one more time.

Sheriff David W. Alexander, September 1855–August 1856

David Watt Alexander was born in Ireland in 1812 and immigrated to America in 1832. He traveled to New Mexico in 1837 and then moved on to California with the Rowland-Workman party in 1841. In San Bernardino he tried his hand at farming on the Rancho Rincon. Farm work did not suit him well, so he moved to San Pedro in 1844 and started a mercantile business with John Temple. Expanding on his business interests, Alexander began operating a stagecoach line with Phineas Banning and then bought into Mellus, Howard, and Company, a general store. It seemed that the young entrepreneur was willing to take a chance on almost any business proposition that came his way.

The Mexican government appointed Alexander to be customs collector, and when the Americans took over, he was allowed to continue his role in this capacity. During the Mexican War, Alexander sided with the Americans and took part in the battle at Rancho Chino. He was captured by the Mexicans and later released. In 1850, he was elected to the Common Town Council of Los Angeles and served his full term. He became a member of the Board of Supervisors in 1853 and was a charter member of the Los Angeles Rangers.[68]

Sheriff David Alexander was a better businessman than he was a sheriff. — SECURITY PACIFIC COLLECTION / LOS ANGELES PUBLIC LIBRARY

In 1855, Alexander ran against J.Q. Stanley, also a ranger, for the office of sheriff. Stanley conducted a poll to see how many people would vote for him, and he wrongfully deduced that he had the majority support. Stanley received only 50 votes in the election. When asked about his lack of support, he commented, "I didn't know that there were so many damned liars in the county!"[69] Alexander was without question one of the most successful and influential businessmen and politicians of early Los Angeles.

Sheriff Alexander's term of office began in September, 1855. Among his claims to fame was Undersheriff William Peterson's arrest of the notorious gambler and cutthroat Henry Talbot, alias Cherokee Bob. Cherokee Bob had recently escaped from San Quentin and was hiding out in San Gabriel where some old gambling buddies recognized him. On December 21, 1855, as Peterson confronted the bandit, Bob reached for his pistol. The lawman was faster, however, and Bob was taken into custody. The gambler was transported back to San Quentin where he continued to serve time until Governor J.B. Weller pardoned him on October 14, 1859.

Upon his discharge from prison on May 15, 1860, Bob continued his life of gambling and crime. The wild times came to an abrupt halt, however, when he landed in the rough mining town of Florence, Idaho. When his girlfriend was refused admission to a town dance because of her social status, Bob became infuriated. He and his friend Bill Mayfield made it clear that they planned to confront dance organizers Jacob Williams and Orlando Robbins regarding the affront to their honor. Williams and Robbins shrewdly prepared for the attack by enlisting several friends as bodyguards.

January 2, 1863, was a cold morning when the gunfighters joined battle on the snow-covered street. Cherokee Bob and Bill Mayfield were soon overcome by overwhelming firepower. The pair was brutally gunned down in a hail of bullets while trying to beat a hasty retreat. No one in the Williams-Robbins party was injured. Mayfield was killed instantly and Bob lingered on for a few days with five bullet holes in his body. He was buried in the old Florence cemetery.[70]

During his brief eleven months in office, Sheriff Alexander had the unfortunate experience of trying to avert an all-out race war between Californios and Anglos. He was also heavily involved in the self-defense case of City Marshal Alfred Shelby.

On April 14, 1856, a very busy Marshal Shelby was summoned to a *fandango* (Mexican dance) regarding a disturbance among partygoers. The marshal was probably not in the best of spirits, as just three months earlier he had to track down and arrest one of his own officers for absconding with $400 in city funds. Upon his arrival at the fandango, the marshal spotted Thomas Taite and Samuel Ayres engaged in an altercation. As Shelby began to break up the fight, one of Taite's friends, William Burgess, told him to stay out of their business. Shelby responded, "If you don't keep quiet, I will arrest you!" Burgess growled, "You can arrest me if there is any cause." The marshal replied, "I'll do so if I attempt it, or wring your neck. You need not think you can run over any officer in this place."[71]

Shelby decided to take Taite and Ayers to Billy Getman's saloon, the Montgomery, where he would be safer. The move would also allow him to keep a close eye on the pair of drunks. Burgess stayed behind and told his friends that he wanted no trouble with the law. As Shelby was walking toward the Montgomery, a drunken Burgess changed his mind and started to follow. The Marshal heard footsteps behind him, turned around, and shouted "God damn you! Why are you following me?"[72]

Fearing that he was going to get shot, Shelby drew his gun and fired at Burgess. The instigator went down with a fatal chest wound. The marshal then re-cocked the hammer on his pistol and spun around to face Taite, who already had his gun pointed directly at him. Shelby fired again and struck Taite in the chest. Taite fell to the ground and returned fire, but he was in too much pain to be accurate, and he missed with four shots. Taite was bedridden in excruciating pain for a month. Before Taite died, Sheriff Alexander arrested Shelby for attempted murder, but Judge Benjamin Hayes cleared all charges, pronouncing that the marshal had killed in self-defense.

Former site of Billy Getman's Montgomery Saloon. – Author's Collection

Constable William Jenkins Sparks Racial Violence

On July 19, 1856, Constable William Jenkins was sent to the home of Maria Candelaria Pollorena to seize a guitar from Antonio Ruiz, who owed another man $50. Maria was sewing in the front room of her house when Jenkins arrived. She invited the constable into her home, where he located Antonio and handed him the writ. Jenkins took the guitar and left. As soon as he was gone, Maria realized that she had placed a personal letter inside the guitar. She sent Antonio to ask Jenkins to return so that she could retrieve the letter. Jenkins apparently thought it would be funny to give Maria a hard time about the letter, so the constable returned but refused to give up the note.

Antonio politely but firmly asked him to return the letter, but the lawman still refused. Frustrated and fed up with the constable's games, Maria grabbed the guitar, and Jenkins pulled away. A struggle ensued, and Antonio joined in by grabbing the constable's arm from behind. The officer panicked when he felt the Californio's grasp on him. He pulled out his revolver, aimed it over his shoulder, and shot the unarmed man in the chest. Antonio died the next day.[73]

Realizing his grave error, Jenkins turned himself in to Sheriff Alexander. Judge Benjamin Hayes released the constable on bail pending trial. Californios became outraged, and when talk of a lynching started to brew, the sheriff jailed Jenkins for his own protection. The constable was tried for murder and acquitted.

At Antonio's funeral, a huge crowd gathered to pay their respects and vent their rage regarding the incident. Surprisingly, not a Latino, but a red-bearded Frenchman named Fernando Cariergue roused the crowd's anger. He urged the mob to attack the town and sack it. The next day, Cariergue gathered a group of 300 Californios and took them to the Catholic priest's house, where they found guns and an old brass cannon left from the Mexican-American War.[74]

Tomas Sanchez, who would later be elected Sheriff, tried to calm the Californios. He asked the mob to abandon their vengeful plans and go home peacefully. Cariergue and his men shouted back at the peacemaker that they would have action, not talk. The Americans congregated by the jail along with Sheriff Alexander, who decided to organize the men into armed platoons in an effort to protect the town. City Marshal and future Sheriff Billy Getman took one of his officers, William Peterson, and six other riders to reconnoiter the situation. He stealthily led them to an observation post near the priest's house. At midnight, Getman saw the Californios commence their advance on the town.

The marshal ordered his men to fall back and alert the platoons, but it was too late. The angry mob was upon them. Cariergue's men, who were also mounted, charged at Getman. The marshal and his posse exchanged fire with the crowd, causing the Californios to temporarily back off. Again, Getman shouted at his men to get moving and sound the alarm, adding that he would cover their retreat. Four of Cariergue's riders attacked the marshal, but he stood his ground, steadily returning fire. One of the attackers' bullets struck Getman in the face and knocked him off his horse. As the riders charged past the prone veteran, they fired more shots at his defenseless body. Getman rolled in the dirt, bullets missing him by inches as puffs of dust exploded all around him.

The marshal's posse arrived in time to warn the militia of the mob's actions. The squad's rapid mobilization prevented Cariergue and his men from destroying the town. Seeing his plans unravel before his eyes, Cariergue fled the pueblo and hid out in San Gabriel. In the morning, thirty-six heavily-armed Americans from El Monte rode into Los Angeles as added insurance to protect the pueblo from a mob resurgence. The Anglos were relieved, as peace was finally restored to the town.

Andres Pico supported Alexander by forming a posse of twenty vaqueros. They rode out and captured Cariergue without incident.[75] The vaqueros brought him back to Sheriff Alexander, who gladly took him into custody. As Jenkins and Cariergue stared at each other in jail, Alexander and the judge tried to figure out how to bring lasting peace to the town. An Anglo jury found Jenkins not guilty and in return, the grand jury refused to indict Cariergue for the attempted murder of Marshal Getman. Both men were released and, with a minimum amount of grumbling, the Angelenos went about their business as usual.[76] Without strong leadership from Californios such as Tomas Sanchez and Andres Pico, Los Angeles would have had much more blood on its hands than it already had.

Completely stressed from the incident, Alexander went to visit his friend James Barton in search of consolation and sympathy. Barton complained to Alexander that he would much rather be Sheriff than County Supervisor, and Alexander explained that he was through trying to chase down criminals and just wanted to return to the pursuit of the elusive greenback. Alexander resigned as the county's chief law enforcement officer and took over the remainder of Barton's County Supervisor's term. James Barton ran for the next term of sheriff. The power swapping deal would work out well for Alexander but not for Barton.

Sheriff Charles E. Hale, August 1856–November 1856

Upon Alexander's resignation in August 1856, the Board of Supervisors appointed Charles E. Hale as interim Sheriff until elections could be held. Hale was no stranger to law enforcement. He had served as a constable in 1854, when he was involved in an exciting incident related by the *Los Angeles Star*:

> On Sunday evening last [March 4], an affray occurred at a Mexican dance house in this city. A Sonorian who kept a butcher's stall in Negro Alley, was stabbed by another and mortally wounded, so that he died almost instantly. Our vigilant constable Hale promptly arrested the murderer, and was conveying him to jail assisted by Mr. Pancho Johnson, when four men overtook them on horseback and commenced firing, probably with the intent of rescuing the prisoner. Mr. Johnson and the prisoner were severely but not dangerously wounded. Mr. Hale promptly returned the fire of these desperadoes, wounding one of them so severely that he died the next morning of his wounds. The man that Mr. Hale shot is recognized by some of our citizens as Dionicio Garcia who killed the Sheriff at Monterey County last summer.[77]

There is very little documentation of Sheriff Hale's tour of duty, mostly because he served for only two months. Hale ran in the November 1856 election against Barton but lost. As a consolation prize, he was offered a job as Justice of the Peace. Apparently, Hale decided that there were safer places to live than Los Angeles. He ran a tin shop for a while, and then he moved "to Mexico where he was reported to have made a fortune."[78]

Sheriff James R. Barton (Second Term), November 1856–January 1857

Even though the citizens of Los Angeles remembered how Barton had interfered with their lynching, they must have found forgiveness in their hearts, because they re-elected him Sheriff for the term beginning September 1857. A proud and jubilant Barton selected Elijah Bettis from Arkansas to be his Deputy.

If Andres Fuentes did indeed go to prison, he would have had completed his two-year term by this time. It is known that Fuentes rode to San Luis Obispo, where he met up with Juan Flores and Pancho Daniel. Flores was probably born around San Jose in the mid-1830s. Horace Bell remembered him well as:

> ... a dark complexioned fellow of medium height, slim, lithe, and graceful, a most beautiful figure in the fandango or on horseback, and about twenty-two years old. There was nothing peculiar about Juan except his tiger-like walk—always seeming to be in the very act of springing upon his prey. His eyes, neither black, grey, nor blue, greatly resembling those of the owl—always moving, watchful and wary, and the most cruel and vindictive-looking eyes that were ever set in a human head.[79]

When Flores broke out of prison on October 8, 1856, he joined forces with Pancho Daniel in Santa Clara. Daniel bragged that he had killed over forty men and was a veteran of the Joaquin Murrieta and Claudio Feliz gangs. Flores called his new gang the *Manillas* [handcuffs]. The name was a cheeky reminder of his time spent in prison. The band rode south and picked up Jose Jesus Espinoza and

Faustino Garcia in Monterey. After the desperadoes joined Fuentes, they rode farther south toward Los Angeles. Along the way they added Francisco "Guerro" Ardillero, Juan Silvas, Jose Santos, Leonardo Lopez, "Piquinni" Galindo, brothers Dolores and Lorenzo Ruiz, Antonio Maria "Chino" Varelas, and Miguel Soto.

The Manillas rode south, past Los Angeles to San Juan Capistrano, so that Flores could meet with his girlfriend, an Indian woman named Chola Martina. On January 21, 1857, some of the renegades entered Michael Kraszewski's store, stole a gun, and began to ride off. Kraszewski ran outside to his horse and galloped after the bandits. He grabbed Varelas's horse's bridle in a bold effort to stop them. Varelas angrily broke loose and headed back to camp.

When told of Krazewski's daring act, Flores became enraged and declared that no man would challenge his gang. He rounded up the men and headed into town to teach the residents a lesson about resistance. As they galloped into the pueblo, the Manillas spotted Kraszewski. The storekeeper ran into a nearby saloon for protection. All of the other patrons had cleared out except for a Californio named Librado Silvas. The two men bolted the door in an effort to keep the desperadoes out. Krazewski told the hair-raising story:

> I heard the bandits outside inquiring after me and making a great noise; Chino Varelas in great excitement kicking at the front door and using threatening language. Silvas and I kept quiet inside the building, holding the side door closed with our hands. Silvas was right in front of me with both palms on the door. When I opened the door a little, Juan Catabo, who was on horseback, saw me and fired his, or my, pistol. By shutting the door quickly with my hand the shot passed through the door and through Silvas' wrist between the bones. Fortunately the wound was not serious and in about two weeks he was well again. Varelas kept up his violent motions and words in front, wanting to get into the shop. One of the residents of San Juan named Pedro Verdugo, said to Varelas, who was asking for me, "He is not inside, he is gone away." All the protection I had when the door was broken away was a small counter about six feet long. The front

part of it had only a piece of common sheeting. I sat down behind the counter with a big Spanish basket covering me. I looked upon myself as lost, but did not lose my presence of mind, and intended, if they rushed into the room, I would slide out through the cloth and out into the street (via an unlocked side door). By the persuasion of Pedro Verdugo they didn't go in, but the chief of them, Juan Flores, said "Lets go into the store." They did and plundered it.[80]

After ransacking the store, the gang went over to German George Pflugardt's store and shot him while he was unarmed. The outlaws then calmly sat down to a hearty, hour-long meal with Pflugardt's corpse at their feet. After they finished, the Manillas took everything that wasn't nailed down, loaded it onto some freshly stolen horses, and rode out of town. Messengers were immediately dispatched from San Juan Capistrano to the Sheriff in Los Angeles.

Sheriff Barton hastily assembled a posse consisting of Deputy Frank Alexander, Constables William H. Little and Charles K. Baker, blacksmith Charles F. Daly, and teamster Alfred Hardy. They departed Los Angeles on January 22 and arrived at Santiago Creek, where they made camp for the night. In the morning they rode into Rancho Sepulveda, where they were told that the Manillas numbered at least fifty men. The sheriff's posse was also told that they were too small to engage Flores' gang and that they should call for reinforcements before attempting to make any arrests. Sheriff Barton thought this to be an erroneous and exaggerated report. He had never heard of a band of desperadoes being so large, so he disregarded the vaqueros' warning and urgently galloped off toward San Juan Capistrano.

When the posse reached a location fifteen miles north of the mission, they spotted a lone rider heading in their direction. Constables Little and Baker charged forward to intercept the rider. Clearing the top of a small hill, they saw the entire gang emerge from the lowlands around them. It was too late for the constables, and they knew that they were in serious trouble. Little and Baker fired at the desperadoes but they were overwhelmed by a heavily armed gang of about fifteen men. Juan Silvas gunned down Little, and Flores killed Baker.

The desperadoes carried shotguns and dual or triple sets of revolvers with extra barrels for reloading. Regardless of the fact that they were outnumbered and outgunned, the sheriff's posse refused to back down; they charged forward into the fray. One of the greatest Western civilian gun battles ever fought on horseback ensued. Three of the renegades were shot and fell from their horses. Barton fought his way toward Pancho Daniel, and the bandit yelled at him, "God damn you, I have got you now!" Leveling his pistol at Daniel, the Sheriff replied, "I reckon I have got you too!" The men pulled their triggers simultaneously; Daniel's bullet struck Barton in the heart but the sheriff's round missed its mark. Barton doubled over and toppled from his mount.[81] Despite the pain, the sheriff managed to prop himself up on one elbow and, in a final act of defiance, hurled his empty revolver at Fuentes' head.[82]

Alexander, Hardy, and Daly fired until their guns were empty. Pancho Daniel was wounded but continued to fight. The three lawmen used their pistol butts as clubs but soon realized that the situation was hopeless. They turned their steeds around and galloped back toward Los Angeles at full speed. Flores and his gang went after them in hot pursuit. Charles Daly had gone three miles before he was overtaken and mercilessly gunned down. Deputy Alexander and Alfred Hardy rode hard for twelve miles, dodging bullets most of the way. They barely escaped with their lives.

When the exhausted lawmen arrived at Rancho Sepulveda, they took on fresh horses and separated to sound the alarm. Hardy rode to Los Angeles and Alexander galloped full speed to El Monte. A panic broke out in Los Angeles. Citizens concluded that a race war was beginning. City Marshal Billy Getman arrested more than forty Californios whom he thought might join Flores' gang. Four companies of militia were organized and deployed to protect the perimeter of the town.

After securing the pueblo, Getman took forty rangers and rode to the scene of the gun battle. Upon his arrival, he found what John Boessenecker described:

The Sheriff had been shot three times in the heart and once in the right eye. Little had bullet wounds in the right eye, head and body; Baker had been shot three times in the head. Daly had bullets in the body and mouth and his face was powder burned (shot at close range). All the men had evidently been shot after they were dead.[83]

The bodies had also been completely stripped of personal effects and valuables. All that was left behind were a hastily abandoned camp and a packhorse loaded with supplies.

Getman sent a small party back to Los Angeles to return the bodies for burial and then pressed on to San Juan Capistrano. The rangers learned that Flores and his gang had ridden through town bragging about their gun battle with the Americans. However, they gave Barton's posse credit for "having fought bravely."[84] The rangers scouted the area for four days, with no luck. They rode back to Los Angeles in a somber mood on January 27. After a solemn funeral procession to the local cemetery called the Campo Santos, the four lawmen were laid to rest. Californios as well as Anglos showed up en

California Historical Landmark # 218 "Barton's Mound" was bulldozed to make way for a freeway. – California State Historical Landmark Archives

*The former location of Barton's mound at the intersection of Highway 133 and the
405 Freeway. –* AUTHOR'S COLLECTION

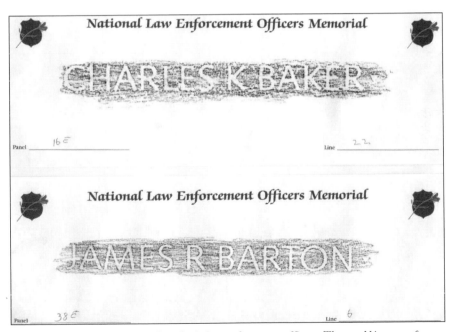

*Fallen heroes are not forgotten by today's law enforcement officers. These rubbings are from
the National Law Enforcement Officers Memorial in Washington D.C. –* AUTHOR'S COLLECTION

Fallen heroes are not forgotten by today's law enforcement officers. These rubbings are from the National Law Enforcement Officers Memorial in Washington D.C. – AUTHOR'S COLLECTION

masse to pay their last respects. The local Spanish language newspaper, *El Clamor Publico,* urged the Latin population to keep the peace and praised the Sheriff for his courage. The editor explained that Flores had robbed native Californians as well as the white man. At the funeral, they removed Barton's badge, for it was of no use to him anymore, and they laid him in the ground (see appendix B). His son, Santiago, was only three years old. Immediately after the sheriff's funeral, one of the greatest California manhunts that the Western frontier had ever seen would begin.

Sheriff Elijah Bettis, January 1857–September 1857

Elijah Bettis was born in Missouri in 1824 after his parents moved there from Kentucky. The family moved again to Arkansas in 1850, where Elijah married Elizabeth Jane Rubottom in the coal mining town of Spadra. Historical records on Sheriff Bettis are limited, and there is no indication that he played a major leadership role in the hunt for Sheriff Barton's killers. The Board of Supervisors appointed him to finish Sheriff Barton's term.

In July 1857, one of Sheriff Bettis' deputies made an arrest of a relatively unknown bandit named Tiburcio Vasquez. Vasquez was a man of average height, weighing about 130 pounds[85]. At the time, no one thought more of him than of any other horse thief. These comments appeared in the *Los Angeles Star*:

> On the 17th, Mr. Wm. H. Peterson, our active and efficient undersheriff, arrested a gentleman who has been dealing quite extensively in horse flesh. His name is Jose Tiburcio Basquez, and he has stolen no less than ten head of horses and mules from San Buenaventura [Ventura]. Information having reached Mr. Peterson, he set out in pursuit, and as usual, succeeded in arresting him.[86]

Vasquez was brought to trial and sentenced to five years at San Quentin. In time, Tiburcio Vasquez would succeed Joaquin Murrieta, Salomon Pico, and Juan Flores to become the state's most notorious desperado.

The Hunt for Sheriff Barton's Killers

General Andres Pico and Tomas Sanchez realized that it was important for them to demonstrate that Juan Flores and his kind did not represent all Californios. They wanted to make it clear to the Americans that they considered themselves loyal and trustworthy citizens of the United States. The future of their ranchos depended on being able to convince the gringos that they were working together for peace and justice. Pico and Sanchez mobilized 51 vaqueros with lances and headed for San Juan Capistrano in hot pursuit of the Manillas. Another posse of twenty-six Anglo men from El Monte joined them en route.

Believing that Flores was headed toward Mexico, the sheriff sent word to San Diego to block border access. The U.S. military cooperated by mobilizing troops along the border. Even Native American leaders such as Geronimo and Manuelito assisted by searching the mountains with a band of forty scouts. Another future sheriff of Los

Angeles County, Jim Thompson, decided that it would be wise to block northern escape routes as well. Thompson took twenty-seven men and closed off all roads heading in that direction. He was assisted by troops from Fort Tejon, which allowed him to rapidly deploy men over the immense area. The troops and lawmen guarded the Simi Valley pass, the San Fernando pass, the pass at Calabasas (El Rancho Escorpion), and the coastal route to Santa Barbara.

Andres Pico asked the San Luis Indians to watch the mountain passes south and east of San Juan Capistrano. On January 29, an Indian scout spotted the outlaws riding through Santiago Canyon in the Santa Ana Mountains. Andres Pico and Tomas Sanchez devised a plan to get insider information from the Manillas gang. The two Dons knew Chino Varelas. They sent word with an Indian runner that, if Varelas would give up Flores' plans, his life would be spared.[87]

The El Monte posse and the vaqueros under Sanchez split up and moved out toward the Flores encampment in a pincer movement. At daybreak on January 30, the El Monte lawmen moved in from the north and the vaqueros rode in from the south. The Californios made first contact and initiated the chase, with the El Monte posse joining in. Several gunshots were exchanged, but the rough terrain and heavy brush made it easy for Flores and his men to evade and move to high ground. The chaparral also worked to Chino's advantage, however, and he managed to escape. The traitor ran from Flores and surrendered to Tomas Sanchez.[88]

Believing that the bandits were lying in wait for them on the high ground, the leaders of the two posses met to decide on a plan of action. Sanchez challenged everyone to follow him up a slope in a brave charge at the renegade gang. The leader of the El Monte posse, Bethel Coopwood, joined him, along with six others. As they crawled up the mountain draw, the lawmen reached the top, only to be disappointed. The renegades had moved on.

Flores' gang had avoided capture by riding up a long sloping hill. When the outlaws reached the peak, they suddenly realized that they were at the top of a 300-foot cliff, with nowhere to go but straight down. Flores used his horse to slide down the first fifty feet to a rocky ledge, and then abandoned his mount. Using strong

Outlaw Juan Flores escaped Tomas Sanchez and his posse by recklessly descending this cliff, which is now called Flores Peak. – AUTHOR'S COLLECTION

chaparral branches as handholds, he desperately worked his way down the cliff. As the outlaw was climbing, his revolver bounced off a rock and exploded. The resulting shrapnel struck him in the arm (see appendix C). The desperate Flores continued to move, shrugging off the pain. Jesus Espinoza and Leonardo Lopez followed their leader down the cliff, shredding their hands on the rough branches. Francisco Ardillero tried to make a run for it at the top of the precipice, but he was easily captured. Juan Silvas surrendered without a fight.[89]

When Sanchez reached the top of the cliff, he realized that Flores had escaped. He also knew that precious time was being wasted. Once again, Sanchez did not hesitate to take action. He shoved a revolver into his belt, secured his Bowie knife, and began to descend the cliff. The Don went as far down as he could and then let go for a long drop into the brush. Seeing that he was not injured or ambushed, the others soon followed. Once the posse reached the bottom, they resumed the chase. The lawmen were soon discour-

81

aged again, however, for the bandit's trail went cold. All they found was Flores' damaged revolver and no sign of the outlaws.[90]

From his prisoners General Pico learned that Pancho Daniel, Andres Fuentes, Jose Santos, and Piquinni Galindo had left camp early that morning and headed for Los Angeles. The weary vaqueros spent the night in the canyon and then moved out early in the morning. The El Monte posse picked up Flores' trail and swiftly moved in. Flores, Lopez, and Espinosa immediately opened fire on the lawmen. Frank Goddard was hit, but the wound was not life threatening. The hunters had now become the hunted. Realizing that they were outgunned, the bandidos made the mistake of running into a nearby cave to take cover. The posse blocked the entrance and showered them with withering gunfire. The cave offered only temporary shelter, and the trio realized that there was no way out. They surrendered themselves and everything in their possession.

Among the articles seized was Barton's gold watch, two Colt Navy revolvers, a Colt pocket five-shooter, two double-barrel shotguns, one musket, and two Bowie knifes. The prisoners were taken to Rancho Yorba, where they were placed inside a small adobe house and put under guard. At midnight, the guard fell asleep and the three escaped under cover of darkness. The embarrassed posse rode back to General Pico and told him the bad news.[91]

Upon learning what had happened, Pico became so angry that he vowed that the two prisoners in his custody, Silvas and Ardillero, would never get the chance to escape. He took them to a nearby tree, where ropes were hastily strung up. Within minutes, the bandits' heels were swinging in the wind. Folklore tells that this tree can be seen today in the vicinity of Hangman's Tree Road and Santiago Canyon Road (see appendix B).

Pico and his vaqueros tracked Flores north. The elusive gang leader stole a horse in Santa Ana and rode toward Ventura, carefully avoiding Los Angeles. After his horse wore out, he stole another one at Mission San Fernando and made for the Simi (Santa Suzanna) Pass. On February 3, the outlaw was traveling through the pass when two soldiers stopped him for questioning. Flores told them that he was a weary rancher named Juan Gonzales Sanchez,

Gangsters Francisco Ardillero and Juan Silvas were hanged near this location by General Pico. – AUTHOR'S COLLECTION

looking for stray horses. The guards saw his injured arm and became suspicious. They took him to their camp, where he was immediately recognized by one of the men.

An hour later, two men came riding up the pass with fourteen horses in tow. When the soldiers ordered them to halt, they refused and galloped off at top speed. A sergeant fired a shot and knocked one of the men off his mount, but Espinoza and Lopez managed to escape, taking eight horses with them. Five of Jim Thompson's men gave chase but they lost the bandits in the pass. Thompson questioned Flores about the other two renegades. The outlaw leader denied any knowledge of the men or the stolen horses. The *Los Angeles Star* reported, "He requested Mr. Thompson to bring him to town, so that he might have the benefit of a clergyman, make confession and then write to his mother—and then he was ready for his fate."[92]

A posse of five, led by Ezekiel Rubottom, traveled through the Simi Pass and arrived at Mission San Buenaventura. They asked around and discovered that the desperadoes had not been seen in town. Rubottom left two men behind and then galloped north to see if the bandits were trying to get to Santa Barbara. The two rear guards decided to set up an ambush, with the hopes of capturing Espinoza and Lopez. They asked a local Californio to go up the road and try to find the two renegades and lead them into the trap. The local man agreed and, soon thereafter, the guards saw two men riding on a single horse. The Californio had led the bandits straight toward the trap. The posse members opened fire and the bandits jumped from their mount and ran. The lawmen captured Espinosa but Lopez got away.

A vigilante trial was held, and Espinosa was sentenced to hang. They took him to Mission San Buenaventura, where Father Domingo Serrano prayed for the boy and took his confession. After the good padre had finished, Jesus Espinosa was lynched. Rubottom and his two posse members returned from Santa Barbara and joined his other two men in Ventura. It was abundantly clear that Rubottom's posse was still seething about Barton's murder, and they were looking for someone on whom to take out their anger.

After inquiring about outlaws and suspicious characters in town, the posse was told that Encarnacion Berreyesa was living in town. Berreyesa was rumored to have given safe passage to Juan Flores and his gang. He also had a scar on his neck from a previous botched hanging attempt. It is unclear whether the attempted hanging was ever really justified. Californios claimed that he was a respectable man and did not cause trouble. Anglos said that he had recently stabbed two men, robbed Raimundo Olivas, and stabbed his wife. Apparently, that was all the information that Rubottom needed. His posse tracked down Berreyesa and ruthlessly lynched him on the spot.[93]

Back down south in Los Angeles, the manhunt continued. On January 29, two Californios were robbing William Stockton, a local vintner, when Cyrus Sanford and two friends accidentally interrupted the crime in progress. The robbers fled, and Sanford and Stockton gave chase. The men fought each other in a running gun battle but no one was hit, except Stockton's horse. One of the bandits escaped and the other jumped off his mount and ran into a swampy marsh. Sanford and Stockton recognized a third Californio, David Navarro, who was galloping his horse toward the pair of robbers. They shouted for Navarro to stop, but he continued to ride away from them.[94]

A posse of men from El Monte arrived to join in the search, and they set fire to the brush around the swamp. The robber was smoked out but he refused to comply with their orders to surrender. A man named King (most likely future Deputy A.J. King or one of his brothers) stepped up and shot the robber dead with a rifle. They cut off the bandito's head and took it to El Monte, where Deputy William Peterson recognized the face as being that of Miguel Soto. Soto still had Sheriff Barton's gun in his possession.[95]

Many of the Anglo town folk were panicked about the Sheriff's murder. Vigilantes began to round up every "suspect" that might in any way be affiliated with the Stockton robbery or the Flores gang. They arrested Pedro Lopez, who they claimed was "never known to work, maintaining himself by cock fighting and cattle stealing." They also arrested Juan Valenzuela, who was suspected of stealing sheep, and Diego Navarro, who claimed that he had nothing at all to do with the robbery. Although all three men had nothing to do with the sheriff's killing, the *Los Angeles Star* claimed that they were "the *banditti* who recently committed the murder of Sheriff Barton and his associates."[96]

The vigilante trial was described as follows:

We met near the veranda of the Montgomery [saloon], and judge Jonathon R. Scott having been made chairman, a regular order of procedure, extra-legal though it was, was followed; after announcing the capture and naming the criminal, the judge called upon the crowd to determine the prisoner's fate. Thereupon someone would shout, "Hang him!" Scott would then put the question, "Gentlemen you have heard the motion; all those in favor of hanging So and So will signify by saying, Aye!" And the citizens present unanimously answered Aye!"[97]

During the execution, Navarro's noose broke and he fell to the ground. While he lay squirming on the ground, he was shot to death.[98]

Faustino Garcia and Dolores Ruiz escaped north to Monterey, where they continued their life of crime for many years. Chino

Varelas was allowed to go free because he had cooperated with Tomas Sanchez and Andres Pico. Pancho Daniel, Andres Fuentes, Piquinni Galindo, and Leonardo Lopez had escaped and were still at large. Juan Flores had been incarcerated in the Los Angeles County Jail for little over a week when, on February 14, after a hasty meeting, an angry vigilante mob started in his direction. Deputy Peterson and Sheriff Bettis offered no resistance. This was partially due to the fact that they, too, wanted revenge. They also knew that if they tried to interfere, the mob would simply brush them aside or kill them.

Juan Flores was taken outside and marched to Fort Hill with two priests by his side. The *Los Angeles Star* reported:

> The prisoner was dressed in white pants, light vest and black merino sack coat. He was a young man, about twenty-two years of age, and of pleasing countenance. There was nothing in his appearance to indicate the formidable bandit which he had proved himself to be.[99]

A crowd of over 3,000 people was present, including the French Militia, Captain Twist's "Southern Rifles" Company, Andres Pico, Tomas Sanchez, Jim Thompson, the vaqueros, and the El Monte posse.

After the priests had taken confession and administered the last rites, Flores made a speech in which he said that he was ready to die and that he had committed many crimes. He said that he did not bear ill will against any man, and he hoped that no man would bear ill will against him. He saw some people whom he knew in the crowd and asked them to make sure that he had a decent burial. He handed a blindfold to the hangman and asked him to cover his eyes with it. A *reata* from one of Barton's murdered deputies was made into a noose and placed around the outlaw's neck. His arms and legs were tied with a rope and, without further ado, they "swung him off."[100]

One can only wonder whether some of these early hangings were "bungled" on purpose. The outlaw's rope was too short and Flores slowly strangled and choked. He managed to wiggle free of his bindings and tried to pull himself back up the rope. The *Los*

Angeles Star noted, "It required considerable effort to release his hold. After a protracted struggle, very painful to behold, the limbs became quiet and finally stiff in death."[101]

On May 8, 1857, Sheriff Bettis helped to prepare the invoice for fees relating to the manhunt for Sheriff Barton's killers. The bill itself tells the story:

$80.00 to Henry Schaeffer for ammunition
$80.00 to Potter and Company for ammunition
$125.00 for support of wounded to Dr. J.S. Griffin
$97.00 for supplies to Thomas Sanchez
$60.00 for supplies to William C. Getman
$10.00 for guard room rent to Victor Beaudry
$34.50 for gallows to Charles Plaisance
$10.00 for coffee to Lugo
$11.23 for freight on arms to Banning and Wilson[102]

A few months after this bill was paid, there was a wild shootout in San Jose. Leonardo Lopez loosed 13 shots in a gun battle with town constables. He was wounded and taken into custody by San Jose Marshal Jasper D. Gunn. Marshal Getman took the steamship up from Los Angeles to extradite the renegade for trial.[103] Although Getman was happy to have Lopez in custody, he was thinking more about his new job as sheriff. "Billy" had just been elected in September. He would not live to see Lopez hang.

California State historical landmark 218 denotes the area where Sheriff Barton and his posse were killed. There is no marker or plaque at the location, and the actual mound where the gun battle took place was destroyed with the construction of the Highway 133 overpass at the 405 Freeway interchange.[104]

Sheriff William C. Getman, September 1857–January 1858

Getman had been City Marshal prior to his election as Sheriff on September 2, 1857. His military experience and his display of courage and dynamic leadership during the roundup of Sheriff Barton's murderers propelled him to the highest law enforcement office in the county.

William Getman was born in Fort Plain, New York, in 1826. His grandfather was a captain in the Continental Army and fought in the Revolutionary War. When war broke out with Mexico, William enlisted on July 15, 1846. He served with Captain C.W. Wessel, Company G, 2nd U.S. Regiment of Infantry. The young soldier was wounded three times in combat. He received his first wound at the battle of Monterey and was again wounded while fighting with "Scott's Line" at Cerro Gordo. During the siege of Mexico City, at the storming of the Belen Gate, Getman was almost killed when he was struck by shrapnel from cannon fire. He was discharged at Jefferson Barracks near Saint Louis, Missouri, and mustered out on August 27, 1848.

As with many young men who return from combat, home was never quite the same. He left his relatives on the East Coast and decided to take his chances out West in the City of Angels. In Los Angeles, Getman found work as a manager at the Montgomery Saloon thereby, like Wyatt Earp, becoming a lawman who was also running a high-class gambling house and saloon. His combat experience and restless spirit also made him a perfect match for the Los Angeles Rangers. He made many close friends in the barracks as they shared adventure stories and made ambitious plans for the future. Getman quickly rose to the rank of Lieutenant Ranger.

In the evenings, Billy and his buddies went to Abdul Mullah's restaurant for oysters on the half shell. The regular customers always begged "Ranger Billy" to play the accordion for their dining pleasure. The boyish, good-natured frontiersman never refused and always delivered a first class performance. As a way to earn additional income, Getman took the job as City Marshal, where he served two dangerous and action-packed years.

The Montgomery and its adjoining gambling room, the famous De-Luxe Parlor, were considered to be among the finest saloons in town. Only the wealthiest gentlemen in Los Angeles could afford to patronize Getman's establishment. The building was located on the west side of Main Street, just a few doors south of the church. The front room was seventeen feet deep and seventy-one feet wide. The bar at the west end had a glass showcase for cakes and pastries. Next to the bar a passageway led to a card room, where "Monte" was the game of choice. Three billiard tables sat in the main salon and another doorway in the back led to a ten-pin alley. The building also contained sleeping rooms and a restaurant. A drink at the Montgomery cost $6.35 in today's money, not much different from what finer pubs charge today.

As City Marshal and proprietor of the Montgomery, Getman kept very busy. One day, a boy ran up to him and exclaimed that Jose Ramon Ruiz had just broken into a house with a large knife and was causing a disturbance. Getman went to his office and pulled a double-barrel shotgun from the rack. The marshal had heard about the troublemaker for weeks but had never actually met him.

Getman entered the house and saw the suspect standing perfectly still, with his back to the door. The Marshal cautiously began his approach with his right finger on the trigger and his left hand on the barrel. When he got within a few feet of Ruiz, the bandit suddenly turned and slashed at him with a huge knife. Getman slammed the barrel of the shotgun into Ruiz's head, dazing him. He reached down, grabbed the troublemaker by the collar, and dragged him off to the *calaboose*. The judge promptly sentenced Jose Ruiz to two years at San Quentin.

On another occasion, Getman was keeping his eye on a local drunk named Gabe Allen, who, like him, was a Ranger and a veteran of the Mexican War. Gabe was a reckless and dangerous man, especially when he had been drinking. Marshal Getman followed the drunkard as he slowly staggered down the dusty street. When Allen came to a building that was under construction, he noticed a carpenter working on the roof. For no apparent reason, Allen pulled out a pistol and took aim at the worker. With lightning reflexes, Getman pounced forward and slammed his fist into the drunk, knocking him to the ground, thus saving the carpenter's life. Allen puffed, "You've got me, Billy!"[105] When the Marshal asked Allen what he was trying to accomplish, Gabe merely replied that he wanted to see how good his aim was. Getman dragged the sharpshooting drunk to jail, where he was safe from the public and vice versa. It is interesting to note that, in 1861, Allen ran for the office of Sheriff against Tomas Sanchez and lost by 617 votes.[106]

Lafayette King and Mr. Reed

In the month that he was elected, Getman chose his best friend, Eli Smith, to become his deputy. He was budgeted for one other position, so he selected future City Marshal Frank Baker to complete the roster. Eli had been on the job for 25 days when his boss was summoned to the Montgomery regarding a dispute. Inside, brothers Thomas and Lafayette King had been drinking hard. Lafayette worked for the stagecoach line; Thomas, who was rumored to have ridden with Pancho Daniel, worked only when he had to. The brothers joined a group of gentlemen for a game of Monte, and everyone noticed that Thomas had a large white-handled knife tucked inside his shirt.

The waiter kept the drinks coming and, by 3:00 a.m., Thomas was roaring drunk. Lafayette decided that he had played enough cards for the night and got up to leave. Thomas stopped him, shouting, "A minute ago I had seven chips, and now I have only six!" Lafayette stared at his brother, who went for his white-handled knife. Lafayette was faster and drew his gun. Pointing it directly at Thomas's face, he cocked the hammer and said, "God damn you! If you draw your knife, I will kill you!"[107]

The other gentlemen at the table pulled the two apart and urged them not to fight. Lafayette walked away and headed to the bar. The men at the table asked Thomas to leave, but he refused and started after his brother. Lafayette heard footsteps behind him and, when he turned around, Thomas attacked him, cutting his throat wide open. Blood splattered everywhere as his jugular was slashed and his windpipe torn. With a surprised look on his face, Lafayette gurgled and slumped to the floor. Men rushed out to notify the sheriff and Dr. Vergennes.

When Smith, Getman, and the Doctor arrived, it was too late. There was nothing they could have done to save Lafayette, anyway. The sheriff picked up the knife, and someone handed Lafayette's pistol to Eli. A coroner's inquest, consisting of William C. Getman, Robert A. Hester, William W. Jenkins, Harvey Rhodes, Francisco de Johnson, D. Marchessault, and E.M. Smith concluded the following:

We find the name of the deceased to be Lafayette King, that he came to his death by means of a knife wound inflicted by Thomas King at the City and County of Los Angeles, on the morning of the 27th day of September, 1857, and that said killing was felonious.[108]

The first jury could not agree on a verdict, but the second trial ended in a conviction for murder.[109] King was hanged on February 16, 1858, along with Leonardo Lopez. Shortly before the Sheriff drew the bolt Thomas said, "We all have to die sometime, but I am to die now and in this manner—Christ have mercy upon me."[110]

James P. Johnson

The deadly combination of alcohol and weapons was truly taking its toll on the citizens of Los Angeles. Jim Johnson was a good man who "received a liberal education and was taught to be moral and honest."[111] He had a happy marriage for six years, until his wife died, leaving him with a small boy. Jim was never able to recover from the blow. He began to drink and gamble, getting into as many as seventy fights. Johnson made several attempts to "go straight," but nothing seemed to work for him. In a last-ditch effort, he remarried and had another son with a "respectable and pious lady." Not long afterward, he got into a horrific saloon brawl with a man named Wagner. A jury convicted Johnson of murder, and he was sentenced to hang.

Unlike Barton, Sheriff Billy Getman was a skilled hangman. In October, 1857, The *Los Angeles Star* reported:

The Sheriff intimated that he must now proceed with his disagreeable duty. The prisoner at once resigned himself to the hands of the officers and assisted them as far as possible in adjusting the fastening of his arms and legs. This being accomplished, he took leave of his friends, his hands were tied behind him, a handkerchief bound around his face and head, and the fatal rope carefully adjusted. The officers then stepped aside and the prisoner was left alone in prayer with his God. His last words were, "Lord, to thee I commit my spirit." The Sheriff drew the bolt and James P. Johnson was ushered into eternity. He died instantly. There was not a convulsive struggle of the body.[112]

Mr. Johnson left behind his wife, their infant son, and the son from his first marriage.

Shootout at the Monte Pio

On the morning of January 7, Sheriff Billy Getman had been in office for four months. He took his daily walk over to the rented sheriff's office at the Bella Union Hotel. Deputy Baker and Officer Hester were there, but Eli Smith had not yet arrived. After breakfast, Getman went to speak with the judge about a man named Reed who had recently arrived from Texas. Reed was said to be mentally ill and causing trouble in town. The judge directed Getman to bring the man in, along with two doctors, to examine his condition. Baker, Getman, and Hester checked their weapons and began to search the streets for Reed.

While the officers were reconnoitering, Reed approached Mr. Cohn, owner of the Monte Pio pawnshop. He handed the shopkeeper a pistol and begged the proprietor to shoot him, saying that he was tired of life. Frightened, Mr. Cohn turned away and asked Reed to leave.

The trio of officers located Reed in the street near the Beaudry Building. Getman contacted him and said, "I want to speak to you." Reed replied, while drawing a derringer, "Keep away from me, don't come near me." The sheriff said, "You don't want to shoot me, I merely want to speak a few words to you—don't shoot." Reed suddenly stepped back and fired point blank at Getman. The sheriff gasped and said, "Boys, I am shot," as he crumpled to the ground, dead.[113]

Reed ran back to the Monte Pio and barricaded himself inside the store. A crowd gathered outside to see what the deputies would do next. When Reed saw Baker and Hester approaching, he began to pepper the crowd with bullets. Everyone scattered, except for the deputies, who immediately engaged the murderer in a vicious firefight. Reed loosed between twenty and thirty rounds—an enormous amount of firepower for that time. Officers Peterson and Jenkins heard the gunshots and ran over to join in the battle.

Realizing that Reed was well barricaded, Jenkins decided to even the odds. He climbed onto the roof and began to fire at the crazed man through an opening in an awning. Reed returned fire and struck the lawman in the leg, wounding him severely. Despite the pain, Jenkins continued to fire, grazing Reed's head with one of his bullets. This caused the mentally ill man to run out of the store, where Peterson, Hester, and Baker all blasted away at him. Reed was struck with ten bullets and knocked backwards; he fell dead on the spot. As the gun smoke cleared, Deputy Baker stared in disbelief at his coat: He counted five bullet holes. The deputy was happy to be alive—a strange feeling, considering the loss of his friend and former boss.

The excited crowd rushed into the shop and recovered two derringers, two pistols, and a Bowie knife from Reed's body. Miraculously, there was no record of anyone in the crowd being hit by stray bullets. The whole town attended Billy Getman's funeral. Buildings were draped in black, and even the saloons closed. As he did with Sheriff Barton a year earlier, the funeral director respectfully removed Sheriff Getman's badge and prepared him for burial.

They took him to Campo Santos on the hill, where he was laid to rest (see appendix B). According to the National Law Enforcement Officer's Memorial Fund, Getman has the dubious distinction of being the first (well-documented) officer in the nation to be killed by a mentally deranged person.[114] It is also one of the earliest documented cases of a syndrome now called "suicide by cop," or "police assisted suicide," a ploy in which a mentally ill person provokes police into killing him because he is unwilling to do the job himself.

The Sheriff left behind a widowed mother and sister in New York. His personal possessions demonstrated his boyish nature: A galvanic battery and an air gun were among his few personal belongings. Wealthy rancher Robert Carlisle bought Getman's five-shooter, very likely the same one that was later used in a bloody gun battle at the Bella Union Hotel.

Sheriff James S. Thompson, January 1858–August 1859

Like that of Billy Getman, the strong leadership that Jim Thompson displayed during the search for Sheriff Barton's murderers helped to pave the way for his appointment as sheriff. Of course, there may not have been many takers for the job, since two sheriffs had been killed within the past year. Horace Bell wrote that Thompson "threw himself into the breach" when no one else was bold enough to step forward.[115] After a round or two of internal squabbling, the County Board of Supervisors appointed Thompson, in a 4-1 vote, to serve the rest of Getman's term.

Thompson was a tough frontiersman from the Texas Llanos. Researcher Eunice Crittenden described him as "not particularly commanding or impressive . . . of fair complexion and with blue eyes."[116] The Californios called him Don Santiago, but the Anglos just called him Jim.

Thompson arrived in Los Angeles in 1849 and married Manuela De La Osa. She bore him five children, of whom only two survived. Manuela died in 1867, not long after bearing twins,

The unmarked graves of Sheriffs Billy Getman and James Barton at Rosedale Cemetery. – AUTHOR'S COLLECTION

although their birth was not cause of her death. Two years later, Thompson married Doña Francisca Sepulveda, whose father, Don Jose Andrea Sepulveda, owned the Rancho San Joaquin. The massive ranch included Tustin, Santa Ana, and the land north of San Juan Capistrano.

Once in office, Thompson selected William W. Jenkins as his deputy. The lawmen continued working the case against the Manillas gang. They finished up where Barton and Getman had left off. By the time Leonardo Lopez was taken to court, vigilante tempers in Los Angeles had actually cooled enough to allow for a proper trial. Lopez was tried by Judge Benjamin Hayes in district court and found guilty of having murdered German George Pflugardt in San Juan Capistrano. The trial went quickly due to the fact that several Californio witnesses testified against him. On February 16, 1858, Lopez was taken to the gallows in the jail yard. Before he was hanged, he insisted to the crowd that he was innocent. In his final address, Lopez pleaded with the Californios to "leave the country, as it was no place for them."[117]

Meanwhile, in northern California, Sheriff John Murphy of Santa Clara County tracked Pancho Daniel to a farm. Murphy found the bandit hiding in a haystack and arrested him.[118] Daniel still had Sheriff Barton's gun belt. He was extradited to Los Angeles to stand trial. The Angelenos expected Daniel's trial to go the same way as the Lopez trial, but this was not to be the case. The wise bandit was lucky enough to receive a capable attorney by the name of Kimball H. Dimmick to aid in his defense.

Dimmick argued repeatedly that there was no possible way that Pancho Daniel could get a fair trial in Los Angeles. He claimed that Sheriff Thompson was biased because he had helped to lead the manhunt, and that all of the jurors whom he had selected were therefore biased, too. Ultimately, the judge agreed with Dimmick and transferred the venue to Santa Barbara. Angelenos protested, fearing that a sympathetic Californio jury in Santa Barbara might acquit him. They also reasoned that the jail "up there" was "leaky" and too weak to hold Daniel.

Just prior to prisoner Daniel's transfer north, Sheriff Thompson picked up a rumor that Andres Fuentes was on the edge of town. A band of 200 vigilantes waited patiently for the sheriff to investigate. As soon as he left, they overpowered the jailer and dragged Daniel out of his cell. The mob took the outlaw to the jail yard gate and forced him to stand on a stool. The vigilantes strung a rope over the crossbeam and put a noose around his neck. They asked him whether he had any last words. Daniel broke down, blubbering. After a short while, he regained his composure and said simply, "No." Just before they hanged him, he blurted, "Tell my wife good-bye."[119] In response to the vigilante action, the *Los Angeles Star* exclaimed:

> "The exhibition of Tuesday last will reflect disgrace upon the community, which years will not obliterate. Our reputation abroad was none the brightest as a law abiding community; there will now be a foundation for such charges."[120]

Andres Fuentes fled south to Baja California where he met Manuel Marquez, a Los Angeles renegade. The pair banded together with several other desperadoes from Alta California, including Chino Varelas and Salomon Pico. They accepted jobs as bodyguards for Mexican General Jose Castro. After Castro was killed in a drunken brawl with Marquez, his successor, General Esparza, ordered the desperadoes to be shot. In 1860, the entire crew, except Varelas, was executed by firing squad. Chino was spared because of his family's wealth and "good name."

Varelas returned to Los Angeles, where he was eventually killed in an altercation. His death brought to a close one of the bloodiest gang rampages in California's history. Some Californios saw the Manillas gang as revolutionary heroes, fighting for the glory of old Mexico against American imperialism. The sad reality is that Juan Flores and his gang were cold-blooded robbers and killers. They did not care what the skin color of their victim was, but rather how much money was in the wallet. The murder of four peace officers in one incident would not occur in California again until the Newhall shootout, north of Los Angeles, in 1970.

After serving the rest of Getman's term of office, Thompson ran for Sheriff in 1859 and was easily re-elected. During the same election, ex-Sheriff Charles Hale was voted Justice of the Peace for Los Angeles, and future Sheriff James Burns was elected likewise for San Gabriel.

During the latter term of his office, Sheriff Thompson became involved in a business deal to build a road from Los Angeles to the San Luis Obispo County line. The proposed road would go through the Santa Suzanna Pass, past Ventura and Santa Barbara, and stretch over the Gaviota Pass, coming to an end at the San Luis Obispo County line. The road covered a total distance of 125 miles and cost $50,000. The highway was sorely needed; after its completion, early travelers testified that it saved them much time. After this construction project was finished, Thompson took a job as county jailer. In 1877, he was elected to the Los Angeles City Council. In the twilight years of his life, he suffered a stroke and was wheelchair bound. He passed away on May 12, 1895.

Chapter 3

TAMING LOS ANGELES:
TURNING THE TIDE AGAINST CRIME

Sheriff Tomas Sanchez, September 1859–February 1867

By the time he was elected Sheriff in late 1859, 33-year-old Tomas Sanchez was known to the entire community as a fearless leader and a patriot of both the old Mexican government and the new American republic. Although he had no formal education, Sanchez was honest and thoroughly capable, with a quick wit and a nose for politics. He had served as a county supervisor since 1857. He was a confident man of medium height, who wore a thick black beard. The Californio Don inherited the large Rancho Cienega o' Paso de la Tijera from his grandfather, Vicente Sanchez. The rancho was located in an area now known as Baldwin Hills. Vicente was the first alcalde of the pueblo and a highly-respected citizen in the Mexican government.

In 1857, the United States officially declared the rancho to be the sole property of Tomas A. Sanchez. Tomas was the first Californio to be elected Sheriff, and there is little doubt that his rise to office was given a boost from the courage and leadership that he had displayed while chasing down the Manillas gang. In addition to name recognition, Sanchez had the undying support of attorney Joseph Brent. The 1860 election campaign for sheriff is considered one of Brent's greatest political accomplishments. Despite his qualifications, Sanchez narrowly won the election,

Fearless Sheriff Tomas Sanchez (left) standing with Mayor Benjamin Wilson's son, John. Sanchez was a courageous peacemaker in times of great strife. Once a wealthy landowner, he died penniless in 1882.
— HUNTINGTON LIBRARY

most likely due to widespread racism.

Sheriff Sanchez's long tenure in office, 1860-1867, not only proved his worth but provided much-needed stability in unstable times. The American Civil War raged during much of his time as sheriff. While northern Californians strongly supported the Union, Los Angeles was a different story. In the 1860 presidential election, 350 votes were cast for Abraham Lincoln and 1,190 for his opponents. The anti-Union sentiment worried the federal government to the point that they established a permanent army post in Wilmington called the Drum Barracks, after Lt. Colonel Richard Coulter Drum.

In the early 1860s, Los Angeles was in the grip of a depression. Prospectors and miners who had given up on their professions were starved for work. Men flocked to the army for the monthly pay of $13, which amounts to approximately $250 in today's currency. The fact that so many men enlisted for this low pay shows how tough the times were and how desperate local workers had become. Luckily, the troops did not have to earn their pay on the battlefield as no major engagements were fought by Drum soldiers. Five days after the war officially ended, anti-Union feelings were still at an all-time high, as witnessed by Bell: "When the news of Abraham Lincoln's assassination reached the pueblo, the Southern 'Patriots' got on a bust; they howled themselves hoarse—they howled and they hurrahed until they fell in the streets dead drunk."[1] By 1871, the Drum Barracks was almost completely abandoned. Wilson College, the forerunner to the University of Southern California, moved in and named the campus College Hill.

Tomas Sanchez was born on Sanchez Street in Los Angeles in 1826, and he lived there during his formative years. When he was sixteen, he married Josepha Maria Sepulveda, who was only thirteen. She bore him nineteen sons and two daughters. The property that Tomas received from her dowry is now called the Casa Adobe de San Rafael, and is currently a museum located in and owned by the City of Glendale (see appendix B).

As a young man, Tomas served under General Andres Pico and fought against the Americans at the battle of San Pasqual. Horace Bell described him as "a true son of chivalry, who wielded a good lance at San Pasqual."[2] By calling him a "true son of chivalry," Bell meant that he was a Southern Democrat and secessionist. Emerson claimed, "It was said of him that he loved a fight, especially in defense of the law."[3] As much as he may have loved fighting, there is little evidence to suggest that he tried to battle against vigilantism during his eight years as sheriff. This may be part of the reason why he was so popular with the citizenry. A high crime rate continued to plague the city of 4,385 inhabitants, and vigilantes were still delivering their own brand of speedy "justice" to desperadoes and cutthroats. The new Sheriff selected Andrew (Jack) King to be his Deputy and right-hand man.

Sanchez figured out a way to earn additional revenue for the County and himself by setting up the first "licensing detail" for the Sheriff's office. He persuaded the Board of Supervisors to let him handle all county business licensing for the nominal fee of 10% per license. However, his greatest legacy was his ability to ease racial tensions between angry Californios and Anglos. Sheriff Sanchez prevented many racial conflicts by acting as peacemaker. His even-handed tactics and cool-headed speech served to de-escalate violence in a way that has been matched by few others, even to this day.

Ironically, the Sanchez reign as Sheriff marked the beginning of the end for many old Mexican and California traditions. A depressing mixture of taxation, crime, drought, small pox, and high interest rates spelled disaster for the powerful land-owning dons, Sanchez included. By 1900, most of the beautiful large ranchos were gone—divided and sold off to pay debts and liens.[4] The story of Mr. Carpenter is just one example of how unfair interest rates could lead to tragedy.

In 1852, Carpenter, who owned the immense and beautiful Rancho Santa Gertrudes, borrowed $50 from banker and later governor John Downey. The interest rate was 12.5%, compounded daily. By 1853, he owed Downey $5,000. The kind and generous Mr. Downey arranged for a new note with 5% interest compounded monthly, payable in three months and secured by the rancho. After that transaction was completed, another note was made for a year and a day. In 1854, a new note was drafted for $9,154 at the same rate. In 1856, the interest was again computed and a second note was written at $4,000 to secure the interest on the other loan. Carpenter's good friend Pio Pico co-signed on this note as collateral. By 1859, Downey figured that he was tired of waiting and foreclosed on Carpenter—he took the Rancho Santa Gertrudes and $4,000 from the rancher. On the day Downey foreclosed, Carpenter went home and shot himself in the head. For a measly $50, Downey took possession of the Rancho, $4,000 in cash and Carpenter's life.[5]

One of Sanchez's first challenges as Sheriff came during a celebration of the Mexican national holiday. During the celebration, a crew of party revelers raised the Mexican flag over the U.S. flag. The Mexican supporters did not think this incident to be a grand offense, but many of the whites became outraged. Seeing that a riot was brewing, Sanchez calmly but forcefully walked over to the flagpole and ordered the flags to be reversed. The Mexicans, along with their Californio compadres, did not take offense at the Sheriff's actions and, after the flags were swapped, the merriment resumed. The Anglos were appeased, and another bloodletting was avoided.

The year 1860 was a busy one for the Sheriff. Much of his time was spent in trying to collect taxes from people who had no money. The rest of his time was spent in trying to pay for and renovate a courtroom. The Board of Supervisors was not much help because the county coffers were empty. The old adobe courtroom was falling apart; rain leaked in from the roof and poured down the wall in buckets. So the County moved the court's offices to a few rented rooms at John Temple's Market House, located where Temple intersected Main Street. The new building was much better suited for their business, and the court resumed its work in style.

The John Rains Murder

One of the more interesting crimes that Sheriff Sanchez investigated was that of the separate murders of two wealthy American business partners. Isaac Williams' body was still warm in his grave when his majordomo (rancho manager), John Rains, started wooing one of his daughters. The proud and beautiful Maria Merced (Lugo) Williams married him on September 14, 1856. It would prove to be a huge mistake for Merced. However, it was a wise move for Rains, because her dowry brought him a small fortune: a large portion of the massive Rancho Santa Ana del Chino. Another southern "gentleman" named Robert Carlisle courted Merced's sister, Francisca. They were soon married, and Carlisle took his share of the rancho as well.

It was not long before Carlisle and Rains started quarrelling about how the property should be managed. When Rains finally had had enough of the bickering, he sold his half to Carlisle. Rains took the profits and made a fresh start by purchasing Rancho Cucamonga, just north of the Chino. He wasted no time in spending Merced's money. The entrepreneur built a mansion on "Red Hill" and filled it with the finest furniture that

Rancher John Rains' murderer was never found. – City of Rancho Cucamonga Archives

money could buy. He planted 15,000 vines and added a winery, a trading post, a general store, and a tavern. Rains hired Ramon Carillo to watch over his cattle, and he spent most of his time trying to figure out new ways to lose money.[6]

Before long, Rains' taste for the good life started to catch up with him and he had to mortgage part of the ranch to keep the cash flowing. On Monday, November 17, Rains went looking for his pistols, which he always carried with him when traveling. He could not find them, so he took his trusty derringer instead. After hitching up his buggy, the Don rode off to Los Angeles for a business meeting with Dr. Winston. The two men were co-owners of the Bella Union Hotel and frequently met to discuss business dealings. The last person to see John Rains alive was a Paiute Indian named Pote. Pote saw the elegant carriage leave "Mud Springs" in a westerly direction. He also noticed three riders heading the same way. They were far away in the distance, but the Indian said that they "rode like Mexicans."[7]

On Wednesday morning, Dunlap, Rains' majordomo, noticed the two horses from Rains' buggy standing next to the barn. They looked exhausted, and one of them had a scratch on its back. Neither the harness nor the buggy could be found. At first, no one was very worried about Rains, since he often went away for several days at a time; the horses returning alone, however, was a bad omen. On Friday, Dr. Winston arrived at the rancho, looking for Rains. When the ranch staff said that Rains had gone to Los Angeles to meet someone, the doctor knew that something was terribly wrong. They sent a runner to Rancho Chino, where Carlisle sent word to Sheriff Sanchez and then immediately began a search. Deputy Jack King and Dr. Myles found Rains' body eleven days later on the road leading to the San Gabriel Mission.

Rains' corpse was found naked, except for one boot and one sock, and his tie still around his neck. Lacerations to his wrists and arms were evidence that the desperadoes had lassoed him and dragged him off of his buggy. There were four bullet holes in his body, but when they checked his clothing they found only three corresponding holes in his shirt. This led the coroner to believe that Rains was not dead after they had shot him the first three times, so, after they had stripped him, they shot him once more to finish the job. The murderers had slashed his stomach open with a knife to hasten the process of decomposition. Rats had eaten his intestines and part of his left thigh. Birds had pecked out his eyes and a portion of his gums.

As the grisly investigation continued rumors began to fly. Many Anglos said that it was Mexican banditos while Californios claimed that Carlisle and his cronies had cooked up a murder scheme in an effort to grab the rancho. Deputy Frank Baker was serving warrants in San Diego when he encountered two Indian houseboys who had recently been employed by Rains. The boys said that vaqueros at Rains' ranch had beaten them in an effort to find out where Mr. Rains' pistols were. The young men said that they did not know, and that they had been fired, anyway. The boys further alleged that on one particular evening Merced had told one of them to go outside and tell Jose that Mr. Rains had just left for Los Angeles. One of the houseboys did as he was told and met up with local ranch-hands Gordo, Ignacio, and Jose. He was astonished to see that all three men's faces were painted with prickly pear juice to disguise them. Before he left, Jose told the houseboy that if he said anything about what he had seen he would be killed.

Sheriff Sanchez investigated further and discovered that each of the three suspects had a strong alibi. There were no further leads until John Rains' funeral. The service was held at the Bella Union Hotel, where the gossip was that Ramon Carillo had done the dirty work, along with Manuel Cerradel and Procopio Bustamante. This information led Sanchez to arrest Cerradel and Carillo in mid-February 1863. Bustamonte was reportedly headed north towards Firebaugh's Ferry. While in custody, Cerradel contracted smallpox and was quarantined in a separate shack under guard. As Cerradel neared death, he told the guards that he had committed the murder, along with Louis Sanchez, Procopio Bustamante, Jesus Asteanes and Tal Juanito. Cerradel said that during the robbery Rains had shot one of them with his derringer. The confession must have cleansed Cerradel's soul for, shortly afterwards, his condition improved and he recovered. Sanchez re-interviewed the bandit and was disgusted when Cerradel told him that he had been delirious at the time and that his confession was not true. Judge Hayes dropped murder charges against Cerradel and Carillo due to lack of evidence; however, Cerradel was charged with assault to commit murder on the officer who arrested him.

In early December, 1863, Manuel Cerradel, was sentenced to state prison for ten years. In the 1800s, the quickest way to travel north was to take the steamship from the port of San Pedro. On December 9, Sheriff Sanchez had his charge in custody when he boarded the *Cricket*, a small harbor boat that took the passengers out to waiting steamships in the open sea. Sanchez noticed that something was not quite right when he boarded the *Cricket*. He recognized several of the "passengers," who were purposefully looking the other way as if they did not wish to be seen.

As soon as the *Cricket* was in deep water and halfway to the waiting steamship, the vigilantes sprung into action. They seized Cerradel from the sheriff and then strung up a rope over one of the yardarms. The vigilantes wasted no time in hanging Cerradel, whom they claimed was John Rains' murderer. After they lowered the body to the deck, the vigilantes pulled heavy stones from their "luggage" and tied them to Cerradel's body. They tossed the body overboard, and the outlaw sank to Davey Jones' locker. Sanchez was probably not too upset as he was spared a long and boring voyage up north.

Tal Juanito had traveled north with Procopio Bustamante to Firebaugh Ferry. Juanito was killed while trying to steal a horse from an Indian near there on April 4, 1863. Procopio Bustamonte continued on with his life of crime, and ended up serving a total of thirteen years in prison in the ensuing decades. During his criminal career he killed one lawman, shot another, and is believed to be the ringleader behind numerous robberies and murders throughout the state. Interestingly enough, Procopio's mother, Vicenta, was Joaquin Murrieta's older sister. When the pressure from California law enforcement got to be too much, Procopio hid out in Hermosillo, Mexico, where he married Juanita Armida Bernal in the 1880s. The couple had a daughter named Margarita, born in 1886. He died sometime around 1890 in Vista Blanca, Mexico.[8] To this day the identity of John Rains' murderer remains a mystery.

Upon his release, Ramon Carillo went back to work on the rancho. There really is no evidence that Ramon was a bad man: He had a wife and family and he was a good friend to Merced and her children. He was a chivalrous man and wanted to help Merced keep the Rancho Cucamonga at all costs. Nevertheless, rumors among the white community were running rampant. Many believed that Merced had her husband killed so that she and Ramon could take over the ranch. Some of the Americans living nearby threatened him, and he was told that vigilantes were organizing against him.

Carillo decided to abandon the ranch and hide in the mountains, hoping that things would cool off. When he returned, Merced asked him to escort her carriage into town. In May 1864, unknown assailants were lying in ambush near the rancho's tavern. The cowardly outlaws ruthlessly shot Ramon off his mount. Carillo died a few hours later, but not before he had implicated two men in the crime. Postmaster G.W. Gillette and a man named R.M. Viall were arrested and interrogated regarding the incident. The judge later released both of them due to lack of evidence.

Merced was lonely and scared. All of her children were under age six and the ranch was mortgaged to the hilt. Growing up spoiled and marrying at age seventeen, she was unprepared to deal with a cutthroat business world dominated by men. A month after Ramon's death, Merced married his brother Jose in a desperate bid to save the ranch and get on with her life. The couple continued living on the ranch until 1870, when there was no more money to pay the bills. The bank foreclosed, and Rancho Cucamonga was lost to history.

Charles Wilkins and the Daimwood Gang

Charles Wilkins was a bad man. He had been raised in a respectable Mormon family in Salt Lake City. The clean living and hard work did not appeal to young Charles, so he decided to strike out on his own at an early age. Charles killed his first victim at age seventeen. He later claimed that he had assisted in the infamous Mountain Meadows Massacre of September 8-10, 1857, in Utah, where 120 pioneers from Arkansas had been slaughtered by Indians and Mormon militia. Wilkins boasted that his share of the loot was several thousand dollars. His next crime involved the murder of a man named Blackburn for his mules and valuables. A life of horse thievery followed, with the occasional murder and robbery tossed in. He was subsequently arrested in San Luis Obispo and sent to San Quentin, where he escaped.

Wilkins then joined up with a Sonoran whom he had met in prison, and the pair decided to rob a couple of cattle buyers. The robbery plan called for the Mexican to take the man on the left while Wilkins took the one on the right. During the attempt, the Sonoran missed his mark and his prey escaped, but Wilkins's man went down in the dirt. The robbers' victim had been prepared to purchase several head of cattle, as shown by the large sum of money that he had with him. After dividing the spoils, Wilkins left his Sonoran amigo and decided to try his luck in Los Angeles.

In the City of Angels he met an 18-year-old street tough named Andrew Wood. Wilkins took a liking to the boy and decided to mentor him in a life of crime. The senior outlaw even went so far as to steal a knife and pistol for his apprentice—Wilkins told the youngster that he would need these tools help him get started. It did not take long for the pair to get into trouble. During a bungled attempt at chicken theft, the Sheriff arrested Andrew, while his untrustworthy partner headed for the hills.

Sheriff Sanchez rarely had much assistance with controlling the jail—very little from the locals and no real help from the local army post commander either—and young Andrew Wood was to become a victim of this persistent problem. In November, 1863, the jail was occupied with members of the Daimwood gang, several desperadoes, and three men and a woman suspected of murder. The Los Angeles vigilantes were on the rampage at the time, and Judge Hayes and the sheriff knew it, as most certainly did the anxious inmates awaiting trial. Sanchez lost control of the jail and he needed federal help, as shown by the following court order:

> It is ordered that the Sheriff immediately take steps for the security of said jail and that the said prisoners and others tryable in this court, and for that purpose summon the *"posse comitatus"* and to the better carrying into effect this order that he be recommended to ask the aid and protec-

tion of Col. James F. Curtis, Commander of the forces of the United States.[9]

Tensions were not eased when Judge Hayes released the woman and her three compadres for lack of evidence. The four rode out of town so fast that no one even knew that they had gone.

Two days after the above court order was written, vigilantes broke into the jail and dragged Daimwood and his three gang members outside. Figuring that they had enough rope for one more, they looked around the jail and spotted Wilkins' 18-year-old protégé, Andrew Wood, languishing there for his recent attempt at poultry theft.[10] It would be the last crime that the young man would ever commit. The vigilantes snatched him and dragged everyone to the Rocha house across the street, where they found a heavy ceiling beam, strung up some rope, and dispatched all five men forthwith.

After leaving his young partner in the lurch, Charles Wilkins went north and wandered around El Tejon. He waved down a ride from a man driving a buggy. The driver, John Sanford, was Phineas Banning's brother-in-law. Phineas and former sheriff David Alexander owned many businesses together, including the stage line. Sanford owned a sheep ranch and, during their brief encounter, hired the wayward Wilkins as a herder. Wilkins did not know the first thing about sheep herding, nor did he care. When Sanford stopped the buggy to get out and relieve himself, he left his pistol on the seat. In a cold-blooded move, Wilkins picked it up and shot the rancher through the neck. Sanford crumpled in a heap on the ground. The bandit jumped out and ran over to the body, where

Colonel James Freeman Curtis was Commander of the Drum Barracks in Wilmington. He was a former vigilante and distrusted Sheriff Sanchez. – UNITED STATES ARMY MILITARY HISTORY INSTITUTE

In 1863, 18-year-old chicken thief Andrew Wood was hanged by vigilantes along with Charles Daimwood and three members of his gang. – DEPARTMENT OF SPECIAL COLLECTIONS, CHARLES E. YOUNG RESEARCH LIBRARY, UCLA

he found $20 in cash and a fob watch. He took the pistol and one of the horses from the buggy and rode to Santa Barbara.

By coincidence, Los Angeles resident Joe Bartlett happened to be in Santa Barbara; he knew that Charles Wilkins was a no-good renegade. He confronted Wilkins regarding some prior crimes, and a fistfight ensued. Wilkins knocked Bartlett to the ground and, as Bartlett fell, he struck his head on a stone. Instead of being injured, the proactive citizen was angered. Bartlett picked up the stone and proceeded to beat Wilkins senseless with it. While he was searching Wilkins' person, Bartlett found several items in the outlaw's possession. Among them was a pistol with the initials J.Y. carved into the wooden grips. Later, during testimony, Los Angeles resident John Young testified that originally it had been his pistol, but he had sold it to Sanford. He said that the gun still had the wooden peg in it that he had used to repair it. Sanford's watch was also recovered.

During his trial, Wilkins admitted to murdering Sanford and then bragged about his other exploits. He said that Sanford looked like a wealthy mark at the time, but he did not realize how many friends and relatives Sanford had around Los Angeles. He added that his only regret was losing his Bowie knife when he cut loose one of Sanford's horses from the buggy. He completed his testimony by stating that he "didn't think more about killing a man than he would about killing a dog."[11]

It was too much for John Sanford's brother in-law, Phineas Banning, to take. He tried to shoot Wilkins, but bystanders

109

Los Angeles businessman and vigilante Phinneas Banning went gunning for Charles Wilkins. – SECURITY PACIFIC COLLECTION / LOS ANGELES PUBLIC LIBRARY

Cutthroat Charles Wilkins bragged about his murders. He was hanged by a crowd of angry vigilantes. – WILLIAM B. SECREST COLLECTION

restrained him. Wilkins was remanded to the custody of the sheriff and told to return to court in two days, on December 19, for sentencing. As Sheriff Sanchez was walking to the calaboose with his prisoner he encountered Phineas Banning, who was leading an angry mob of armed vigilantes. They took Wilkins from the Sheriff and hanged him, using the usual corral gate. The judge and the sheriff could only shake their heads.

The Murder of Mr. Edward Newman

In January 1864, Edward Newman and Mr. Tischler were driving their buggy from Rancho Cucamonga toward San Bernardino. Six miles from Cucamonga, they were ambushed by three bandidos and Newman was shot in the shoulder. The horse was spooked and Tischler was thrown from the vehicle. A short way down the road the buggy overturned, trapping Newman beneath it.[12]

Celestino Alipaz and Santiago Sanchez rushed forward and attempted to finish off Newman with their knives. Tischler retrieved his shotgun from the side of the road and began to advance on the outlaws. The bandits ordered him to give up his money, promising that they would not hurt him. Tischler disregarded their demands and continued to advance, pointing the barrel of the gun directly at them. The desperadoes lost their nerve and fled.

Tischler righted the buggy, placed his severely wounded friend inside, and took off at full speed back to Cucamonga. The outlaws continued to pursue the buggy in the hope that they could gain an advantage on Tischler, but gave up when another wagon came into sight. Newman died before reaching town.

Sheriff Sanchez organized a posse and rode out to the Alipaz house on the Santa Ana River. They took him by surprise while he was sleeping in bed. As he was being escorted away, Alipaz broke free and ran back into his bedroom, where he grabbed a pistol and Bowie knife from under his pillow. The deputies responded by shooting the bandit down.

On February 4, 1864, Santiago Sanchez was in the Calle de Los Negros when he got into an argument with Los Angeles tinner Manuel Gonzales. Santiago went to the front door of Gonzales' house and called out for him. When the tin worker answered the door, he was greeted by two bullets from Santiago's gun. Sanchez was hanged for murder on June 3, 1864. Sheriff Sanchez was serious about going after killers and, sometimes, as in this case, two of his suspects were brought to justice—the hard way.

Shootout at the Bella Union

Benjamin Hayes was the attorney representing the estate of the deceased John Rains. He was celebrating at Solomon and Caroline Lazard's wedding with many of the good townsfolk at the Bella Union, when he noticed that Robert Carlisle was there, also. Carlisle took on a nasty disposition when he was drunk and, seeing that he had recently won a judgment against him, Hayes figured that it would be wise to take leave of the hotel. It truly was a smart decision, for the ensuing argument sparked what was to be one of the bloodiest gun battles in the town's history. Before it was over, two gunfighters would be dead, a third badly wounded, and a bystander struck by an errant bullet. Not even the horses were safe.

In later years an extra story was added to the Bella Union. This hotel was the scene of one of the bloodiest gunfights in Los Angeles. — SECURITY PACIFIC COLLECTION / LOS ANGELES PUBLIC LIBRARY

The wedding celebration had begun on July 4, 1865, and Robert Carlisle was liberally partaking in the libations. He was conveniently staying at the Bella Union so he could sleep off his intoxication and continue with the celebration in the morning. On the evening of July 5, he began to complain about the King brothers (not related to the aforementioned Thomas and Lafayette King). Carlisle probably knew that the King brothers were no strangers to violence. In 1855, Micajah Johnson killed their father, Sam Houston King, in El Monte. At their dying father's request, the boys tracked Johnson down to a barricaded house. They smashed down the door and put four bullets in his body.[13]

Robert Carlisle believed that Jack and his brothers, Frank and Sam Houston, Jr., were out to get him and take away his livelihood with the help of Attorney Benjamin Hayes.[14] After John Rains' mur-

der, Carlisle obtained power of attorney over the vast Rancho
Cucamonga and had been running it ever since. Judge Samuel Bell
McKee of the Third Judicial District Court in San Jose ruled that
Carlisle had defrauded property owner Merced Rains for personal
gain. The judge further ruled that Jack King would be the new
receiver, replacing Carlisle. More gasoline was tossed on the fire
when the King brothers openly implied that Carlisle was the master-
mind behind the Rains murder.[15] Carlisle was in a foul mood. He
began to wave a large Bowie knife in the air and he fired a shot from
his pistol, saying that he was not afraid of the King brothers: "Let
them come and get me."[16]

City Marshal's Deputy John Evertsen heard the shot and went
inside to investigate. Deputy Evertsen made an attempt to arrest
Carlisle for riotous behavior but backed off when the rancher waved
a knife at him. He went to his office to get his gun and take Carlisle
to jail, but then decided to seek a warrant from the court and tackle the problem the next day. This would prove to be a fatal error.

314 N. Main Street, where the Bella Union Hotel used to stand. – AUTHOR'S COLLECTION

Deputy Sheriff Jack King, who was Deputy Evertson's brother-in-law, entered the bar, and heard Carlisle spouting insults towards him and his family. King slapped Carlisle across the face to shut him up. The two began to fight but were broken up by the crowd. Jack left the bar and headed for the ballroom. After a few more drinks, Carlisle could no longer resist the temptation to attack. He staggered over to King. The deputy turned in time to see a razor-sharp knife arcing through the air. King put up his arm to ward off the blow and the blade slashed his hand and bounced off his ribs, injuring him severely. Blood splashed everywhere. The deputy reached for his pistol and fired a round, missing Carlisle by inches. King stumbled outside in order to get away and to recover from his wounds. Dr. Griffin skillfully patched up the undersheriff that evening. Robert Carlisle staggered over to his hotel room and fell fast asleep. The next morning at the sheriff's office, Jack told his brothers, Frank and Houston, what had transpired. He told them that Carlisle had threatened to kill all three of them. Houston replied, "Let's go call on Carlisle and see if he is goin' to do it!"[17]

The morning was bustling with activity in the muddy street. The stage would be arriving soon to take passengers to San Pedro for the steamship trip to San Francisco. It was 8:00 a.m., and Carlisle had already been drinking for an hour. As drunk as he had been the

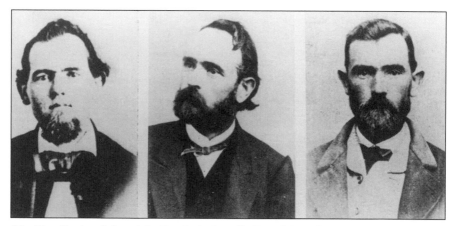

The King Brothers left to right: Frank, Andrew (Jack) and Sam shot it out with wealthy rancher Robert Carlisle. – SEAVER CENTER FOR WESTERN HISTORY RESEARCH, LOS ANGELES COUNTY MUSEUM OF NATURAL HISTORY

night before, he vaguely remembered that he had injured a deputy sheriff, and he knew that someone would probably come after him. Carlisle asked another patron, named Phillips, for a favor. Phillips complied by retrieving Carlisle's shotgun, loading it with buckshot, and handing it over to the wealthy drunk. Carlisle checked his pistols and his knife. He placed the shotgun behind a nearby door, ordered another drink, and waited patiently.

Andrew Henderson, the jailer, noticed the King brothers walking in the street. He ran to the courthouse to tell Sheriff Sanchez that there was going to be trouble. The Sheriff calmly walked over to the Bella Union and looked around. Carlisle was there, but the King brothers were nowhere to be seen. Sheriff Sanchez went over to Lazard's store to buy a cigar and wait. Before long, Houston King walked into the store, and the Sheriff asked him what he was up to. He told Sanchez that he was just buying supplies for a trip to Wilmington. The sheriff eyed him carefully and noticed that Houston did not appear to be wearing a gun. The King brother left and Sanchez continued to wait, chatting with his jailer to kill time.

At high noon, the sun was blazing directly over the dusty street. Frank and Houston King watched the stage pull up in front of the Bella Union. People were preparing for their journey, loading luggage and saying their last-minute goodbyes. The King brothers checked their weapons and walked toward the Bella Union. Inside, Carlisle was sipping his whiskey and watching the entrance via a mirror behind the bar. He was sitting with his good friend and lawyer James H. Lander, while being tended by a skittish bartender. As Frank and Houston came through the door, the bartender ducked while Carlisle drew his pistol and fired. The explosions could be heard up and down the street. One of the stagecoach horses was shot and dropped dead.

Sheriff Sanchez came running out of Lazard's store. A furious gun battle raged inside the hotel. The King brothers returned fire and struck Carlisle in the chest with four bullets. Carlisle fired back. Landers, who had run outside, was struck in the hip by a stray bullet. He screamed and flipped over a hitching post. Several bullets whizzed past innocent bystanders. Glass shattered, wood splinters and brick adobe chips flew everywhere. A slug punctured

Houston King's lung, passing through his right breast and exiting his left shoulder blade. He stumbled outside, trying desperately to return fire.

Frank King rushed at Carlisle, firing all the way. He grabbed Carlisle by his collar and dragged him outside the hotel. Frank then pointed his gun directly at him and pulled the trigger. The gun clicked—empty. Frank improvised and used it as a club to bash Carlisle in the head. The rich man reeled from the blow—the force was so powerful that it bent the trigger guard. Frank was about to bash Carlisle again when Sheriff Sanchez grabbed his arm and stepped between the two men. The sheriff told Frank to drop his gun, and he complied. Meanwhile, Carlisle, realizing that he was dying with four bullets in his torso, and with one last bullet left in his gun, staggered into the doorway. The rancher took careful aim with both hands and pulled the trigger. His last chance bullet zipped through the sheriff's clothing and struck Frank King, causing him to tumble backwards and out the door where he died in the street, lying next to his brother.

As the smoke began to clear, doctors were summoned. They took Carlisle over to a billiard table, where Dr. Griffin took one look at him and told him that he was going to die. The rich man swore revenge on the Kings, saying that he had a young son who would grow up and avenge his death. He told his friends "good bye all."[18] Dr. Griffin had heard many foul mouths in his time, but never had he heard a man swear like Carlisle did on that day. They took him upstairs to a room, where he died 3 hours later. Carlisle's widow, Francisca, was left with four small children just as her sister Merced had been three years earlier. Sadly, due to the land disputes, murders, rumors and suspicions, the sisters were now estranged, and Francisca would have to manage on her own.

Houston was rushed to the Lafayette Hotel across the street. The blood spurted out of his chest as Dr. Gelsich operated; the citizens figured that he would probably die, too. Landers had taken a bullet through the thigh but recovered. To the amazement of the townsfolk, Houston also recovered. He was tried for murder and acquitted by the court. Deputy Jack King recovered from his knife wounds. He became a judge, never to forget that violent and bloody day at the Bella Union. The hotel was torn down in 1940 and a plaque at the Los Angeles Mall marks the spot where it once stood (see appendix B).

Dueling, Mr. Bell, and Michel Lachenais

Although dueling was illegal, Sheriff Sanchez had little time to intervene in such disputes, especially when the parties involved were determined to do battle. Wesley Scalf and S.S. Smith, both from El Monte, found themselves in the middle of such a dispute. Scalf's challenge note read as follows:

> El Monte California, January 13, 1866. Mr. Smith, you have talk around that you would fight me any way that I would fight name. I will fight you on Friday morning at 10 o'clock at the Old Mission Hill. Navy sixes (Colt Navy six shooters). If that don't do, we will end with knives. For that name you call my mother was a lady. I want satisfaction and I must have it. Give me satisfaction let me know today. Signed, W. Scalf.[19]

A seemingly insignificant entry in the minutes of the Board of Supervisor detailed the outcome: "Coffin and funeral expenses for Wesley Scalf, $15.00."[20]

Los Angeles City Marshal William C. Warren was Eugene Biscailuz's grandfather. Gene Biscailuz would become the 27th and one of the most popular sheriffs of Los Angeles County. On March 24, 1867, Warren arrested Los Angeles Ranger Horace Bell for murder. Bell was traveling along the old orchard road when he encountered a very drunk Tomas Miranda. Mr. Bell feared highway robbery and took the offensive. He viciously lashed out at the Californio's head with his pistol, knocking him unconscious. The wound was three inches long and four inches wide. Five weeks later, Miranda died. The jury found Bell not guilty of murder.

This incident by itself is not particularly noteworthy given the times. When analyzed carefully, however, it reveals much about the prejudice and unilateral nature of the legal system. If the roles had been reversed and Horace Bell had been murdered, there would most certainly have been a lynch mob looking for Miranda.

As it was, Horace was considered *gente de razon,* a respectable citizen. He was both a ranger and a well-known lawyer in the community. Who in town would think him capable of any wrongdoing? Even if he had done something wrong, his vigilante buddies would most likely have not let anything happen to him.

This incident, and many others like it, would lead one to believe that being an uneducated non-English-speaking Californio in 1860s Los Angeles was not a desirable identity. It must have been extremely difficult for Sheriff Tomas Sanchez to see his people suffer during those turbulent years.

Michel Lachenais did not know it, but his criminal career would place him at a critical turning point in the history of Los Angeles and the Sheriff's department. After his well-documented lynching in 1870, the vigilante practice of "quick justice" in Los Angeles would grind to a halt. Other changes during the 1870s would irrevocably steer the sheriff's office in a new direction.

In September 1865, Frenchman Michel (Miguel) Lachenais returned to Los Angeles to see whether people had forgotten him. The Rangers gave him hard looks when he walked down the street and rumors started flying about the Frenchman's past evil deeds. Accordingly, Sheriff Sanchez went into the court archives to check the suspect for warrants. He dug out an old indictment regarding Lachenais. It read as follows:

> . . . on October 1, 1861, shot Henry DeLaval with a certain pistol of the value of two dollars, with leaden bullets charged with gunpowder, in the left side of the belly. A wound of the depth of four inches and a half an inch in breadth . . . of which said wound Henry DeLaval then and there died contrary to the Statute and against the peace and dignity of the people of the State of California.[21]

Sanchez picked up the wanted man and dragged him into court for a proper hearing. Throwing himself on the mercy of the judicial system, Lachenais said that he was just a poor ignorant farmer who did not speak English. He stated that he did not know that he was supposed to show up in court for a trial. The judge took mercy on the miserable wretch and found him not guilty of the crime. Narrowed eyes watched the Frenchman as he rode back to his farm in an area that is now called Montebello.

It was not long before the Sheriff had to ride out to the Lachenais farm to take him into custody again. This time, Lachenais was accused of murdering Pablo Moreno, one of his Indian workers, by bludgeoning the native in the head with an iron club. Michel had calmly loaded the body onto his wagon and drove to the public cemetery. He then dug a grave and buried the man as if he had died from natural causes!

A trial was held, using Indian farm laborers as witnesses. After a short deliberation, the jury found Lachenais guilty of manslaughter. The defendant's attorney filed a stay of judgment because Indians had been allowed to testify in a case against a white man. The judge ruled in favor of Lachenais, for indeed, the law at the time was clear that Indians could not be used as witnesses because they were thought to be non-Christians, and as such were not capable of understanding the oath "to swear before God."

When a new trial was held without the Indian eyewitnesses, the jury could not find enough evidence to convict Lachenais. The jury found him not guilty and he was once again released. The vigilantes were still watching but, to them, the murder of an Indian did not matter much, so they let him go about his business, which, in Lacenais' case, was murder. All of this was of no great concern to Sheriff Sanchez. His final term of office was drawing to a close, and he was tired of the endless parade of death and violence.

Sheriff Tomas Sanchez had faithfully served the citizens of Los Angeles throughout eight of the most dangerous years the County has ever seen. Droughts, disease, depression, vigilantes, criminal violence, and a civil war marked his time in office. He had been shot at, punched, kicked, and attacked by countless felons, desperadoes, and renegades. Miraculously, he was still alive to talk about it. Sanchez was a hero who should have retired in grand style, to be praised forevermore by his successors. Sadly, this was not be the case.

Like many of the great Rancho Dons, Tomas Sanchez enjoyed the lifestyle that his land and livestock afforded him. However, he often required cash to pay for the day-to-day expenses of the rancho

Tomas Sanchez's wife
Josepha bore him 19
children. She lived on for
33 years after his death.
— HUNTINGTON LIBRARY

Sheriff Sanchez's Rancho Cienega o' Paso de la Tijera
was located in an area now known as Baldwin Hills.
He sold the rancho to pay off debts. – SECURITY PACIFIC
COLLECTION / LOS ANGELES PUBLIC LIBRARY

The Sanchez adobe in
Glendale, California is now a
museum and park open to the
public. – AUTHOR'S COLLECTION

and to make payroll for his vaqueros and servants. The sheriff
became a persistent borrower, and the high interest costs began to
eat away at his fortune. In 1875, he sold half of his rancho for
$60,000. Not long afterward, he sold another quarter of it, and soon
afterward, the rest was foreclosed upon. His house in town was also
sold, and he moved to the Verdugo property, which had been given
to him as dowry upon his marriage many years ago. Sanchez told his
good friend Joseph Widney, "If I were a younger man, I would take
my boys and go to Mexico. Our civilization has been so different,
that we cannot compete with the rush and the complications of a
civilization so unlike our own."[22] He died penniless on June 24,
1882, at the age of fifty-six. Josepha followed thirty-three years later.

Sheriff James F. Burns, March 1868–February 1872

Sheriff Tomas Sanchez ran against 37-year-old James F. Burns for the term of office beginning in March, 1868. Both men were popular among the citizens of Los Angeles, and even Burns had to admit that Sheriff Sanchez was "beloved and respected by all."[23] The voters could see that Sanchez was exhausted, however, and ultimately they felt that it was time for a change. Voting laws had changed, and the new sheriff would now serve a term of 2 years instead of the traditional 1 year. Besides the legal differences, there was an unprecedented advancement in the field of communication: The first telegraph system had come to Los Angeles County. Information that used to take weeks to send could now be transmitted in seconds.

The county had grown to a population of 10,000, and the sheriff's office was collecting more than $123,000 a year in taxes.[24] Another noticeable change in the City of Angels was the emigration of Chinese laborers into the Calle de Los Negros. The influx of immigrants would play a major role during Sheriff Burns's tenure in office—not just locally, but internationally.

James Franklin Burns was born in Clifton, Ontario County, New York, on September 27, 1831. His parents moved to Kalamazoo, Michigan, where young James was raised and educated. He attended college and began a career as a teacher, but then joined the Hazard party wagon train to travel to the Golden State. Along the way, he met and married Miss Lucretia Burdick. In 1853, the newlyweds' convoy passed through Utah where they were attacked by Indians more than once and the entire group was lucky to make it through alive.

A former schoolteacher turned lawman, Sheriff James Burns put a stop to vigilantism in Los Angeles County. – LOS ANGELES COUNTY SHERIFF'S DEPARTMENT ARCHIVES

Lucretia Burns bore one son. The family continued traveling west and finally settled in San Gabriel in 1854. Burns opened a children's school, and business was booming. His skill at teaching earned him much respect and elevated him to the office of Superintendent of Schools in 1856. In 1858, his career took a different path when President James Buchanan appointed him U.S. Marshal for the southern district of California. In 1865, Burns was elected Treasurer for the City of Los Angeles and served in that capacity for two years prior to running for sheriff in September, 1868.

Jim Burns did not have the appearance of a typical lawman. Crittenden wrote: "He was short and chubby with a kewpie-like expression on his round face. He was partially bald and wore a neat 3-inch fringe of ginger-colored beard descending from his lower lip."[25] Like others before him, Sheriff Burns had assisted in the hunt for Sheriff Barton's killers. Throughout the 1860s, whenever volunteer deputies called for help, Burns had always made himself available.

After a successful first term as sheriff, Burns decided to run for a second term. During his re-election campaign he received 1,312 votes, while 1,166 votes were cast for William R. Rowland, for a total of 2,478 votes. This is an interesting figure since the number of registered voters in the county was only 2,400. Apparently, the polling places were in need of tighter security. During September and October of 1869, general security did come, however, in the form of lighting: The city was proud of its five new gas streetlights, which helped to deter crime in the evening.

Despite the lighting, however, crime in Los Angeles was still prevalent. In regards to an order from the U.S. Attorney General's Office for communities nationwide to supply crime statistics, the *Star* claimed that Los Angeles had a volume of crime that would match or exceed any other community in California. "We feel no hesitation in asserting that Los Angeles in proportion to population will do as much to give this report the voluminous character usually appertaining to "Pub. Docs." as any portion of the state."[26] When the 1870 crime statistics were sent to the U.S. Census office, the Superintendent thought that there must have been a mistake. He wrote back, "An impression very unfavorable to your section might be created by the publication of these statistics."[27] Vigilante senti-ment remained strong. One year after completing the first Los Angeles railroad, Phineas Banning commented, "There has been no one murdered there for three or four days. But there are at least 500 there who are suffering for a good hanging."[28]

Sheriff Burns was the type of leader that the county desperately needed. He believed that he could bring about change in both crime and the vigilante problem. In 1870, a large lynch mob went to Wilmington to seize one of the sheriff's prisoners. Sheriff Burns arrived with a heavily armed posse and the mob backed off. Historian Remi Nadeau noted, "The would-be lynchers evidently had no taste for encountering cold lead."[29] Watershed moments like this were clues that the county was beginning to come of age. Los Angeles was far from becoming civilized, however, as a drastic chain of events involving the Chinese population would soon foretell.

Marshal Warren and Joseph Dye, October 31, 1870

By the 1870s, the Calle de Los Negros was almost entirely populated by Chinese. Chinese men organized into "Companies" that exer-cised control over the neighborhood. These companies frequently fought with each other over turf. Young women were purchased in China and brought to America as slaves. The luckier ones were bought up by wealthy men and became concubines, sometimes even wives; the rest were put to work in the town brothels.

The Hong Chow *tong* stole a beautiful woman, Ah Hit, who was worth as much as $2,500. The Hong Chows took her from the Nin Yung clan and started for San Francisco. The Nin Yungs went to the police and complained that the Hong Chows had stolen some very valuable "jewelry" from them. A $100 reward was put up for her safe return.

Marshal William Warren and Officer Jose Redona rode to Santa Barbara to stop the "thieves" while Officer Joseph Dye telegraphed the Santa Barbara Constable's office regarding the incident. Upon their arrival, the constable had Ah Hit in custody. The lawmen returned her to Los Angeles on the stagecoach, disembarking to find both tongs facing off in the street. Although there was no vio-lence at that particular moment, the tension was mounting.

Warren collected the reward money and started to walk away. Officer Dye became upset and demanded a share of the money, claiming that the only reason they had had such an easy time in Santa Barbara was because of his quick work at the telegraph office. The Nin Yung clan also demanded the money because they had reported the crime. Warren laughed it off and told both of them that the money was his and he would take no further action on this matter.

The animosity between Dye and Warren was longstanding, based chiefly on the fact that Warren was a strong Union supporter and Dye was a secessionist. When Warren was allowed to select a new officer, he chose a northerner instead of one of Dye's friends. Dye was outraged and made his anger known to anyone who would listen.

On October 31, 1870, during the Hong Chow court trial, Dye again demanded money from Warren, but Warren simply brushed him off and walked away. Dye chased after his boss, who was walking with Officer Redona in the middle of the street just outside the courthouse near the corner of Spring and Temple. Dye continued to pester Warren for the money. He was relentless and Warren, fed up with Dye's charades, told him "any man who says I have taken things which do not belong to me is a liar."[30]

Those were fighting words and Dye raised his cane as if to strike. Warren was already prepared for the brawl and had concealed a derringer in his left hand behind his back. He fired. Dye was struck over the left eye by a glancing round as he simultaneously dropped his cane and drew his pistol to return fire. The marshal dropped his derringer and commenced firing with his six-shooter. Officer Robert Hester and another innocent bystander were wounded in a hail of flying lead. One bullet slammed into Warren's silver pocketwatch saving him temporarily until another bullet punched into his groin. He staggered and fell to the ground calling out, "I am killed."[31] When Dye's gun was out of bullets, he tackled his boss, and the two grappled in the street. Onlookers broke up the fight, but not until Dye had taken a vicious bite out of Warren's ear. They took the marshal to his house and called the doctor, but it was in vain for the lawman died the next day.

Dye was charged with murder and released on bail of $2,000. After being found not guilty by reason of self-defense, Joseph Dye

Eugene Biscailuz served as county sheriff from 1932-1958. His grandfather, William C. Warren, pictured here, was gunned down by one of his own deputies. — SEAVER CENTER FOR WESTERN HISTORY RESEARCH, LOS ANGELES COUNTY MUSEUM OF NATURAL HISTORY

would leave the City of Angels for a while. He made his way to Ventura County, where the ever-watchful eyes of Los Angeles vigilantes would not follow him. In Santa Paula, Dye often dealt with his business partner's intermediary, a man named Haines, whom he introduced to his wife. Mr. Haines soon became enamored with Mrs. Dye and tried to pressure her into having an affair with him. That was Haines' first mistake.

Dye was a jealous man and easy to anger. On September 2, 1886, he confronted Haines. Haines also had a temper, which he demonstrated by retrieving a rifle with which to shoot Dye. No stranger to a gunfight, Dye reached for the pistol which he always carried. Haines pulled the trigger and heard a "click" but no report—his second mistake. Dye smiled, and sent the man to his grave without even flinching. He was sentenced to life in prison, but, in typical Dye fashion, he appealed and was acquitted for the second time.

Once again, Joseph Dye saw the eyes of townspeople watching him and heard their whispering in the shadows as he went about his business. Realizing that it was time to move on again, he returned to Los Angeles, where he hoped things had "cooled off." Dye had several oil and mining claims in the Sespe oil fields in Ventura County, and it was there that he met a man named Mason Bradfield. The two quickly became good friends and decided to go into business together, leasing a small piece of land in the hopes that it contained oil. The "Kentuck" claim was on one side of their property and a vacant lot was on the other. Dye cut a deal with the California "Oil Spouter" Company to drill for black gold on their property.

When the oil workers, called "roughnecks," arrived, Dye directed them to drill on the vacant lot. He led the men to believe that he and Bradfield owned the property. Before long, the well was producing 100 barrels a day. Not long thereafter, Mr. Irland from the California Oil Company found out that they were not drilling on Dye and Bradfield's claim, but on someone else's property. When Irland confronted Dye, he was indignant and told him that everything was 100% legitimate. He would never try to hoodwink anyone, especially the prestigious California Oil Company! Joe Dye assured Irland that everything would be just fine, and then he went immediately to speak with Bradfield.

Bradfield was upset when he found out about Dye's unscrupulous business practice. Dye shot back a glaring look and told Bradfield that he needed to go immediately to the assayer's office and file a claim on the land. He figured that it was at least worth $100,000, and Dye wanted the oil company to continue pumping oil. When Bradfield refused, Dye shouted, "You dance to my music or I'll make it so hot for you, you won't be able to stay in the country." Referring to the men he had killed, he said, "You know Haines? You know Billy Warren, you remember the son-of-a-bitch in the vineyard? You do as I tell you or I will give you some of the same medicine!"[32]

Bradfield backed off and walked away. He was so angry at Dye that he decided to get revenge. He researched the title for the vacant lot and then discreetly located two investors. Next, he went to the assayer's office and filed three claims—one for himself, one for Mr. Hendly, and one for John Thompson—covering a total of sixty acres. He then cut a deal with the oil company and transferred all three claims to them; in exchange, Bradfield received the deed to a rock quarry on the property. He then brokered an agreement with the Mentone Stone Company whereby they would pay him to quarry rock from his land.

About a month later, Joseph Dye was watching workers quarry rock from the property and inquired about their business. They told him that a man named Bradfield owned the land and had purchased it with money he had made in the oil business. Dye flew into a rage and went to Los Angeles searching for Bradfield. He found the businessman in Linde's jewelry store, where he confronted him: "I gave you a chance to make a stake, to make $10,000, and you have thrown me down for a lot of tenderfeet sons of bitches? This will cost you your life. I have a mind to kill you right now!" Dye's hand went for his pistol, testing Bradfield's nerve. "Don't draw on me!" Dye exclaimed as he poked Bradfield in the face. Dye was wearing a sap glove (a type of glove reinforced with iron), and he struck Bradfield in the face with it, causing him to bleed. The angry killer continued to provoke the petrified Bradfield by poking him in the ribs with his six shooter. The frightened entrepreneur fled from the jewelry store with every intention of avoiding Dye for the rest of his life.

On May 1, 1891, Bradfield was riding the cable car past Dol's Restaurant when he spotted Dye. Dye was chewing on a toothpick, when his eyes locked with his old partner. The killer put his hand on his gun but he did not pull it out. He continued to follow the cable car, trying to find a way to kill Bradfield or, at the very least, to terrorize him. Whenever Dye ran into some of Bradfield's acquaintances, he told them that he was going to kill their friend. One evening, Bradfield thought he saw a man hiding in the shadows near his home on Hope Street. He had become so frightened that he could barely function. In early May, Bradfield finally cracked.

Mason Bradfield bought a shotgun. He trailed Dye in a clandestine fashion, noting that his nemesis lived in the Mott Building on Commercial Street and Alameda. He also noticed that the killer took several walks a day up and down Commercial Street. Dye was never without a gun, and Bradfield was surprised that the gunman did not notice that he was being followed. On May 7, Bradfield calmly entered the New Arlington Hotel and asked for a second-story room facing Commercial Street.[33]

Hotel worker Peter Haack arranged for the room and gave him the key to suite 27. Bradfield was satisfied with the window that faced the street. He watched Dye take his daily walk on Commercial Street and calculated the exact time that he needed to make his move. On May 14, at three o'clock in the afternoon, Bradfield entered his room, carrying a pistol, a knife, and a double-barreled shotgun.

He opened the window and then waited until his target passed directly across the street from him. Bradfield called out to Dye, and when the killer turned in order to see who had yelled out to him, Mason pulled the trigger. The explosion shattered the afternoon silence. A secondary explosion followed soon after. Nine buckshot wounds perforated Dye's chest. He threw up his arms and collapsed in a heap in front of Germain's Saloon.

Bradfield dropped the smoking shotgun on the floor. He grabbed his pistol and ran out of the Wilmington entrance of the hotel. Police Captain Roberts heard the gunshots and was responding when he saw the assassin running down Wilmington toward Requenna. He intercepted Mason, who had a pistol in his hand and a huge knife in his pocket. Bradfield was arrested and jailed to stand trial for the murder of his old business partner. The jury listened to the evidence and found him not guilty on account of self-defense. This was perhaps a fitting end for a man like Dye, who never cared much for anyone's life but his own.

Joe Dye is buried at Evergreen Cemetery. His grave marker is a small concrete circle in the ground (right foreground).

The Notorious Dick Fellows

Dick Fellows was a down-on-his-luck alcoholic who had spent all of his money in the Calle de Los Negros. His real name was George Lyttle, and he had been born in Clay County, Kentucky, in 1846. His father, who was a prominent lawyer, judge, and businessman, gave George the best education and family support that could be afforded to a young man in his situation. At age seventeen, George enlisted in the Confederate army and served in the 10th Regiment, Kentucky Infantry. He was captured after less than five months of service and sent to an Ohio prison camp. After serving only one month as a prisoner of war, he was released, and he went home to study law with his father.

It did not take young George long to realize that he had an embarrassing drinking problem. Not being able to face his family, he headed west, ending up on the mean streets of Los Angeles. In 1869, he took on the assumed name of Dick Fellows and attempted to hold up a stagecoach by himself. At 1:00 in the afternoon, six miles from San Fernando, he waited on his horse by the side of the road to rob the northbound stage out of Los Angeles. As related from a newspaper article that Dick wrote:

> Presently the cloud of fine dust preceding the stage on the wind, which is set in our direction, began to envelope us, and springing to my seat in the saddle I shouted, "Hold on there driver!" "All right," he called through the cloud of dust and stopped his team. At the same instant I saw a man dressed in partial uniform of a United States soldier step out of the stage on the opposite side from me and secrete himself quickly in the cactus, drawing as he did so a pistol. I sprang on my horse because out of the road a horse could not turn around or be maneuvered properly because of the dense cacti. Immediately placing myself on the same side of the road with my soldier antagonist, I knelt down to peep under the cactus to locate him, where the branches of the plant become fewer nearer the ground. My bold soldier had been a little before me in making this maneuver, and as I stooped down to peep, he took a shot at me.

Springing to my feet I called out, "Hurry up Bill, you and John go on around one side, and I'll take the other," as if the rest of my party had just appeared on the battlefield. Instantly he called out "I will surrender, don't shoot, boys." I lost no time in getting around to where he was, but proceeded cautiously, pistol in hand, and disarmed him. When he shot at me, which was the next instant after I had stopped the stage, the horses became unmanageable, or the driver, availing himself of the opportunity, sped on, sweeping my horse away with them on the road. As I had not asked the stage driver to throw off the box, he kept it aboard and by the time I had disarmed the belligerent passenger the whole fleeting outfit had passed the wash and was safe from all pursuit.[34]

After his bungled robbery, Dick relieved the stranded, unarmed soldier of his money and then went on to try his luck again by robbing the evening stagecoach; this time, he was successful. Only a few days later, he was shot in the foot during a struggle with some Angelenos who had heard of the robbery and recognized him. Sheriff Burns took Fellows into custody, where he was later convicted and sent to San Quentin for eight years. He was a model prisoner at San Quentin and, for his excellent behavior, he was released on April 4, 1874, after having served only half of his sentence.

Fellows spent the rest of his life in and out of prison, mostly in. He continued to rob stagecoaches, but his other exploits took place north of Los Angeles in the Bakersfield, San Luis Obispo, and Santa Clara areas. On March 8, 1908, Dick Fellows received a final pardon. The 62-year-old outlaw was tired of the gangster lifestyle. He quietly assumed a new life, and no one ever heard or saw him again.[35]

The Last Lynchings

Michel Lachenais had escaped justice one too many times. After killing five or six men and being charged with murder twice, his luck had run out. In late 1870, Lachenais got into a heated argument with a fellow farmer named Jacob Bell over the use of water from the *zanja madre*, a brick aqueduct that supplied the city with water from the Los Angeles River. Michel initially backed away from the argument, but then returned with his pistol. He shot Bell dead and then decided it was time for a drink. After spending time at one of the local watering holes, Michel's tongue started to loosen. He bragged about shooting Bell and the ridiculous look that the man had on his face when he died. Lachenais even mentioned where he had left the body.[36]

A sheriff's deputy arrested the drunken man and tossed him into jail. It did not take long for the vigilance committee to gather on Stearns' block to discuss their options. Felix Signoret and his fellow vigilantes decided that Lachenais had gone free one too many times and they were not going to take a chance on the legal system again. In the next day's newspaper:

> One by one our citizens are dropping into their graves, sent hither by the bullet or knife. . . . Almost ere one victim is coffined we hear the ringing of the shot which sends another unprepared into the presence of his maker. . . . This state

Vigilantes overpowered Sheriff Burns and hanged Michel Lacenais on December 17, 1870. This was the last lynching in the City of Los Angeles. – HUNTINGTON LIBRARY

of affairs is interfering with the growth and progress of our city and county. . . . We are no advocate of vigilance committees [but] . . . we warn the authorities that if the flowing tide of crime which is now sweeping over us is not checked, a terrible vengeance will be meted out.[37]

At 11:00 a.m. on December 17, 1870, Signoret, accompanied by 300 armed men, marched to the jail and demanded the keys. Sheriff Burns tried to stop the mob, but they would not listen to him. When he refused to give up his prisoner, they took sledge hammers and began to pound on the jail door (which had been reinforced due to many previous lynchings). It took the vigilantes half an hour to smash the two heavy security portals and jail gate. But they succeeded, and they took Lachenais to Tomlinson's corral and prepared to hang him.

A priest administered the last rites. Michel was allowed to speak his final words; in Spanish, he said: "I am guiltless of murder, if I had not killed Mr. Bell, he would have killed me. . . . It was done in the excitement." He then turned to the priest and said "Good-by, Padre."[38] The vigilantes kicked away the box, and the accused man was no more. Michel Lachenais was the thirty-fifth man to be lynched by Los Angeles vigilantes, and the last to be lynched in the city.

The distinction of being the last person to be lynched in Los Angeles County went to a man called "Romo". His extralegal execution occurred in June 1874, conducted by an angry crowd of El Monte residents because he had seriously injured a shopkeeper and his wife during a robbery. Vigilantism had finally come to an end.

Buckskin Bill

Sometime in the winter of 1871, Allanson Gardner, Alfred Henry, and David Stevenson paid a visit to the Bilderbeck twins at their cabin in the mountains near the Rancho Verdugo. David Stevenson was also known as Stephen Samsbury, Steven Samsbray, Six Toed Pete, Pata de Oso (Bear's foot) and, most famously, Buckskin Bill. He was a notorious outlaw who had admitted to killing at least seven people.

Oscar and Henry Bilderbeck were clearing brush from their property and selling it in town. They planned to use their profits from the wood sales to buy livestock. According to court records, Gardner stood by during the robbery while Alfred Henry and Buckskin Bill shot the twins. The outlaws headed north and were last seen far from Los Angeles, in Lone Pine, Mono County.

On January 16, 1871, Deputy Jonathan Dunlap went to visit the twins to see how they were coming along with their project. He was shocked to discover their bodies at the bottom of a canyon near Tujunga Pass. They had been covered with a bloody blanket and placed in a shallow grave, apparently having been shot and then beaten to death with an axe. After some investigation, Dunlap found that the three aforementioned outlaws had just been seen leaving town; however, the sheriff's office would not pick up the trail until that summer. The story of the pursuit is told in Sheriff Burns' own words:

When I went into Mexico in the summer of 1871 for Buckskin Bill, I found an entirely different situation from that the Americans have discovered in later years. I was shown every courtesy and consideration, and got all the necessary authority and cooperation from Governor Pasquela and other officials of Lower California. In those days the Mexican people and government respected American citizens.

After Buckskin Bill, whose other name was Stephen Samsbray, the confessed slayer of seven men, had killed the Bilderbeck brothers of Los Angeles, I, and deputies from my office, trailed him in various parts of California, from February to June 1871. After Jonathon Dunlap, a deputy in my office, lost the bad man's trail up near Lone Pine and returned to Los Angeles, I later discovered the trail and traced him to a point in the mountains, eighteen miles from Temecula in Riverside County. I sent another deputy after him, but without success.

One day a young man who came to Los Angeles from Fort Yuma told me that he could find the trail taken by the bandit. I paid him fifteen dollars and he returned to Riverside County, and then came back with the information that the bandit and his squaw and her infant had crossed the international boundary line into Lower California, the bandit riding on a horse and the woman on a mule.

I made up a party and went to San Diego, where I was joined by the Under-Sheriff of that County, and we crossed the line on one of the most trying trips I ever took. With the help of natives across the border, we located the outlaw in a rugged region around Real de Castillo, about two hundred miles below the border.

I had requisition papers from Judge Ignacio Sepulveda of the Superior Court of Los Angeles County to Governor Pasquela. The Governor and his men were very cordial and gave me prompt assistance. At Real de Castillo, I had the assistance of Felipe Zarate, Jefe de Policia de Frontera [Chief of Police of the border country].

When I learned that Buckskin Bill had taken the trail over the mountains at the head of the Gulf of California, I entrusted his capture to a party composed of four Mexicans and two Indian guides. I promised to give the men fifty dollars apiece if they brought other evidence that he had been slain.

It was generally known that the outlaw had six toes on his left foot, and in four days these men returned with his six toed foot, which I accepted as unmistakable evidence that the desperado had been killed. The outlaw and his squaw camped at a spring in the mountains, and the men crept up and surprised them. In a struggle with the outlaw, he was shot in the abdomen with his own rifle by one of the Mexicans. Realizing he was mortally wounded, the outlaw begged to be shot in the head (the Mexicans refused). The squaw who came originally from the Agua Caliente in Kern County, and who had remained faithful to him through many desperate vicissitudes, and was nearby when he was wounded and died, was left in the wilderness by the party. The captors thought she would be able to make her way back home but in this effort she failed. A few months later I learned that the dead bodies of herself and infant were found in the mountains about a hundred miles of where she was last seen.

I brought the outlaw's telltale foot, preserved in mescal, back to Los Angeles. With this evidence, I went north and applied for the reward offered by the state, and in ten days had received the money.[39]

Before he died, Buckskin Bill admitted to killing men in San Francisco, Stanislaus, Merced and Kern Counties. It is not known what happened to Alfred Henry, but Allanson Gardner was brought to trial. The court agreed to change the venue to San Bernardino, where he was found not guilty.[40]

The Chinese Massacre

By fall 1871, anti-Chinese feelings had grown to a fever pitch. Although there were fewer than 200 Chinese immigrants in Los Angeles, their culture and religion were strange to Anglos and Californios alike. There was much misunderstanding and a complete lack of knowledge about the Chinese in general. In an article titled "Ye Heathen Chinee," The *Los Angeles Star* wrote, "We venture the assertion that many a dark and terrible deed has been perpetrated by these heathen in their secret dens, which will never come to the knowledge of the Christians whose places they are usurping."[41]

The Hong Chow Tong, run by Yo Hing, was still doing battle with the Nin Yung Tong, which was operated by Sam Yueng. Once again, the beautiful and very expensive prostitute, Ya Hit, was at the center of the controversy. Ya Hit had either run away or had been stolen from the Nin Yungs. Yo Hing's prize was not long in his custody when Yueng went to the Marshal, claiming that Ya Hit was a thief who had stolen jewelry from him. One of Yueng's men was conveniently waiting at the jail to bail her out, and the poor woman was now back in the hands of the Nin Yungs. Yo Hing was not to be outdone. He arranged for a secret marriage, claimed Ya Hit for his wife, and took her back. The Nin Yungs were outraged and put a $1,000 price tag on Yo Hing's head. The shooting started soon afterward, around 5:30 p.m. on October 24.[42]

There are several versions of how the massacre started, but two of them stand out as the most plausible. In the first version, Deputy City Marshal Jesus Bilderrain was having a drink at Higby's Saloon when he heard the gunshots. He ran over to the Calle de Los Negros to investigate and found Ah Choy's body. Ah Choy, the leader of the tong that originally owned Ya Hit, had been shot through the neck. The warring tongs continued to exchange gunshots, and Bilderrain was accidentally caught in the crossfire, struck in the wrist and shoulder. The officer called for help; a man named Robert Thompson started to come to his aid. But as Thompson passed in front of a doorway by the Coronel building he was fatally shot in the chest.[43] According to Sheriff Burn's memoirs, Thompson was a Deputy Constable in the discharge of his official duties.[44]

The second version of the story begins with the courtroom testimony of Sam Yeung. Sam had been arrested by Marshal's Deputy Emil Harris as a suspect in one of the Tong shootings prior to October 24. His bail had been originally refused because the judge said that he did not have enough money. Mr. Yeung had objected,

stating that he had plenty of money locked in a chest behind his store. The bond was accepted after Harris went to Yeung's establishment and verified $7,000 in gold coin.[45]

Jesus Bilderrain was a gambler and a deputy marshal. He and Robert Thompson got wind of the large amount of money and decided to rob

A Chinese dragon proceeds through the streets of Chinatown. Fear and ignorance of Chinese people and their culture would lead to a horrible massacre. – HUNTINGTON LIBRARY

Judge Robert Widney saved the lives of several Chinese residents by threatening rioters at gunpoint.
— HUNTINGTON LIBRARY

Yeung. They entered the old Coronel house with a fake warrant and bullied their way to the back. Mr. Yeung was suspicious, and he sat on his money chest, refusing to budge and yelling for help. As Thompson was trying to yank Yeung off the chest, Yo Duc entered the room with a large pistol and began to fire. The two bandits made a break for the door. Thompson fell dead outside the Coronel house and Bilderrain, who was shot in the leg, barely escaped with his life.[46]

Whatever the actual initial cause of the shooting, the sentiment was the same among the Anglo citizens who were drinking in the nearby saloons: The Chinese were slaughtering white people in the Calle de Los Negros! A small but angry crowd began to gather in Los Angeles Street. Suddenly, several panicked Chinese men exited the Coronel building and fired into the crowd. A 15-year-old boy was struck in the leg and another bystander was hit in the hip. Within minutes, an angry drunken band of 500 people was marching toward Chinatown. Some wanted to loot and pillage, some wanted to kill the "heathens," and some just wanted to watch the for the "excitement."

Even local businesses joined in. Broderick and Reilly's bookstore donated a rope, and a housewife offered her clothesline to use for hanging. Attorney, Judge, and former Deputy Andrew King heard the ruckus, which interrupted his dinner. He grabbed his gun and checked to see whether it was loaded. In his haste, he accidentally discharged the weapon and blew off the tip of his finger.

By the time the mob had reached Chinatown, all of the gang members except Ya Hit's brother, Ah Choy, had left town. His body was still lying in the street. Many of the innocent Chinese who were left behind barricaded themselves inside the Coronel building.

Judge Wilson Gray, Judge Robert M. Widney, and Sheriff Burns began to rally what little support they had left in the City of Angels. They placed themselves in front of the Coronel building and urged the crowd to stop the madness. Burns stood on a dry goods box and addressed the crowd, ordering them to disperse. He said that he would guard the building and arrest the Ch inese who were responsible for the shootings. However, before he could finish his speech, the box gave way and the officer fell to the ground. The crowd roared in laughter as the embarrassed sheriff crawled out from the debris.

Unwavering in his resolve to stop the crowd, Burns posted his few volunteers around the building and continued to address the mob. He realized that he was losing control when he could hear the shouts: "Damn the Sheriff! Shoot him! Hang him!"[47] Burns realized that the only way to stop the mob was to go for help. He hurried off, leaving the city marshal in charge.

The doors of the Coronel building slowly opened and the officers hoped that the Chinese would surrender, thus ending the standoff. However, the mob disagreed and refused to allow anyone to be taken into custody. When an Asian appeared in the doorway, more than forty bullets slammed into the house. One Chinese man who decided to make an escape by running away was instantly gunned down. Another tried to escape down the back alley, but the mob seized and hanged him. At first, the crowd wanted to burn them out, but the handful of officers on the scene made it clear that the first man to light a match would be shot. The mob then tried to wash them out with a water hose but, when that failed, they gained access to the roof by ladder. The hoodlums cut a hole in the roof and began to shoot at the occupants. This caused most of the Chinese to panic and run outside, where they were captured by the rioters. Historians Thompson and West wrote, "For three long hours the 'Angel City' seemed possessed by the powers of hell. Yells, curses, screams, prayers, and pistol shots rent the air continuously. It was a carnival of blood; murder was rampant."[48]

A group of the mobsters took the innocent and highly respected Dr. Chien Tong to their makeshift gallows. He begged for his life, saying that he would give them all of his money. The hoodlums showed him no mercy. They hanged him, took his money, and even went so far as to cut off a finger that held a valuable ring. The sick nature of the crowd was truly disturbing. The rioters' anger was compounded by the fact that Chinese laborers would work for lower wages than white men, a fact that upset many Anglos. After hanging two 19-year-olds, one of the lynchers danced a jig and shouted, "Give me some more Chinamen boys, patronize home trade!"[49]

Rioters were breaking into Chinese homes and stealing everything of value. Robert Widney, local real estate baron, lawyer, and judge, realized that the situation was worsening. When the jurist first tried to interfere, he was told, "A good lot of white men ought to be hung, too."[50] At Widney's request, his brother handed him a Colt Navy pistol and, with it, the judge began to take matters into his own hands. Widney approached the leader of one gang, jerked him backwards, stuck the gun in his face and said, "You won't do any more hanging!"[51] After realizing that the judge was deadly serious, the gang backed off and released their captive. The judge asked a group of armed supporters to take the shaken victim and lock him in the jail under armed guard in order to protect him. Widney then systematically approached other lynch mobs with his pistol and continued to order the release of captives. The county's prosecuting attorney, C. E. Thom, saw the judge with a gun in his hand and asked him what he was doing. The judge replied, "I am stopping a massacre!"[52] In all, Judge Widney is reported to have saved the lives of twenty-two Chinese citizens in this manner.

After much cajoling and browbeating, Sheriff Burns swore in a posse of twenty-five men and proclaimed that everyone in the Coronel building who did not live there would be placed under arrest unless they dispersed immediately. Officer Emil Harris later testified:

> I heard some shots fired and ran toward them to Los Angeles Street, and saw an excited crowd in front of Negro Alley . . . [The Sheriff] requested me and all citizens willing to obey the laws to stand alongside of him. . . . The excited multitude got the upper hand. . . . One Chinaman came running out [and I] heard a cry of some white persons,

Formerly home to native Americans, the Calle de los Negros became populated by Chinese immigrants in the 1860s. – SECURITY PACIFIC COLLECTION / LOS ANGELES PUBLIC LIBRARY

"Here is one! Here is one!" and I succeeded in capturing him . . . when some parties . . . about 100 or more took him from me, held me and took me to Temple Street . . . they cried "Hang him!"[53]

After four hours of mob rule, the crowd had finally had enough, and they began to disperse. Nineteen men had been ruthlessly murdered. After the dust settled, Sheriff Burns had time to count the losses: five men hanged from upended wagon tongues, four men shot, and the remainder either hanged from the iron beam at Slaney's Boot and Shoe Store or from Tomlinson's Corral gate at Temple and Buena Vista. All nineteen victims had been stripped and their valuables had been removed.

The massacre would forever stain the name of Los Angeles. Many people living on the east coast had never even heard of Los Angeles until this time. It is unfortunate that this would not be the last riot that Los Angeles would experience.

Sam Yueng was indicted for the murder of Robert Thompson, and the grand jury indicted thirty-seven people for participating in the lynchings. The list of witnesses was much longer. Many of the witnesses claimed that they had trouble remembering who did what and exactly how things happened. District Attorney Thom prosecuted fifteen, of whom eight were found guilty of manslaughter and sentenced to serve two to six years. Defense attorney Edward J. C. Kewen successfully appealed the case to the California Supreme Court on the grounds that the original indictment claimed that people were "killed" but it did not actually say that anyone was "murdered." All eight prisoners were released from San Quentin after completing less that a year each.

By the end of his four years in office, Sheriff James Burns was worn out. He had sent many criminals to San Quentin and had seen much bloodshed. Burns had not only stemmed the tide of vigilante justice; he had stopped it. Historian Remi Nadeau commented, "When Burns gave up his sheriff's badge in 1872 he left Los Angeles County relatively safe for new waves of settlers. Debauchery and corruption would continue, but murder was no longer excused."[54] Burns continued to serve the County of Los Angeles long after his term as sheriff.

Lucretia divorced the ex-sheriff in 1872. Burns left for Nebraska, where he became a state senator for a short while. Then he returned to California and campaigned for Henry Hazard, who eventually became mayor of Los Angeles. Mayor Hazard appointed Burns Chief of Police in 1889, a post he held for four months. According to Burns he was asked to leave the post due to "political machinations." He then found a position with the Santa Fe Railroad as an agent with their Claim and Law Department.[55]

In 1889, Burns married his best friend's widowed daughter, Josephine Hill. He moved from his job at the Santa Fe Company to a position with the Los Angeles Electric Railway. His final career move was to the O'Melveny, Stevens, and Milliken Law Firm, where he worked as a "Defense and Evidence" expert. Before he died, Burns gave the bottle of mescal with Buckskin Bill's foot in it to his best friend and father-in-law, Frank Carpenter. James Burns passed away at his home on Burns Avenue on January 5, 1921. He was eighty-nine years old.

Chapter *4*

THE LAST OF THE GREAT CALIFORNIO OUTLAWS

Sheriff William R. Rowland, March 1873–February 1876

In 1870, William Richard Rowland inherited 3,000 acres of land and 1,000 head of cattle from his father, John Rowland (who was the leader of the Workman-Rowland Party that had emigrated to Los Angeles from Taos, New Mexico, in 1841). William was born on his father's La Puente Rancho on November 11, 1846.[1] His mother, Encarnacion Martinez, was from Taos. Her father, Santiago, was also a member of the Workman-Rowland Party. William, whom everyone called "Billy," had a passion for life in Los Angeles County, and he almost never left it, except to transport prisoners as sheriff.

Young Rowland was seriously interested in politics and was an avid member of the Democratic Party. He studied at Santa Clara College from 1858 to 1860. His first job for the county was to transport mentally ill patients to Stockton, California. He married Doña Manuela Williams, from the magnificent Rancho Chino, who bore him three children. They lived in a brick home that Billy built on the east side of the Portrero Grande. His interest in politics and law enforcement led him to run for Sheriff at the young age of twenty-five. Billy Rowland was elected to serve the 1872-1874 term, becoming the county's eleventh sheriff.

Sheriff Rowland selected Albert Johnson to be his Undersheriff and Henry M. Mitchell to be his Deputy. The county spent a few dol-

Sheriff Billy Rowland was half-Mexican and half-White. He loved Los Angeles County and only left it when work demanded it of him. – LOS ANGELES COUNTY SHERIFF'S DEPARTMENT ARCHIVES

lars on three pairs of shiny new handcuffs to aid the deputies with detaining suspects. This was the first documented purchase of "modern" law enforcement equipment (other than badges or weapons) for the fledgling office. The sheriff and his two paid deputies made good use of the handcuffs until eleven months later when they were lost, having been left behind in someone's overcoat. After a tongue lashing by the board of supervisors, the county purchased new ones.

Sheriff Rowland's first two years in office were marked with the usual duties of Sheriff, including tax collection, locating witnesses, keeping the jails in order, and tracking down criminals. During his heated 1873 re-election campaign, Rowland was told that none other than the notorious Joseph Dye was telling deliberate lies about the sheriff in an effort to smear his good name. A fuming Billy Rowland confronted Dye in front of the Orient Saloon on Main Street near Temple. "Dye, I have heard that you have been talking about me." When Dye started to give a lame excuse, the sheriff punched him and called him a liar. Dye grabbed Rowland by the beard, and pointed a cocked revolver at his head saying: "take it back." Rowland gripped Dye by the wrist and stared directly into the killer's eyes. A crowd, which had gathered nearby, waited in silence for the sheriff to answer. "I have nothing to take back," said Rowland. A trembling Joe Dye backed down, he could not pull the trigger. Rowland pulled free and made it clear to everyone that he was not afraid of Joe Dye or any man.[2]

The Capture of Tiburcio Vasquez

Sheriff Rowland was re-elected in 1874 to serve for two more years. The year 1874 was to be an extremely exciting one for the office. The sheriff and his deputies would capture the most famous California desperado of the age, Tiburcio Vasquez. Vasquez, after whom the famous southern California rock formations are named, was born in Monterey County in 1835. He had many brothers and sisters, but he may have been the only one to learn to read and write both English and Spanish. He was a natural-born leader, Vasquez started his criminal career at an early age by robbing peddlers; by age nineteen he had moved up to murder.[3]

One evening in 1854, Tiburcio and his friends Anastacio Garcia and Jose Higuera attended a fandango. Anastacio was seven years older than Vasquez and married to his cousin, Guadalupe Gomez. Folklore tells us that at the fandango, a beautiful, slender dancer named Antonia Romero began to dance *"La Son."* In this traditional dance, men attempt to toss their hats onto the woman's head as she dances close to them. On this particular evening, Antonia allowed an American sailor to throw his hat. When the Californios saw this, they became jealous that a gringo would be allowed such an honor. Whatever the reason for the fight was, when Constable William Hardmount arrived to break it up, he was stabbed to death.[4]

During the ensuing investigation it was discovered that the only two men missing from the

Outlaw Tiburcio Vasquez was a snappy dresser and a ladies man. He was also a ruthless murderer.
— Robert McCubbin Collection

scene were Vasquez and Garcia. Higuera was immediately taken into custody and lynched not long afterward. Tiburcio escaped with Anastacio and, together, they stayed away from Monterey for two weeks. Garcia was indicted for the murder of Constable Hardmount.[5]

Anastacio Garcia was a known killer and a dangerous man, admired as a skilled horseman and a proficient fighter. He taught the young Vasquez how to use a weapon and how to commit robbery. After leaving their hideout in the Gabilan Mountain Range, the outlaws returned to town to see whether anyone was still looking for them. The police heard that they had returned and immediately attempted to round them up. Another struggle ensued, and Vasquez escaped again. This time, he decided to avoid Monterey completely, but not before saying goodbye to his family. He told his mother that he was "going to suffer and take chances," thus declaring his intention to become an outlaw.[6]

With nothing to lose, the 19-year-old Tiburcio rode through the countryside with Garcia on a plundering expedition. Garcia was captured in February 1857 and transported to Monterey where he was lynched in jail for Constable Hardmount's murder. Tiburcio continued his life of crime until August of that same year, when Undersheriff Peterson arrested him in Ventura for stealing a mule and nine horses from Luis Francisco. The young criminal was sentenced to serve five years at San Quentin.

In June 1859, Vasquez escaped with several other inmates but was recaptured a month later. In September, he and several fellow inmates tried to escape again, this time using a boat. After prison guards killed several of his compadres, Vasquez gave up and was sent back to the penitentiary. Soon after his release in August, 1863, Tiburcio began to roam Mendocino, Contra Costa, and Sonoma counties looking for easy prey and beautiful women.

Vasquez was a notorious womanizer, which often got him into trouble. One rancher shot Vasquez in the arm while he was running off with the rancher's daughter. When the rancher came looking for her, she had to be dragged off, because she said that she was in love with the desperado. Being constantly on the move, Vasquez found that it was easier to ride with one or two compadres and then enlist local men when planning a raid.

Soon afterward, the outlaw and one of his cousins, Faustino Lorenzana, were suspected in the murder of a Santa Clara County butcher. The sheriff could find little evidence to convict, so the men were not pursued. Tiburcio's luck ran out when he was caught breaking into the Sargent and Barnes store in Petaluma with an Anglo burglar named Horace Dade. On January 8, 1867, he found himself cooling his heels in San Quentin once again.

Upon his release three years later, he met up with his friend Abelardo Salazar, who harbored him and provided shelter from the law. Tiburcio repaid Salazar's kindness by seducing his wife! Upon learning that he had been cuckolded, Salazar shot Vasquez in the neck and then tried to have him arrested for attempted murder. Tiburcio was badly wounded and in need of a place to recover. Once again, he galloped off to the coast mountain range, where he hid near Cantua Creek.[7]

After recuperating, he joined forces with Francisco Barcenas and Narciso Rodriguez. In mid-August 1871, the trio rode to Soap Lake near San Jose and robbed a stagecoach. The *San Francisco Bulletin* reported:

> The first thing they did was to capture a gentleman named Moore. . . . He was riding in a buggy. They took him aside privily in a road near the field, tied and blindfolded him, and robbed him of $55. By this time the two horse stage came along. The robbers then fell upon it, and ordered the drivers to go through an opening they made in the fence. The stage was stopped at the point where [Moore] . . . lay "horse de combat." The passengers were four men and a woman. The men were compelled to alight, keep their eyes on the ground, while each was securely bound, searched and blindfolded. . . . The robbers secured something over $500 from the stage company, and a gold watch or so.[8]

In Santa Cruz, Vasquez shot it out with Officer Robert Lidell, whose bullet struck Tiburcio in the chest. Barcenas and Rodriguez managed to help their leader to escape, but three days later, Sheriff Charles Lincoln's posse cornered Barcenas in the Lorenzana Barn near the Branciforte part of Santa Cruz. When Barcenas tried to make a run for it, he was gunned down. The *Santa Cruz Sentinel,* September 16, 1871, related the following story:

> Haynes leveled his gun—a double barreled shotgun—and snapped three caps while the revolver of his desperate assailant [Barcenas] cracked away at him, it also being a miss shot, by about two inches, rendered such by the deadly aim of Majors, who fired at him the ball striking him square in the mouth thus making his aim unsteady. Not 'til he had received another shot, which entered below the right eye and penetrated the brain did he drop, and even then in his death struggle, he grasped for his revolver, now useless in his hands. Another shot from the pistol of Majors put an end to the desperado's earthly career.[9]

Narcisco Rodriguez was captured the day after the shootout and sent back to prison. Vasquez barely escaped with his life. The renegade headed for his usual hideout in the Arroyo Cantua to recover and heal his wounds.

Upon his recovery, Vasquez gathered together a new gang, consisting of Clodoveo Chavez, Abdon Leiva, Teodoro Moreno, Romulo Gonzales, Frenchman August DeBert and several others. They hid out at Abdon Leiva's ranch in Cantua, where they plotted their next move. While at the ranch, Vasquez made sly advances toward Leiva's wife, Rosaria. Tiburcio's charm must have been powerful, for it was not long before she, too, fell in love with the renegade leader. The pair carried on a discreet but passionate affair.

On February 26, 1873, Vasquez and five of his men galloped into Firebaugh's Ferry, where they planned to rob a $30,000 payroll from wealthy cattleman Henry Miller. They entered Hoffman's store, bristling with guns, and systematically robbed every one of the twelve occupants. Next, they plundered the safe, but the payroll had not yet arrived. When the stagecoach did pull in, however, they robbed that, too. The outlaws rode off into the hills and were not pursued.

The gang tried to rob a train in June 1873, but after bungling the attempt they decided to take down a hotel, the "Twenty One

Mile House," instead. Afterward, Vasquez, Romulo Gonzales, Moreno, Leiva, and Chavez rode into Tres Piños in San Benito County. The gang went to rob Andrew Schneider but panicked; they killed three innocent bystanders before galloping out of town.

John Utzerath, one of Schneider's clerks, raised the alarm. Sheriffs from Monterey and Santa Clara counties responded and tracked the bandits south. Later, Sheriff Morse from Alameda County organized a posse and received state funding to track Vasquez and his gang.

It finally dawned on Abdon that his wife was sleeping with Tiburcio when he accidentally walked in on the two of them one day. Abdon became so outraged that he betrayed Vasquez by turning himself into the Sheriff, knowing full well that he would go to prison. He did not care, however, for he wanted revenge on Vasquez so badly that he gave up the gang's secrets to the lawmen. The authorities used this information to arrest and convict Teodoro Moreno. He was given a life sentence.[10]

With the law hot on their trail, the outlaws moved on to the San Joaquin River, where they robbed Jones' Store on November 10, 1873. The store, located a short distance downriver from Millerton, was very large. It was a two-story structure, with a hotel upstairs and a general store and saloon downstairs. At 6:00 in the evening, Vasquez and his men crashed through the doors and ordered the patrons to put up their hands. There were about twelve men in the saloon at the time, all of whom were ordered to lie on the ground.

The gang tied the victims' hands behind their backs and, in their usual method, systematically robbed every one of them. They ordered the clerk, Smith Norris, to open the store safe. The bandits took $1,000 from the safe and then decided that they were in no particular hurry, so they stayed an hour and a half, had drinks, and joked about the day's work. The desperadoes rode off into the night, after exclaiming "Adios, caballeros."[11]

A month after the robbery of Jones' store, on the day after Christmas, the Vasquez gang rode into the small river town of Kingston, on the Kings River. The current roster of gang members included Blas Bicuna, Clodoveo Chavez, Ramon Molina, Ysidro

Padilla, Ignacio Rangel, Francisco Gomez, Procella Anamantoria, Refugio Montejos, Manuel Lopez, and a handful of others.

This time, the confident outlaws robbed the entire town of thirty-five people, plundered several stores, and pillaged more than a few safes. A brave rancher named John Sutherland saw what was happening and grabbed his repeating rifle. He took up a sniper position and opened fire on the desperadoes. The outlaws were taken completely by surprise and were subsequently routed.

By this time, the State of California had had enough of Tiburcio Vasquez and his gang. Governor Newton Booth hired Alameda County Sheriff Harry Morse and several others to track the renegade and bring him to justice.

Sheriff Harry Morse wrote to Governor Booth:

Sir:—I rode 40 miles through the mountains today to get to the outside world and a post office. Three of the Vasquez party were wounded at the Kingston robbery, one of them, Refugio Montejos has since died. Another named Manuel Lopez was shot through the neck, and the worst man of the gang, to wit, Chavez was shot through the leg.[12]

Anamantoria and Rangel were captured, but Chavez made his escape with the others. The gang went their separate ways for a short while, but then rejoined in southern California.

In the central valley, they held up the Bakersfield stagecoach at Coyote Holes in the Mojave Desert. They were in the process of robbing twenty men when one of the victims started to resist. The brave but foolish man was promptly shot in the leg for his efforts.

The lawmen surmised that the outlaws had gone to the area around Lake Elizabeth in northern Los Angeles County. Tiburcio had many hideouts in that part of the county, including his brother's place near Soledad Canyon. Morse traveled over 2,700 miles searching for the renegades, but his efforts were in vain. Vasquez and his crew always managed to avoid capture.

In Los Angeles, Sheriff Rowland received word that Vasquez was in his jurisdiction. Like Morse, he organized a posse and went out on the trail. Rowland came across smoldering campfires, footprints, and evidence of recent crimes but never the gang itself. Sheriff Billy put the word out that there was a state's reward for the capture of Vasquez: $6,000 dead or $8,000 alive.

In April, 1874, Vasquez received information that a grossly over-weight and wealthy sheepherder named Alexander Repetto had just sold $10,000 worth of livestock. Repetto lived on his ranch with his young nephew, whom he was looking after. Early in the morning of the 16th, Vasquez, Isidro Padilla, Clodoveo Chavez, Francisco Cantua, and Lebrado Corona rode to the ranch on the outskirts of San Gabriel, where they met with Repetto and claimed to be looking for work. Repetto recognized one of the Vasquez men, Lebrado Corona, as a good sheep shearer, so he agreed to hire the entire group. The men smiled at Repetto, went back to their horses, pulled out their weapons, and demanded $10,000 in cash.

A shocked Repetto told them that he had deposited some money at the Temple and Workman Bank in Los Angeles but that he had spent most of his profits in buying more land. Vasquez became angry and demanded $800 for his trouble. Again, Repetto told the bandit that he had no money in the house, but he promised to send the boy into town with a withdrawal note to get the cash. Vasquez agreed and sat down to help himself to a hearty breakfast at the fat man's expense.

At the bank, the nephew looked so nervous that Mr. Temple became suspicious. Temple called for the Sheriff and, after a short talk with the lawman, the boy broke down and blurted out that he had to have the money or his uncle would be killed. Rowland asked Temple to stay with the boy while he organized his posse. The Sheriff sent word to the El Monte Posse to prepare to ride, while simultaneously alerting his deputies. While Rowland was away, Temple became worried about Repetto. He reconsidered and decid-ed to give the lad $500. Vasquez took the money but was not satis-fied. He was thinking of a way to get more, when he saw plumes of dust rising from the road.

Tiburcio and his men mounted their horses and galloped away from the ranch at top speed. In a daring move, they fled across the open plains toward the Arroyo Seco and the Rancho San Pasqual. On their way, they came across a wagon team consisting of John

Osborne, Charles Miles, and two workmen. The bandits never passed up an opportunity to relieve the public of their belongings, so they robbed Miles of his watch and the others of their meager possessions. Rowland's posse was hot on the trail of Tiburcio's gang and, at one point, they almost had him. In a May 15, 1874, interview with J.M. Basset from the *Los Angeles Herald*, Vasquez stated:

> Rowland is the one I've been looking out for. He has taken more risks than any of them. The pursuit after the Repetto robbery was very close. Rowland passed within ten yards of me as I lay in the brush after abandoning my horses in Lajunda Canyon. I had by my side two Henry rifles and two revolvers.[13]

Perhaps Rowland was lucky that he had failed to engage the desperadoes at that moment. The El Monte posse also failed to make contact.

On the morning of the 21st, Sheriff Morse came to meet with Sheriff Rowland. Morse offered up a plan to Rowland in which he and his men would disguise themselves and hide out by Greek George's place, west of the Cahuenga Pass in what is now West Hollywood. Morse had learned that Greek George was harboring Vasquez. Billy Rowland, still seething from his recent failure, refused the Alameda County Sheriff's plan, telling Morse that he had many spies in Los Angeles and that the northern lawman's information was not accurate. Secretly, Rowland knew that Morse's information might be good, but he was angling to collect the $8,000 reward for himself. A disappointed Morse left the city and rejoined his posse in the Tejon pass. They left the county and headed north in the belief that Vasquez too might be heading that way.[14]

After Morse left, Rowland formulated his plan. He, too, knew that Vasquez liked to visit Greek George—but he knew the whole truth. Greek George was originally from Smyrna (now called Izmir), Turkey, and although his real name was George Caralambo, he changed his name to George Allen when he became an American citizen. He was an eccentric man who had been hired by the War Department to lead a pack of camels to America as part of a U.S. Army experiment. The camels had been thought to be ideal pack

George Caralambo a.k.a. "Greek George" was sheltering Tiburcio Vasquez at his home. Did he turn the bandit in for a share of the reward money? – HUNTINGTON LIBRARY

animals for the harsh California desert climate. Unfortunately for the Army, the camels did not agree, and the experiment failed.

It has never been proven who turned Vasquez in, but there is little doubt that Rowland used Sheriff Morse's information to enable him to prepare an attack on Greek George's adobe. Utilizing Deputy D.K. Smith as a lookout, Rowland confirmed that Vasquez was indeed staying at the adobe. Sheriff Rowland then confidentially notified his seven most trusted men that he was planning a raid. The officers surreptitiously hid weapons, ammunition, and supplies in a cache at the Jones Corral on Spring Street and Seventh to prepare for their mission. On the evening of May 13, Rowland went about town as if business was as usual. Some reports say that when the posse was ready to ride, Rowland shanghaied Greek George and kept him under close guard. He may have done this to ensure that Caralambo would have no chance of double-crossing him at the last minute.

At 2:00 a.m., Undersheriff Albert Johnston, Deputies Henry Mitchell and D. K. Smith, Constable S. J. Bryant, Chief Benjamin F. Hartley, Officer Emil Harris, Palace Saloon owner W. E. Rogers, and George Beers from the *San Francisco Chronicle*, rode quietly out of town.

The men arrived at the mouth of Nichols Canyon and made camp in a location two miles from Greek George's property. At daybreak, the undersheriff took Deputy Mitchell with him to reconnoiter Greek George's house. The two men worked their way over to a ridgeline that overlooked the property. The little house was located in an area close to Santa Monica Boulevard near La Cienega

Boulevard in what is now the city of West Hollywood. A heavy fog prevented them from seeing clearly until about 10:00 a.m. At noon, Deputy Mitchell saw a man, who looked like Vasquez, mount a white horse and ride off toward Los Angeles. He also noticed that at least one other desperado was still at the house.

While the undersheriff and his partner were watching the Vasquez gang, Smith and his five companions were trying to figure out a way to approach the house, knowing that even the smallest mistake could result in their death, or at the very least, the loss of their prey. From Greek George's house there was a clear field of vision, and approaching it in broad daylight seemed like a hopeless plan. There was no easy way to get close enough to the structure without being noticed. The men became dejected and cursed their fate upon realizing their situation. Suddenly, the creaky wheels and stomping hoofs of an approaching horse-drawn wagon could be heard.

The posse turned their heads to see two Californio men driving a box wagon pulled by four horses. The wagon was headed right past their location. All six men quietly watched the teamsters passing by, and a slow grin broke out on Deputy Smith's face. He ordered the posse to seize the wagon, complete with drivers. The other men chuckled when they caught on to the deputy's clever plan. They stopped the wagon and then waited impatiently for the undersheriff's return.

Shortly past noon, Johnston and Mitchell met the posse. Johnston agreed with Smith's plan, but he was afraid that it was Vasquez who had ridden off toward the city on the white horse. He sent Mitchell and Smith to track down the rider, while he and the others planned to capture whomever was in the house. Johnston and his five remaining posse members climbed into the back of the wagon. The teamsters were told to act normal and drive past Greek George's house at their usual pace. They were also advised that, if they tried to give any sort of warning to the occupants, the posse would fill them with lead. Seeing that they did not have much choice, the teamsters complied and drove toward the house. As the wagon neared Greek George's residence, the posse jumped out and surrounded it.[15]

Greek George's wife, Cornelia, heard footsteps outside and went to the front door to investigate. Suddenly, the barrel of Emil Harris's shotgun forced its way across the threshold. She screamed and tried to slam the door, but the barrel blocked the way. Vasquez and Corona, who were in the middle of eating their lunch, leaped from their chairs as the shotgun fired. Buckshot slammed into the far wall as the outlaws dived for cover. Harris shouted "there he goes through the window!"[16] Vasquez scrambled out a back window, where Beers and Hartley were waiting with their guns. Lebrado Corona stayed in the house and rushed to protect Cornelia's children.

As Vasquez was running away at top speed, Beers shot him in the shoulder. At the same time, Hartley loosed a flurry of buckshot, striking the renegade in the chest, left arm and leg, and left side of the head. Tiburcio's luck had run out. He threw up his hands and surrendered, saying, "No shoot, No shoot."[17] Bleeding from the buckshot wounds in his shoulder and back, Vasquez reminded his captors that they would receive an extra $2,000 for allowing him to live. After a 21-year criminal career, the notorious Vasquez was taken into custody.

The posse entered the cabin and found Corona with the children. They sent the children to Cornelia and then arrested him. The lawmen searched the house and found Tiburcio's vest. In it was Charles Miles' watch. Vasquez claimed that it was no good, anyway, because he could not get it to work. They hauled Tiburcio and his partner to the calabazo in Los Angeles, where the bandit became an instant celebrity.

On May 16 at 4:10 p.m., Sheriff Rowland proudly sent the following telegram:

> To his excellency Newton Booth [Governor of California], I have the honor to report the capture of Tiburcio Vasquez alias Ricardo Cantua. This county has delayed announcing the capture until his identification could be certain, the nature of his wounds fully ascertained and his statement reduced to writing. His wounds are not necessarily serious. He has been identified by at least one hundred persons and

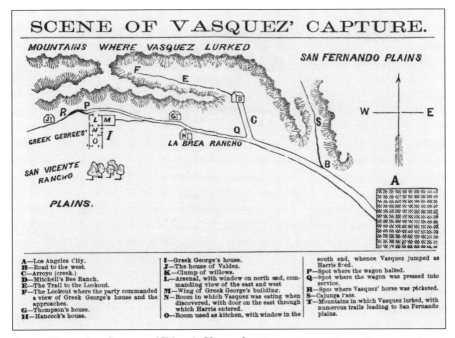

A map illustrating the scene of Tiburcio Vasquez' capture. – SECURITY PACIFIC COLLECTION / LOS ANGELES PUBLIC LIBRARY

his confession places his identity beyond all doubt. I shall proceed to deliver him to the sheriff of Monterey County as soon as his wounds will permit unless you shall otherwise direct. I have the honor to remain your obedient servant, Wm. R. Rowland, Sheriff.[18]

A photograph of the famous desperado was taken, and entrepreneurs did brisk business selling copies for twenty-five cents each.[19] A Los Angeles businessman went so far as to advertise in the *Los Angeles Star*: "Vasquez says that Mendell Meyer has the finest and most complete stock of Dry Goods and Clothing in the City of Los Angeles."[20]

A flurry of requests came over the wire demanding Vasquez' extradition to various jurisdictions. Rowland coordinated these claims with the court, which ultimately decided that he should be tried in San Jose for the murders committed at Tres Piños. On the

A poster commemorating the men who captured the famous bandit. – HUNTINGTON LIBRARY

23rd of May, nine days after his capture, Vasquez was transported to San Pedro for his steamship trip north. Upon his arrival in San Francisco he was taken to the city jail, where large crowds gathered to see him in his cell. There were so many people waiting in line that Theodore Cockrill, the Chief of Police, considered a plan to put several Vasquez impersonators in the jail to help move the queue along. The plan was never implemented; Vasquez was soon transported to the Santa Clara County Jail in San Jose to await trial.

While languishing in jail, the outlaw gave a deposition for an ongoing court case back in Los Angeles. His old partner, Lebrado Corona, was asking for corroboration from Vasquez. Corona wanted to explain to the court how the bandit leader had forced him to be in the gang and commit crimes. Vasquez dictated his testimony, which was sent to Los Angeles via Wells Fargo courier.

When asked about his injuries, Vasquez replied that he had been shot once in the chest by the Santa Cruz posse, once in the neck by

Salazar, once in the hand during the San Quentin escape; he reported that he had received eight buckshot and rifle wounds during his capture. He also said that he had never shot anyone, and that a life of crime was no good.

On January 23, 1875, Tiburcio Vasquez was found guilty of murder by the San Jose jury and sentenced to hang on March 19. Judge Belden stated: "Vasquez' record was one of unbroken lawlessness and outrage, a career of pillage and murder, his name, a synonym for all that was wicked and infamous."[21]

A special gallows was imported from Sacramento for the occasion, and printed invitations were handed out to the public. The undertaker's office showed him the casket he was to be placed in. After feeling the silky smooth lining he said, "I can sleep here forever very well!"[22] The officials asked Tiburcio if he had any last words. He said that children should obey the teachings of their parents and that his followers should not seek vengeance on the lawmen, who were just doing their jobs. After the death warrant was read from the gallows, Tiburcio looked over at Sheriff Adams, who was adjusting the noose. "Pronto!" he called. The trap door swung and the rope was yanked taut.[23]

The Vasquez gang was not the same without their leader. Clodoveo Chavez fled to Mexico but returned early in 1875 to form a new gang. This gang headed for the south fork of the Kern River, where they robbed William Scoby's Tavern. A Bakersfield newspaper wrote:

> On Sunday night last, he with his band of outlaws, appeared at the store of Mr. Scoby on the south fork of the Kern River. They captured five horses, a large amount of store goods and $800 in money. Sheriff Bowers heard of them again afterward and on Monday telegraphed to the Sheriff of Los Angeles County, as Chavez was evidently shaping his course in that direction.[24]

A local posse chased them for hundreds of miles into the Mojave Desert, where the lawmen finally gave up.

The band continued on to plunder roadside inns at Little Lake and Granite Springs. After a stagecoach holdup in Indian Valley, a squad of soldiers on patrol pursued them so closely that they had to ditch their heavy loot in order to pick up speed. The outlaws lightened the load by hastily burying a Wells Fargo box containing over $45,000 in cash. Not one of the desperadoes would ever return to claim it, and eighty-six years later it was discovered by a band of treasure hunters. The state of California posted a $2,000 reward for Chavez, and posses everywhere were looking for him. He and his gang decided to steal a herd of horses and then cross into Mexico, where they hoped that they would not be hunted. After the locals nicked his stolen horses, Clodoveo split up the gang and abandoned his life of crime for a quieter existence working as a cowboy in Arizona.

In a freak coincidence, one of Chavez's boyhood friends, Luis Raggio, was working on the Woolsey Ranch, which happened to be adjacent to the ranch where Clodoveo was working. Luis's brother, Vincent, was working on the Baker Ranch with Chavez. One day, Luis was delivering some cattle when he saw Chavez, who was working under another name. Luis talked to Vincent and found that Chavez was teaching his younger brother the ways of a criminal life. Luis was angered and decided to take action. When he learned about the $2,000 price tag on Chavez's head, he secretly organized a posse with Clark Colvig and Harry Roberts. The trio confronted Chavez on the ranch. Luis told the story in a letter to his father:

> Next morning we rode over and I told my men to ride ahead and go to the house and wait for me. But as soon as they saw Chavez they told him to surrender and he ran and my partner shot him in the back and he fell dead.[25]

At Fort Yuma, a surgeon removed Clodoveo's head and placed it in a jar, so that Harry Roberts could transport it to California for the reward money. The three men split the reward, which totaled $2,199.42.

In Los Angeles, Greek George was charged with being an accessory to the Alexander Repetto robbery, and Lebrado Corona was charged with two counts of robbery. Lebrado claimed that he was innocent and that Vasquez had forced him to take part in the criminal acts. He anxiously awaited the reply from Vasquez, which to his surprise read as follows:

> I know Lebrado Corona about two months. I met him first in the Tejon. For two or three weeks he had been with me around the place where I was arrested. He had been in my employ. He came to me of his own accord and said he would do anything I asked. We went to rob Repetto and Corona went as a member of the gang. He was the only one of us Repetto knew or recognized. He never said anything about leaving me. I never forbade him leaving. He could leave whenever he wanted to. I never threatened him. All his acts were of his own accord. I never used any compulsion. While he was under me, he did nothing but go with me to rob Repetto. He never took part in any other act.[26]

Corona was not happy with Vasquez' deposition; he was found guilty of the Repetto and Miles robberies and sentenced to twenty-five years in state prison. Thus ended the saga of the Vasquez gang. Sheriff Rowland desperately wanted to join the posse during Tiburcio's arrest at the foot of the Cahuengas, but his wise decision to stay in town, coupled with careful planning and patience, paid off with the greatest arrest of his career. Not since Flores' Manillas gang had a band of desperadoes so thoroughly terrorized the state of California.

Sheriff David W. Alexander (Second Term), March 1876–February 1878

Towards the end of Rowland's second term, an attempt was made to rid the city of prostitution. Every year, the influx of churchgoers, women with children, and families helped to put pressure on the pimps, bordellos, and saloons that engaged in or encouraged the world's oldest profession. Late in 1875, John J. Jones was made to appear in court for operating houses of prostitution. The prosecutor accused him of renting rooms to "Belle," "Rachel," and "Cora" on Bath Street and "Rosa" on Olvera Street. Jones claimed innocence, stating that he was merely a landlord collecting the rent from Belle and her friends. He said that he had absolutely no idea what was going on behind their closed doors. The case was dismissed, and the "angels" went about their business as usual.

It was in 1875 that Sheriff Rowland shrugged off a great burden: that of tax collecting. No longer would the Sheriff and his deputies ride throughout the county to collect taxes; that responsibility was now delegated to the new office of the Tax Collector. The same year also marked the end of the City Marshal's office and the beginning of another famous law enforcement agency, the Los Angeles Police Department.[27] Sheriff Rowland chose not to run for re-election this time, although he would later return to serve yet another term. Former Sheriff David Alexander won the election and took office on March 1, 1876.

By the time of his second election to Sheriff, Alexander was 63 years old and one of the wealthiest men in the county. He owned over 21,000 acres on the Rancho Tujunga (including Flintridge) and Rancho Providencia (Burbank). This was in addition to ownership in the shipping and mercantile business as well as property in San Pedro and Wilmington. He had a great love for politics, and this passion, along with his business interests, led him to the office of Sheriff once more. His first action as Sheriff was to appoint Henry M. Mitchell as Undersheriff.

Although the City Council appointed the first Board of Police Commissioners and selected Benjamin Franklin Hartley as Chief in 1875, the *Los Angeles Star* was already calling him Chief by May of 1874.[28] With a new department and a new chief came the first LAPD regulation uniform: a hip-length, blue serge coat and felt hat. Officers were asked to purchase their own silver, 8-point badges for $6. Emil Harris, who participated in the Vasquez arrest along with Hartley, succeeded the second chief, Jacob Gerkins, in 1877. The fact that the city now had its own professional police force did not reduce the Sheriff's workload, because all that changed were the titles of the officers and the name of the department. The number of lawmen and their jurisdiction basically remained the same.

The Sotelo Brothers

In the case of the Sotelo brothers, city and county law enforcement would have to work together to bring these outlaws to justice. A dark streak ran through the Sotelo clan, dating as far back as 1805 when Ramon Sotelo had first settled in Los Angeles. Ramon was known by the locals to be a bandit, and he was killed at Purisma in 1824. He had five grandsons, three of whom would, unfortunately, carry on in his footsteps.

Miguel, who was older than both Francisco and Santos, was arrested for stealing horses. In November 1869, he was arrested by Sheriff Burns and sent to San Quentin for six years. While in prison, Miguel met Tiburcio Vasquez, and the two of them plotted many a robbery. Upon his release in February, 1874, Miguel immediately joined up with the notorious outlaw. When Sheriff Rowland's posse arrested Vasquez, Miguel Sotelo escaped, but he was alone and on the lam— sheriff's posses from all over the state were constantly on the lookout for him. Meanwhile, his younger brothers, 18-year-old Francisco and 25-year-old Santos, were just starting their lives of crime.

As they were growing up, the pair was always getting into trouble. Santos used the alias "Chico Lugo," perhaps in reference to the real Chico Lugo who had battled against the gringos for his innocence during Sheriff Burrill's term. Francisco sometimes used the last name alias of "Olivas." For reasons that are not exactly clear, there was growing animosity between Francisco and his cousin Ramon. In the middle of June 1876, Ramon and Francisco got into a fistfight, and Ramon knocked his cousin down. Later that evening, Ramon was leaving a funeral in the Calle de Los Negros when Francisco ambushed him and shot him down in a narrow alley. Francisco Sotelo's lone horse returned to town, but he was nowhere to be found.[29]

Realizing that he was now a wanted man, Francisco hid out in the San Bernardino Mountains. He waited until the pressure was off and then joined his brother Santos and a friend named Jose Tapia. In late December, the trio rode northwest, past Mojave to Red Rock Canyon. There they camped out and made plans to rob the Darwin Stage. On January 6, they robbed the stagecoach and then hid out in the Tehachapi Mountains. On January 20, they held up the

Newhall Ventura stage and then galloped over to a little pueblo near Bakersfield called Panama. Another outlaw, named Francisco Romero, joined the gang, and they proceeded to steal six horses in preparation for their next heist. At the edge of Tulare Lake, they went into S.A. Lovell's store, struck him on the head with a pistol, and took $500 in cash and other merchandise.

As they were heading back south, the outlaws came across some canal workers who recognized the stolen horses. The workers opened fire on the bandits, but no one was hit; the bandits galloped off toward the Tehachapis, with Constable Harry Bludworth and two other posse members in relentless pursuit. The lawmen pushed so hard that the outlaws abandoned their stolen horses and made an all-out run for their freedom.

Francisco Romero could not keep up with the pack and bailed off his horse to hide in the brush. The lawmen seized the horses and returned to Bakersfield. Early the next morning, the authorities were back on the Sotelo brothers' trail. They captured Romero, who was still hiding in the bushes and sent him back to the Bakersfield jail under guard while they continued the chase for an entire week. After an exhausting search they lost the Sotelos' trail and turned back home. On their way back they stopped at George Reig's ranch, hoping for some hospitality. When Reig did not answer, they became uneasy. They went inside the ranch house and found him dead. He had been shot through the head. The lawmen believed that they knew exactly who had committed the crime.

The Sotelos made their way back down south to San Francisquito Canyon, where they robbed fourteen Chinese miners of $260 in gold dust. Sheriff Alexander's men had been notified via telegraph about the Sotelos and so the deputies had many posses searching the hills. Jose Tapia was captured, and Santos and Francisco were starting to feel the pressure. A San Bernardino posse consisting of Constable Thomas, Luis Lopez, Guadalupe Lugo, D. Bustamonte, and Thomas Warden trailed the outlaws into the San Bernardino Mountains. They found Francisco alone and quietly encircled him. The posse suddenly stepped free of the heavy brush and leveled their pistols at him. The *Los Angeles Star* wrote: "He was surrounded before he had a chance to use his weapons or fly."[30]

The posse's next move was to find Santos. They had heard that he was enjoying himself at a fandango house in San Bernardino. When the posse arrived, they carefully checked the occupants, but failed to find Sotelo; Santos had shaved off his beard and was not recognized by the lawmen. When they were looking in the opposite direction, he quickly stepped out the front door, right under their noses. The same San Bernardino posse that had captured Francisco was not about to give up on Santos. They trailed him to Lake Elizabeth. On July 19 the *Los Angeles Star* reported:

> The last member of a desperate gang of horse thieves, stage robbers and suspected murderers, Santos Sotelo has at last fallen into the clutches of the law, and will doubtless do the state some labor for the next few years of his life. . . . On Friday last while riding in the mountains of Elizabeth Lake, Rafael Lopez, a young Californian, espied a horse hitched to some bushes quite a little distance ahead of him, and a closer observation showed the form of a man lying in the shade of a tree, quietly smoking a cigarette. Lopez recognized the outlaw at once, and quietly made preparations for his capture. . . . Lopez softly crept towards the robber, keeping the tree on a line between them, until he had approached within a few steps, when he suddenly presented the muzzle of a formidable six shooter at Sotelo's head.[31]

Santos was tried in Kern County for robbing a stagecoach and received fifteen years in prison. Jose Tapia and Francisco Sotelo were tried in Los Angeles and received seven and ten years, respectively. A Tulare County jury sentenced Francisco Romero to five years for his part in the Lovell store robbery. When Francisco was released from San Quentin in 1883, he went back to Los Angeles. Three years later, he was going by the name Pancho Olivas, when he was caught stealing and was sent back to prison for three more years. A few years later, an aggressive new Los Angeles County Sheriff would track down Miguel Sotelo.

July 4, 1876, marked the 100th birthday of the United States, and Los Angeles celebrated by having a grand parade down Main

Street. The entire city was beautifully decorated in red white and blue, and a sign over the elegant Pico House Hotel read, "1776. 1876. Now for 1976! To the patrons of the Pico House: May you live 100 years! No North, No South, No East, No West!"[32] The parade included Mexican War veterans, firemen, police, deputy sheriffs, vaqueros, the French Benevolent Society, the German Turneverein Club, floats with the Statue of Liberty, and many others. Undersheriff Mitchell presided over the event as Grand Marshal.

In addition to the celebrations, 1876 ushered in a technology that would further change the isolated city of 10,000. The railroad had finally come to Los Angeles. On September 5, the entire town turned out to watch the first train pull into town. It had come from the north, past Bakersfield, chugging through the Tehachapi Pass and winding its way through the San Fernando Valley tunnel and into the city. While much land was still available in Los Angeles, it was very arid; there was a drought, and smallpox was ravaging the county. Most travelers from San Francisco preferred to exit the train far north of Los Angeles.

In June 1877, Yo Hing, who was still running his "Company" in the Calle de Los Negros, had pushed his luck too far and had finally angered the wrong men. Ah Hok and Wong Chu Sut confronted him in the street and split his head open with a hatchet. Yo Hing lingered in agony for four days, and then died. No reason was given for the crime, but it was most surely over "business." Officers John Fonck and John McFadden were dispatched to search for the killers. They found Ah Hok easily enough, and Wong Chu Sut was found hiding in an attic crawl space. The two men were arrested and went to trial, where, after several appeals, they were found guilty and sentenced to life in prison by the affirmation of the Supreme Court on September 9, 1878.

David Alexander's term as Sheriff was marked by a relatively quiet period in office. At age fifty-two, twelve years before he was elected the second time, he had married Doña Adalaid Mellus, his former business partner's widow. He died in Wilmington at the age of seventy-five. The fact that Alexander was able to keep his large land holdings up until the time of his death is a legacy that most pioneer Angelenos found difficult, if not impossible, to emulate. It is a

164

fine example and the surest proof of his knack for paying attention to detail and his wise use of business planning principles to obtain wealth and financial security.

Sheriff Henry Milnor Mitchell, March 1878–February 1880

By the time he was elected to office for the term beginning in 1878, Henry Mitchell had accumulated an impressive resume, which demonstrated that he was amply qualified for the job of sheriff. He was born in Richmond, Virginia, on December 14, 1846. His father, Samuel P. Mitchell, was a wealthy businessman in the woolen industry and president of the Planter's Bank of Richmond. His mother, Rebecca Klapp, was the daughter of a Philadelphia physician. Henry had a bright and carefree future ahead of him until the Civil War broke out; the war changed his life forever.

Mitchell's plans to attend the well-respected Virginia Military Institute (VMI) were put on hold when Union troops under the command of General David Hunter burned the college to the ground. In December, 1864, VMI re-opened, operating out of a temporary headquarters at the Alms House in Richmond.[33] Only a few weeks before his arrival, one of Mitchell's classmates wrote the following letter to his friend John E. Roller:

> I scarcely have time to write a letter, so busily are we occupied drilling and having dress parades. Soon after you were at Camp Lee, we moved to this place and it seems impossible, although we have procured the Almshouse for us to get away, we are anxiously expecting a furlough of two weeks to prepare etc. When we will be relieved from duty here I cannot say, we are daily expecting a fight on this line, certainly before the end of this week.[34]

Mitchell entered not only as a cadet for the class of 1868 but also as a private in Company G, 3rd Regiment, Virginia Local Defense Troops. The Confederates were getting so desperate for fighting men that they enlisted 16-year-olds like Henry to help defend Richmond. Classes were interrupted and by early April the Corps of Cadets was disbanded. Mitchell is said to have been present at the

Sheriff Henry Milnor Mitchell tracked down outlaw Miguel Sotelo, one of the last remaining members of the Vasquez gang.
— LOS ANGELES COUNTY SHERIFF'S DEPARTMENT ARCHIVES

Appomattox Courthouse when General Lee surrendered to General Grant on April 9, 1865[35]. He most likely resigned from VMI to help his family rebuild after the war.

After mustering out, Mitchell returned to Virginia and tried his hand at raising wheat and tobacco. Two years later, Henry tried teaching school in North Carolina, but he was too restless. He quit his teaching job and worked his way to Los Angeles, where he arrived via Nicaragua in 1868. In Los Angeles, Mitchell became a surveyor, a reporter, and a law student. He passed the bar in 1872 and practiced law for a short time, until he realized that he could make more money as a Deputy Sheriff. While working as a Deputy for both Rowland and Alexander, he earned extra cash as a notary and as a Major in the National Guard under General John M. Baldwin. At least part of the reason for Mitchell's successful election campaign was his fame as one of the men who had helped to capture Tiburcio Vasquez. Upon taking the oath of office, Mitchell selected James C. Kays as his Undersheriff.

On June 17, 1878, Sheriff Mitchell received word that one of the old members of the Tiburcio Vasquez gang, Miguel Sotelo, was hiding out in Verdugo Canyon. Sotelo was one of the last of the "old time" California outlaws to still haunt the Southland. The court issued a bench warrant, and Mitchell began the usual preparations for service. He checked his weapons, saddled up his mount, and took Deputy Adolfo Celis with him to serve the warrant. Sotelo was drinking at a roadside inn when he saw the dust clouds from Mitchell and Celis, who were riding his way.

Knowing that he was wanted, Sotelo wasted no time in making his escape. The bandit jumped on his horse and galloped off at full speed. He tried to repel the officers by firing at them, but they pressed ever closer, returning fire. The three men went over two miles at high speed, exchanging pistol fire most of the way. Sotelo was rusty and rode slower than he had when he was with Tiburcio. The sheriff and his deputy closed the gap, which allowed them to get in more accurate shots. They struck Sotelo several times. Finally, the last member of the Vasquez gang toppled from his mount. They took him into custody, where, after a night of excruciating pain, he died from his wounds.[36]

In 1879, Mitchell was invited to practice law before the California Supreme Court. In that same year, he married Judge Andrew Glassel's daughter in Los Angeles. After he left office, Mitchell practiced law until 1887, when his former undersheriff, James Kays, selected him to be his undersheriff. Mitchell served in that capacity for two years, and left office at the same time as Kays.

On December 7, 1890, Mitchell went hunting with his friend, City Attorney William Dunn. The two were up at Vasquez Rocks and had separated for the hunt. Suddenly, Dunn saw what he thought was a deer. He fired, and tragically struck Mitchell with a single shot. The ex-sheriff died immediately, and was taken back to the city for burial.

Sheriff William R. Rowland (Third Term), March 1880–December 1882

Billy Rowland returned to office in 1880 to experience a much less exciting term than his previous adventures with the Vasquez gang. Nevertheless, Rowland found ways to keep busy. He began to search for oil with business partner William Lacy. In one of the first successful drilling operations in Los Angeles, they discovered black gold on Rowland's land and piped it to Chino, where it was used in a sugar refinery. The enterprise was profitable enough for the Shell Oil Company to buy the well from them in 1906.

In the 1880s, criminal science was in its infancy, and law enforcement officers were looking at better ways of identifying suspects. They were paying closer attention to physical characteristics such as foot size, length of limbs, distance between joints, size of skull and other distinguishing marks. French criminologist Alphonse

Bertillion had incorporated these physical characteristics into a system to help officers to identify suspects, and the Bertillion System was widely used until the advent of fingerprint identification.

By this time, the county jailer was so busy that he asked the sheriff for some relief. Rowland overstepped his bounds with the board of supervisors by immediately hiring a new assistant jailer without obtaining prior approval from the board. They admonished him, but allowed the addition with the caveat that he notify them prior to spending the county's money.

Progress was making its way to the county, and there was excitement about the first telephone to be installed in the courthouse. The streets were still unpaved, however, and in the rainy season they filled with muddy water and horse manure. Woe be to the pedestrian who did not pay attention when a carriage rolled over one of these "fishing holes"![37]

Sheriff Rowland served an extra two months as Sheriff because the legislature had adjusted the voting date from September to November. After he left office, Rowland continued to work on his petroleum research and exploration projects. He also became involved with the state reform school called the Whittier State School for Boys, where he took a position as manager. Rowland helped the boys learn how to lead productive and useful lives. He kept his home in Los Angeles but, as he neared retirement, the old lawman spent more and more time on the Rancho Puente. He truly enjoyed looking after his land, livestock, and oil wells.

After a five-year illness, Billy Rowland died of a heart attack at his Los Angeles home on February 2, 1926. He was eighty years old. His shotgun, complete with its original case, can be viewed at the Sheriff's Museum in Whittier, California (see appendix B). Billy Rowland will forever be remembered as the man who masterminded the capture of Tiburcio Vasquez, one of the most notorious desperadoes California has ever seen.

Sheriff Alvin Tyler Currier, 1883–1884

Alvin Currier ran against Sheriff Rowland for the 1883-1884 term of office. He was backed by popular support from a strong Republican Party platform, which helped him to take the election from

Rowland. Like his predecessor, he was also well-known and respected in the community. Los Angeles was now a thriving county of more than 30,000 residents, with more coming every day. By 1900, the population would increase to over 100,000.

Alvin T. Currier was born in Franklin County, Maine, on April 13, 1840. His grandfather, Samuel Currier, was a Maine State Senator who held many influential offices. Young Alvin went to public school and then attended college at the Farmington Academy. Like Sheriff Burns before him, Currier was an educator. He taught in the Maine public school system near his home. By 1861, Currier had saved enough money to travel. He took a sailing vessel to Panama and up the west coast of California. Currier settled for a while in Shoshone County, Idaho, where he tried his hand at gold and silver mining until 1867.

After a visit back home to Maine, he decided to return to California. In 1868, Currier traveled the entire state on horseback, looking for a place to settle down. He ultimately decided on the Pomona Valley, where he purchased a vast 2,500-acre ranch in 1889. The ranch came complete with cattle, hogs, large fruit orchards, and fields of grain and alfalfa. Because the property had its own artesian wells, Currier did not have to worry about droughts. The farm prospered and, in 1881, he married Susan Glenn Rubottom, who lived three miles west of Pomona near the Southern Pacific Railroad.

His first action as Sheriff was to appoint former Sheriff James Thompson as jailer. It seems that selecting his deputies was about the only action the new sheriff would take. Currier was more interested

Sheriff Currier preferred to let his deputies fight crime while he attended meetings and furthered his business interests. – Los Angeles County Sheriff's Department Archives

in politics and personal financial gain than any of his predecessors had been. In that respect, he was most like Sheriff Alexander. Although there was still plenty of crime and lawlessness, Currier preferred to let deputies George Gard and Adolfo Celis handle the day-to-day business of law enforcement. This was not uncommon, however, as many California sheriffs were not professional lawmen.

Currier joined and became active in a plethora of organizations. His titles included Director of the First National Bank of Pomona, board member of the San Antonio Fruit Exchange, board member of the University of Redlands, President of the Mutual Fire Insurance Company, board member of the San Antonio Canyon Water Company, and board member of the Walnut Fruit Growers Association. He was also a member in good standing of the Union League Club and the Los Angeles County Pioneers Society.

When Sheriff Currier was not attending meetings, he was busy managing his many properties and businesses. Besides owning property in the city, Currier built an office building at 212 West Third Street. He was also the majority shareholder in the Pomona/North Pomona Motor Line Company.

While county politics suffered its share of corruption, the City of Los Angeles was experiencing an epidemic of graft. Police officers were accepting as much as $2,000 a month in bribes and payoffs. They had apparently been appointed to office in relation to the number of votes they could bring in for a particular candidate. Gamblers and prostitutes would regularly pay the police to look the other way so that they could continue to rake in large sums of illegal profits. The old Los Angeles Ranger Horace Bell started a small newspaper called the *Porcupine*. He took every opportunity to use it to slander what he felt were corrupt city officials and policemen. In one article he wrote:

> The Police are always drunk on duty. One policeman in Sonoratown lay on a bench to sleep it off. A bunch of boys took off his badge and fastened it to the seat of his pants and pinned back the long coattails. When he woke up he missed the badge and the boys informed him the Chief had come by and finding him asleep had removed the badge. They fol-

lowed him all the way back to headquarters yelling and making fun of him.[38]

The *Porcupine* reported that Chief Henry King himself was said to receive $200 a month to protect the gaming between Pico House and Headquarters, and an additional $35 a month from *Fan Tan* games in Chinatown.

On April 18th, 1883, Deputy Adolfo Celis was killed in a tragic accident. Deputies Celis and Gard were traveling with two other men in a wagon. They were attempting to recover some stolen livestock about a quarter of a mile from the San Fernando Mission. As Deputy Celis was adjusting the wagon seat, his rifle accidentally discharged and he was killed instantly when the bullet tore through his chest. Celis had worked as a peace officer for thirteen years. He may have not been a perfect citizen, as he was one of the men indicted in the Chinese massacre,[39] however the *Los Angeles Times* claimed that, "He was intrepid, brave and persistent, and he rarely failed to bring in his man when he went for him. Celis has been shot at numerous times without number, but has never been scathed by a bullet from anyone else's gun."[40]

By the end of 1884, Sheriff Currier's term of office had come to a close. The Republicans selected George E. Gard as their new candidate for the 1885-1886 term.

Sheriff George E. Gard, 1885–1886

George Gard was born to Dr. William and Mrs. Lucretia Gard in Warren County, Ohio, in 1843. His mother was a well-educated teacher at a renowned private school in Middletown. Both of George's parents died when he was young, so he went to live with his grandfather, Garret Williamson, in Hamilton, Ohio. After finishing high school, Gard moved out west with his uncle. They brought with them herds of thoroughbred horses and cattle. The pioneers settled in San Jose for two years, and then George moved to Mariposa County, where he worked in his uncle's sawmill as a manager.

The Mariposa Mining Company saw raw talent in young George and hired him as superintendent for their mills. Looking for a job with more action, he enlisted in the Union Army late in the war and was appointed First Sergeant in H Company, Seventh California Infantry. The unit served in Arizona and New Mexico until March of 1866, when they were mustered out.

Gard worked in various Wilmington businesses for two years and then formed his own firm, The Los Angeles Ice Company. He partnered with Mr. Queen to form the Queen and Gard Corporation, which built an ice storage house on Main Street. The ice was brought in from the Truckee River and transported via steamer down the coast to San Pedro. By April 1868, Angelenos were keeping their perishables cool and frosty for the first time. In 1869, he married Kate A. Hammel, Deputy William Hammel's sister. The couple had two children, William Brant and Georgette Miles.

After three years in the ice business, Gard sold off his share of the company and went to work for the office of the county clerk. He later switched to the city Marshal's Office where, in 1871, he worked for $80.00 a month as a deputy marshal. It was in this capacity that he met his good friend and partner Emil Harris. Harris was a rugged lawman who emigrated to the United States from Prussia at age fourteen. He was a leader in the Jewish community and enjoyed keeping physically fit.

The two officers worked well together and solved so many cases that the city council appointed them as the city's first detectives in 1873. In 1874, Harris ran for Chief and was defeated. Gard was not re-appointed so he found work with the County's Chief Deputy Recorder and stayed there until 1879. Harris succeeded in obtaining the post of Chief of Police in 1877. Gard followed in his friend's footsteps and became the Chief of Police on December 12, 1880. In 1882 he worked as a deputy for Sheriff Rowland. In 1884, the Republicans selected him as their candidate for Sheriff. He was elected to serve the 1885-1886 term of office, winning with 2,408 votes.

Gard appointed two outstanding men, Martin Aguirre and William Hammel, as deputies, both of whom would later become sheriffs themselves. On January 19, 1886, Deputy Aguirre had just completed serving a warrant in the Newhall area when he noticed dark rain clouds beginning to form. By the time he reached Los Angeles at 5:00 in the evening the city was inundated. Levees were carried away as if they were grains of sand on the beach. The parts

Sheriff George Gard was an aggressive lawman who pursued outlaws with relentless vigor.
— LOS ANGELES COUNTY SHERIFF'S DEPARTMENT ARCHIVES

hit hardest were between Wilmington Street and the hills on the east side.

By midnight, the Los Angeles river had begun to overflow its banks and was still rising. Aguirre mounted his powerful gray horse and rode all night, warning residents who lived near the river to evacuate. At daybreak, despite his warnings, many persons were trapped and in danger of drowning.

Aguirre immediately began to charge through the waters to effect rescues. He saved the lives of nineteen people, several of them children. His courage and physical endurance amazed many Angelenos. On his last rescue, where First Street ran into the river, he attempted to save Mrs. Whitney's little girl, Theresa. He reached Theresa and managed to pull her from the window of her house. After helping her up onto his big horse, they started for land. Suddenly, they struck a half submerged picket fence. Martin tossed the girl onto the fence just as he was dragged into the freezing water. He tried desperately to reach her, swimming as fast as he could back to the fence. When he finally reached the fence, Theresa was gone. Martin barely managed to save himself by swimming across to Seventh Street before he collapsed on the riverbank in an exhausted heap. Other helpers rescued the mother, but the little girl was lost.[41] Aguirre would regret not being able to save the girl for the rest of his life. For his valor and bravery, the Los Angeles County Bar

Association awarded him a gold watch, which he highly prized and always carried with him.

A New Jail Is Built

By 1886, the county's population demanded that a larger and more sophisticated jail be constructed. The 1886 Grand Jury commented on the old 1853 brick jail: "The accommodations are entirely insufficient, but this will soon be remedied by the new building now in course of construction."[42] The new lockup was called the New High Street Jail; it was nearing completion in December, 1886, when Deputy Sheriff Hammel began to transfer prisoners there. On December 2, the *Los Angeles Times* reported:

> At 3:45 . . . Deputy Sheriff Hammel having charge, and being assisted by Bill Stoermer and a dozen policemen. The prisoners were taken up handcuffed two and two, surrounded by officers. There were fifty-six of them in all. . . . All went without trouble, and all were pleased at the change and new comfortable quarters from the old wretched ones. All their old blankets were left behind and they found comfortable new ones. The beds in the jail were also a pleasant surprise. They are flat hammocks of canvas stretched from wall to wall by straps, and apparently very comfortable. The bathtubs and sanitary appliances in the new quarters are admirable.[43]

On the second floor of the jail, a trapdoor was built for the purpose of executions. In 1891, the responsibility for executions was transferred to the state prison system.[44] There is no doubt that the new jail, with its many separate cells and modern design, helped to make Sheriff Gard's job much easier.

The Evans-Sontag Robberies

The zenith of Gard's law enforcement career would not be reached during his tenure as sheriff but rather while he was serving as a U.S. Marshal. After he left the sheriff's office, Gard started an orange farm in Azusa, where he worked for four years until President Harrison appointed him U.S. Marshal for the Southern District of

In 1886, the Los Angeles County Sheriff's Office moved 56 inmates to the newly constructed High Street Jail. Today the jail population can reach 20,000 on any given day.
— SECURITY PACIFIC COLLECTION / LOS ANGELES PUBLIC LIBRARY

California. During his four-year term he worked closely with railroad detectives and local sheriffs to apprehend the notorious train robbers Chris Evans and John Sontag.

It is one thing to take down a stagecoach, but robbing a train is a much more complicated job. Where Tiburcio Vasquez and his experienced henchmen had failed, Sontag and Evans managed to succeed. Twenty-seven-year-old John Sontag was working for the Southern Pacific Railroad Company in 1887 when he was seriously injured in a train yard accident. He abandoned railroading and met 42-year-old rancher and family man Chris Evans. The two soon became close friends and Sontag moved in with the Evans family. The pair opened a livery business in Modesto, but four months after the grand opening, a fire burned the building to the ground.[45]

While Sontag may have held a grudge against the railroad for what he claimed was poor medical treatment, scholars and historians still ponder why Evans, who had a wife and children, turned to a life of crime. Perhaps he did not really understand it himself. Maybe it was the thrill of getting away with the loot. No matter what

175

the reason, the pair began robbing trains near the California towns of Pixley, Goshen, and Visalia. In the three robberies, more than $20,000 in cash was taken and four people were killed. It did not take long before Pinkerton detectives were hot on their trail and watching every move they made.

On August 3, 1892, the pair included John Sontag's younger brother George in the Collis train robbery near Fresno. The three outlaws took $50,000 from the Southern Pacific train. Detective Will Smith and Deputy Sheriff Witty arrested George in Visalia. The two investigators felt that they had enough information from George to contact Chris Evans and John Sontag for questioning. When they arrived at the Evans house, the bandits opened fire on the lawmen and then escaped into the hills.

Evans's wife was shocked at his behavior. Apparently, she did not know that her husband was a train robber. A reward of $10,000 was posted for the bandits' capture, and bounty hunters and lawmen from as far away as Arizona came pouring into Visalia. The pair was tracked to a mountain cabin owned by Jim Young in eastern Fresno County, where Evans and Sontag had decided to put up a fight.

Vic Wilson, a deputy U.S. marshal from Tucson, Deputy Sheriff Frank Burke from Yuma, and two Indian guides, Pelon and Camino, also from Yuma, arrived in Visalia to take up the chase. They joined with Detective Will Smith, Constable Warren Hill, Andy McGinnis, and Al Witty. Later, *San Francisco Examiner* reporter Petey Bigelow took down Chris Evans' story in his own words:

> We waited until the first two men came within fifteen to twenty feet of the door, then we thrust our shotguns through the window panes and blazed away, one barrel each. Both men reeled and fell, and as I swung open the door swiftly and came out through the smoke towards them, McGinnis cried out to Sontag "For God's sake, don't John!" We dashed by the two fallen men and opened fire on the balance of them. Witty fell and bellowed like a calf. Burke tumbled over the fence to the right of the gate, and I sent a Winchester bullet after him to increase his speed. He flew down the gulch and we saw him no more.

Sprinter Smith with a wild cry, wheeled his horse, clapped spurs to its flanks, dropped his head against the horse's neck and flew back up the trail, scattering his gun, his belt, his coat, and for all I know everything that he had along the road. One Indian bawled for him to stop, but that only increased his terror. The Indians meanwhile had taken to the rock pile at the left of the gate and were fighting in true Indian fashion. I did not mind them so much, because I had fought Sioux and Cheyenne and I knew their tricks. These fellows simply thrust their rifles above the rocks and blazed away without taking any aim, so they failed entirely to hit us. Pretty soon I made it so hot for them that they thought distance would lend enchantment to the view and dashed away down the road. Warren Hill started to run away with his horse, but a Winchester bullet dropped the animal and Hill took Burke's horse.

All this occurred within the twinkling of an eye, and it was with a jump that I discovered that we were attacked from the rear. John Sontag suddenly dropped his right arm and cried out that it was broken, while a bullet sped past my right eyebrow, leaving the scar. Whirling about we saw that McGinnis had revived and had turned over on his back to fill me with lead from his Winchester rifle. I was compelled to put another bullet into him to stop him.[46]

The pair managed to escape into the woods, where they hid from the law and tried to recover from their wounds. Posses looked tirelessly for the bandits but their searches always met with negative results. Wells Fargo Detective John Thacker knew that a different approach had to be taken if they were ever going to catch these outlaws. He called in ex-Los Angeles County Sheriff and U.S. Marshal George Gard.[47]

The two men secretly put together a small posse of four men, including Gard, Nevada lawman Fred Jackson, private detective Tom Burns, and Fresno County Deputy Sheriff Hiram Rapelje. The posse rested during the day and patrolled at night. They made no fires and ate cold food the entire time they were on the hunt. Nine months after the shootout at Young's cabin, their hard work paid off. This time, it was the lawmen who surprised the desperadoes as they were walking toward Visalia on the evening of June 11, 1893. Again, Chris Evans later told the story:

> The first intimation I had of danger was a bullet. John and I was walking leisurely down the trail and were just sitting down upon the old manure heap near the cabin. Suddenly there was a report and a bullet flew past Sontag's head. Then we knew we were in for it. It was the worst fight I ever was in; worse in fact, than a big battle with the Sioux Indians I was in once upon a time.
>
> The manure heap was small and only two feet high. It served as a death trap because of its flimsy protection. We flung ourselves behind it, however, kneeling on the ground, and proceeded to pump lead into the cabin. It was about half an hour before sundown. The door of the cabin was aslant and we could not see exactly where our adversaries were placed at first, but presently after the first four shots, we could tell that they were not inside, but round the corner of the house. I directed my fire toward that point and presently was hit in the middle of the right eyebrow, the bullet plowing a hole across the bridge of the nose. This splashed blood across my eyes and blinded me so badly that I could not see the sights on the rifle. They must have fired 200 shots into that dung heap during the battle. We had plenty of ammunition, but the whizzing bullets came ripping through the straw and caught me in the forearm, shattering it badly. Next, my other arm went by the board and I was helpless. John Sontag, however, kept up the return fire bravely. He is always exceedingly cool when under fire, and he never lost his nerve a minute, although repeatedly hit. He did not give up heart though til just before dark, then a bullet striking him in the forehead knocked him backward like a tenpin. He cried "My God, Chris, I'm done for this time."
>
> It's a wonder that the wound in the chest that he had received ten minutes before had not floored him, for the

blood was flowing through his shirt fearfully and his face was a dreadful sight. He begged me to blow his brains out, but I had not the heart to do it.

I waited until the stars came out, and then knowing that John's case was hopeless I helped to cover him with straw and resolved to make a break for high land. You see they did not fire from behind the cabin all the time, but would flank us firing at long distance. Why, at one time they fired at 200 or 300 yards range. Well, when I made up my mind to leave, I slid on my belly, Indian fashion through the grass. It was then that a man running along the fence took a quick shot at me and plowed my back with a bullet. I rose to my feet with a jump and dashed up the slope over a low hill. The man did not follow me.[48]

Fred Jackson was seriously injured during the ferocious gun battle. He was rushed to a doctor in Visalia, his lower leg was amputat-

This famous photograph depicts the capture of train robber John Sontag (on the ground bottom left). Before he died he is quoted as saying "I am only sorry I did not make a better job of killing myself." Former Sheriff Gard is third from the right with the handkerchief on his head. – NATIONAL ARCHIVES AND RECORDS ADMINISTRATION

ed but he recovered. Sontag, on the other hand, was mortally wounded. He was taken into custody in the morning. Before John Sontag died of his wounds, he said, "I am only sorry I did not make a better job of killing myself."[49] Beating the Fresno officers to the scene, Tulare County Undersheriff Hall found Chris Evans a few hours later, eight miles away at a relative's house.

Chris Evans went to Folsom prison missing an eye and an arm. His cellmate was Dick Fellows, the notorious Los Angeles stage-coach robber. The two got along well together, for they both enjoyed reading and writing. Evans was pardoned in 1911 and ban-ished from California. He died in Oregon six years later, surround-ed by his family.

Tulare County Sheriff Eugene Kay picked up $5,000 in reward money for Chris Evans's arrest. The other $5,000 for Sontag was split four ways: $1,500 to George Gard, $1,500 to Fred Jackson and $1,000 each to Tom Burns and Hiram Rapelje.

Gard's reputation soared after the shootout with the bandits. He accepted a position with the Southern Pacific Railroad as chief of detectives. The jurisdiction was extensive, running from Ogden to San Francisco and from Portland to El Paso. When the opportunity presented itself, Gard opened his own detective agency and settled down closer to home. He continued orange farming until his death on March 10, 1904.

Chapter *5*

FRONTIER STYLE LAW ENFORCEMENT FADES: THE SHERIFF'S OFFICE MOVES TOWARD THE 20TH CENTURY

Sheriff James C. Kays, January, 1887–December, 1888

Late in 1886, Sheriff Gard ran for re-election against James Kays and lost. Kays' story is a rags-to-riches tale of which many of his father's fellow Irishmen could only dream. James C. Kays was born in Santa Barbara, California, on May 5, 1850. His father, John Kays, immigrated with his wife, Josephine Burke, from Roscommon County, Ireland. Tough financial times in the Kay family meant that young Jim, at age thirteen, had to leave school and work for his uncle, who owned a general merchandising store in Santa Ynez, a neighbor town of Santa Barbara. At age fifteen, Kays was able to work part-time in the store while he attended Christian Brothers College. However, he could not afford to complete his education because of the family's continuing financial burdens, so he returned to work full-time.

At age nineteen, James struck out on his own and tried his hand at mining in Nevada and Inyo counties. In 1870, he settled in the small mining town of Cerro Gordo near Lone Pine and opened up a general store. On March 26, 1872, a series of earthquakes rocked the town: twenty-four people were killed and sixty adobe houses collapsed. When tremors and quakes continued to besiege the area, Kays decided that he had had enough. Believing that a larger city

would offer him greater opportunities and more stability, he went to Los Angeles in 1874, where he found employment at Harper and Long's Hardware store.

In 1875, he took a position as deputy county clerk and, in 1877, Sheriff Mitchell appointed him as undersheriff. He served in that capacity for five consecutive years. In 1883, he married Alice Benedick of Booneville, Missouri. They had five children: Cecilia, Catherine, Florence, Francis, and Walter. Walter was tragically killed in an automobile accident in 1922.

Kays was elected treasurer of the City of Los Angeles, where he served until 1886. The federal government offered him a job as a United States Revenue Agent, but he had to resign shortly after he took the position because he was elected Sheriff of Los Angeles County. His first appointment was Henry Mitchell, whom he selected to be his undersheriff. Kays instituted a new policy for the office. Each of the eight deputies was required to post a $5,000 personal bond. The bond was supposed to ensure the "faithful performance of their duties." The grumbling deputies were Henry Mitchell, Charles Cruz, John Griffin, Terrance Cooney, Edward Smith, Richard Barham, John Cline, and former Sheriff James Thompson, who served as jailer.

Jail Break

James Thompson and the inmates were more than happy to move to the New High Street Jail on December 1, 1886. The new jail was spacious and allowed for a more sophisticated classification system of inmates. Thompson was getting old, however, and the sloppy jail records from that period indicate that he was not paying attention to detail.[1] On January 14, 1887, the *Los Angeles Times* reported two escapes within a week, both the results of Thompson' careless jailing. Three months later, the largest escape in the history of the Los Angeles County jails occurred. Fortunately for Thompson, he could not be blamed for this incident.

The escape took place in April, 1887, when Assistant Jailer Bob Clark was on duty and Thompson was off duty. An inmate lured Clark into a hallway, where a gang of waiting prisoners attacked the jailer. They overpowered him and took his keys, enabling several of them to escape. A black cook identified simply as "Joe" saved the day by rescuing Clark. Joe threatened the remaining inmates with his meat cleaver, thus preventing further escapes. Clark called for help and the jail was finally secured, but not before fifteen prisoners had escaped. Despite Sheriff Kays' efforts, only five of the inmates were recaptured. The county's next largest jailbreak would not occur until more than a century later, when, on April 30, 1995, eleven inmates escaped from the "North" facility at the Pitchess Detention Center in Castaic. All but two of these inmates were recaptured.[2]

The Remainder of Sheriff Kays' Term

Kays was known to be somewhat of a strange character with many quirks. He was socially aloof but a wily politician, a charitable man but not a kindly soul. He was a religious worshipper, yet greedy. These traits may have stemmed from the fact that, while he was fairly well-educated, he came from a very poor family. Never having had money, it must have been important for him to make as much as he could and then hoard it. It is perhaps no wonder that Sheriff Kays had more of his deputies resign from office than any other sheriff, except John Cline.

One of the wisest decisions that Sheriff Kays made during his term of office was to hire Juan Murrieta, a young and energetic deputy. Murrieta would become a legend, retiring in 1927 after serving forty years as a deputy sheriff—a record that no other deputy of the time, not even ex-sheriff and jailer James Thompson, could match.

Murrieta was the antithesis of the notorious outlaw Joaquin Murrieta, who had ravaged the California countryside thirty-five years earlier. Like Sheriff Sanchez before him, Deputy Murrieta stood for everything that was good about the Californio culture and heritage. He was highly-respected by every sheriff who met him, including Eugene Biscailuz, who took office in 1932. All of them considered Murrieta a friend, counselor, and advisor. For this reason, he is known as the "Father of Sheriffs," a legacy that no other deputy has been able to claim.

In 1887, a land boom took place in Los Angeles. Crooks from the east coast were selling plots of land, sight unseen, to gullible investors. The county registrar recorded claim after claim, some of which were on cliffs in the desert with no potable water for miles. There was even a group of swindlers who sold land based on other real estate agents' advertisements. "Paper" towns sprung up overnight. They had names such as Widneyville by the Desert, Chicago Park, Sunset, Manchester, Santiago, Nadeau, St. James, and many others. Conservative estimates of the land boom ranged to 200 million dollars. One of the towns that actually transcended "paper city" status and became a reality was Inglewood, thanks to its reliable source of water from the Centinella Springs. There was not much that Sheriff Kays could do for the victims of these crimes, as the transactions were usually made in cash; by the time the victim realized that he had been swindled, both the crook and the money had long since vanished.

By the late 1800s, the city police department had grown to be much larger than the sheriff's office. The department consisted of a chief of police, a captain of patrol with fifty foot patrol officers and ten mounted officers, and a captain of detectives with four investigators and two sergeants.[3] Rapid growth of the sheriff's department would not come until the twentieth century, when the outlying areas of the county would start to develop.

Early one morning in 1887, a Los Angeles legend came to a crashing end. Jacob Kurtz, a demolitions contractor, had been paid to level the Calle de Los Negros. The city had to destroy the street in an underhanded way because the old adobe businesses were still producing large amounts of cash for the owners, and for years the proprietors had used lawyers and injunctions to halt the urban renewal process. Kurtz accomplished his job with great efficiency. First, he moved the Chinese out of the old, rotting adobes and then he smashed the buildings to the ground as quickly as possible.

From that day forward, the "Calle" was known simply as an extension of Los Angeles Street (see appendix B). When Sheriff Kays and his deputies went to view the destruction, they were more than a little melancholy. The lawmen realized that the end of Los Angeles as a frontier town was now complete. Never again would there be shots fired from the saloons of the "Calle" while whiskey flowed from the bottle and fandango music played in the background. Never more would gold coins clink on the gaming tables and ladies of the evening ply their wares to lonely vaqueros and gamblers in search of something more from their dusty, dangerous lives.

After retiring from the office of sheriff, Kays managed the Citizens Water Company, which supplied water to the "Hill" section of Los Angeles. In 1902, he entered the banking business and became a board member of the Riverside Bank and Trust Company of Los Angeles. He ultimately became president of the bank, which was renamed Park Bank in 1907. While Kays was working as a banker, he held positions as director and treasurer for the Los Angeles Chamber of Commerce. He died in Los Angeles of pneumonia on March 27, 1917.

Sheriff Martin G. Aguirre, January 1889–December 1890

James Kays did not run for re-election as he was already focused on other business pursuits. Martin Aguirre, who was riding a wave of popularity and hero worship from his brave deeds during the 1886 floods, won the election and started his term on January 1, 1889. At thirty-one, Aguirre was the second youngest man to occupy the office, and the energy and enthusiasm showed.

Martin's father, Don Jose Antonio Aguirre, was a sea captain. He came to Mexico City from Madrid, Spain, when he was sixteen. Captain Aguirre worked as an importer, shipping goods to Mexico from ports in China and Manila. When Mexico won its independence from Spain, Antonio moved to San Diego, where he married Rosario Estudillo. Their son Martin was born on September 6, 1858.

Antonio died when Martin was two, and at age nine he was sent to live with a relative, Joseph Wolfskill, who took young Martin into his spacious Los Angeles home at Alameda and Third Street. Aguirre attended school at Professor Lawler's Institute and ultimately graduated from St. Vincent's College, the predecessor of Loyola Marymount University.[4]

Martin's best friend was William Hammel, the son of a German immigrant. The two were fond of practical jokes, and they played them often. The boys once dammed up the *zanja madre*, a canal which diverted water from the Los Angeles river to the city for drinking and irrigation purposes. The dam created a spot for a perfect swimming hole, and neighborhood children would frequent the place to splash around and cool off. One day, Aguirre and Hammel gathered up a bunch of stinging nettles and anchored them to the bottom of the swimming hole. It did not take long for the swimmers to realize that a joke had been played on them. They jumped out of the water, screaming and itching all over. The pranksters, who were watching nearby, took off, stumbling through the brush and clutching their bellies from laughing.[5]

To Martin's great misfortune, sometimes the children played too wildly. When he and his cousin were practicing with bows and

Sheriff Aguirre was a superb rider and a caballero in the truest sense of the word. He took many a crook to jail and saved many lives during the flood of 1886. – Los Angeles County Sheriff's Department Archives

arrows, Martin was accidentally struck in the eye. The wound left him blind in that eye for life. Today, a disability of that nature would most likely have disqualified him from applying for work as a fireman or policeman, but in the 1880s there were no such restrictions.

Young Martin started working as a public servant at an early age. He became a volunteer firefighter with the Confidence Engine Company No. 2. When pistol shots in the air sounded the alarm, Aguirre would jump on his pony and gallop over to the station. He used his small horse to pull the hose cart by fastening a rope from the cart's tongue to his saddle horn.

Aguirre worked on the Wolfskill ranch and became a skilled horseman and proficient ranch manager. He was elected as a Los Angeles Constable in 1885 and was involved in several harrowing incidents. One evening, after coming home from work, he heard an old man calling for help. Aguirre called, "Hold it, I'm coming," and ran to the sound of the voice. Aguirre ran headlong into two robbers, whom he subdued with his bare fists. He handcuffed the outlaws and tied them to a tree. After escorting the old man home, the constable returned and dragged the two bandits off to jail.[6]

On another occasion, Constable Aguirre's stepmother answered the door and recognized a local ruffian whom Martin had arrested two years prior. The man asked to see the constable. In a wise move, Mrs. Wolfskill told the man that she would check to see whether Martin was home, and she asked the stranger to wait outside. She told Aguirre about the stranger and warned him to be careful. Martin cautiously answered the door and was greeted by a loaded pistol. As the outlaw fired, Aguirre slammed the door, deflecting the bullet that lodged in his arm instead of his chest.

Rather than deter the lawman, the wound only served to anger him. Aguirre charged headlong into his would-be assassin and tackled him. After a short scuffle, Aguirre handcuffed the desperado and placed him under arrest for attempted murder. The outlaw went back to prison, this time to serve a life sentence.

Martin Aguirre also worked as one of Sheriff Gard's deputies. He was very strict with regard to the enforcement of laws and regulations. The *Los Angeles Times* exclaimed, "He was not a very large man, but he had a fine physique, muscles like iron. He was always very neatly dressed and conducted himself with the manners of a born gentleman. When he rapped for order in his courtrooms, there was order."[7]

When on patrol, Aguirre preferred carrying a razor-sharp Bowie knife in a sheath under his arm, rather than a gun. He once told his friend Harry Carr, "You see, if anything starts, I don't know where bullets might go or whom they might hit, but I know where this knife is going."[8] Aguirre's friend Henry Carr wrote, "Aguirre could throw a knife fifty feet and pin the spot on the ace of spades." [9] When he did carry a gun, Aguirre toted a Remington six-shot revolver that had been given to him by Sheriff Gard. The weapon had originally been given to Gard as a gift from condemned murderer Billy McDowell.[10]

Like all law enforcement officers, Aguirre was fallible. Without first carefully checking out the legality of his orders, he was sent to evict Rogerio Rocha and his family of ten from their home near the San Fernando Mission. Rogerio had lived on the property for eighty years and, by Spanish land grant law, was entitled to the plot. The order to seize the property came from scheming former state senators and real estate barons Charles Maclay and George Porter.

Deputy Aguirre thought that he was doing the right thing when he forcibly placed the old man onto a wagon and told the family that they had to leave. The rest of the family quietly joined Rogerio on the wagon, and they were dropped off on a country road, along with their few meager possessions and some chickens. Angelenos complained to the newspapers, and their opinions were printed. Deputy Aguirre learned to pay closer attention to court warrants and to use common sense as well as compassion when enforcing the law.

As Sheriff, Aguirre appointed A.M. Thornton as his Undersheriff and seven other trustworthy men as his deputies. He told them, "Bring back your man, I don't want a report!"[11] Aguirre was also a smart detective; he knew that a case could be lost if a tight lid was not kept on criminal investigations. One reporter complained:

> Sheriff Aguirre and his able deputies are about the hardest set of officials that the average reporter ever ran across for

information. While they are very courteous to the newsgath-
erer, they have a happy faculty of keeping the secrets of the
office to themselves, especially if they think that the ends of
justice might perchance be thwarted.[12]

Aguirre's jails kept the staff very busy, as they now housed
between 250 and 300 men on a daily basis. Orange County was
formed, and the Los Angeles County Board of Supervisors lost
almost a thousand square miles of territory. The upside to this
secession was that the county gained the ability to better manage
the remaining land.

Six months after he took office, Aguirre was almost killed during
an attempt to arrest a rape suspect. Mary Simmons had recently
filed charges against Benoir Renault, claiming that he had forcibly
raped her. On May 2, 1889, Deputy Constable Dawes went to
Renault's house to serve an arrest warrant when shots rang out.
Dawes pulled out his pistol and immediately returned fire, shooting
into the house where the suspect had barricaded himself.[13]

Dawes called for help and Undersheriff Thornton arrived with
deputies Kemp and Brady. More shots were exchanged and a standoff ensued. Sheriff Aguirre took deputies Kearny and Dorsey along
with several boxes of ammunition and supplies to the scene of the
shooting. Aguirre entered the house and worked his way to a door
behind which he believed Renault had barricaded himself.

The Sheriff called out to the suspect but received no answer. He
was slowly turning the doorknob when Renault fired his weapon.
The bullet punched through the door and smashed into Aguirre's
left arm. A second shot would have killed him if it were not for a half
dollar that he carried in his vest pocket. The bullet struck the coin,
causing the lucky sheriff to stumble outside. His deputies bandaged
his wounds, but as the lawmen were dealing with Aguirre's injuries
Renault made his escape from the house, which had caught fire during the shootout. The next day, officers found Renault hiding
behind a coal bin in the Bunker Hill section of town.

Renault chose none other than the famous Los Angeles attorney
Horace Bell to represent him in court. Bell claimed that no warrant
had been read to his client and that Constable Dawes had fired first.

He even went to far as to say that Sheriff Aguirre "ought to have been shot" because Renault was only protecting his property. The trial ended in a hung jury, and a new trial was set for August 20.

During the second trial Renault's attorney claimed that his client was mentally ill and that he thought that members of a secret society, who were out to cut his throat and bury him at sea, were chasing him. The jury found Renault guilty of the lesser charge of assault and the judge fined him $350 or 350 days in jail. Many Angelenos were angry, and the *Express* commented, "It is a sad state of affairs when an officer is not protected by the law."[14] Renault appealed the decision and lost, so he went to jail and served his 350-day sentence.

The Sheriff found his own private way to protest the verdict. Not long after the trial, the grand jury ordered him to bring an unruly witness to the courtroom for testimony. When Aguirre located the man at a local watering hole, he decided on a unique plan of action. The sheriff took off his badge and pulled out a white flag. After making sure that he had plenty of witnesses, he entered the bar with his flag and sat down next to the man. Aguirre bought the angry drunk several beers and then kindly asked him to accompany him to the courtroom. The drunk said that he would go "when he was damn good and ready!"

Aguirre took his white flag and marched back over to the courthouse where the grand jury was waiting. Upon seeing him, they asked where their witness was. Aguirre told them his story, and they agreed that it was best if he continued to do business using conventional methods. Seeing that he had made his point, the sheriff smiled and politely left the courtroom, as he had further business to attend to. Two years later, Benoir Renault was arrested while attempting to rape a woman in Boyle Heights. This time, a housewife captured him and held him at bay with a loaded revolver. The victim of the attempted rape begged the housewife for the gun so that she could shoot her aggressor, but Police Officer Gridley arrived in time to save the criminal's life. Gridley took him into custody and booked him into jail.[15] Renault was convicted of criminal assault on June 29, 1891, and sent to San Quentin for three years.

While in office, Aguirre learned that he had an extreme dislike for the distasteful job of hanging criminals. The very thought of it turned his stomach, and he felt that the responsibility for executions should be taken from the local authorities and assigned to the state. Along with several other California sheriffs, he lobbied Sacramento to change the law; and was eventually successful.[16]

Some of Aguirre's greatest challenges came from maintaining jail security. During one jailbreak attempt, the sheriff was forced to fire a gun over the inmates' heads in order to stop fourteen of them from escaping.[17] Bullets ricocheted off the bars, and the inmates backed down. Help arrived, and jail operations went back to normal.

Another problem surfaced when complaints arose regarding appropriate medical care for inmates. The sheriff explained to both the media and the board of supervisors that the county hospital had refused to accept them, and so he was doing his best to care for them. Problems like this continue to exist today, where the Sheriff of Los Angeles County is responsible for the health of up to 20,000 inmates on any given day.

In early 1890, Sheriff Aguirre rode into the Castaic foothills to investigate a double homicide. William Chormicle and W. Gardner had shot down George Walton and Dolores Cook in a dispute over railroad land. After the shooting, the two men panicked and rode off into the mountains. Aguirre teamed up with Sheriff Riley from Ventura County to hunt down the killers.

On March 11 1890, the *Los Angeles Times* wrote:

The pursuit of the two men (William C. Chormicle and W. Gardner) shows that they were not, as it had been intimated, thoroughly determined to give themselves up. When Sheriff Aguirre and Deputy Sheriff Brady left Los Angeles they went straight to the scene of the murder. Then they followed the trail of the men up Castac [sic] Canon. They went on and crossed over to the Marengo Canon by the mountain trail, a wild and precipitous route. It was Sheriff Aguirre's determination to follow up and trace the fugitives if possible. . . . It is probably the case that they were driven out of Piru Canon by Aguirre into the arms of Sheriff Riley.[18]

In one of the longest trials the county had ever seen (four months), both men were acquitted of murder on the grounds of self-defense.

After completing his two-year term, Aguirre ran for re-election against Edward Gibson. The Republican Party, the *Los Angeles Times,* and the *Express* all supported the sheriff. Even the grand jury declared that he had conducted the affairs of his office in a proper manner. Despite this strong support, Aguirre could not hold against the *Los Angeles Herald* and their mudslinging editorials. The *Herald* claimed that Aguirre had made false arrests, kept sloppy records, and even let Renault's house burn down during the standoff incident. Gibson won the election in a hotly contested race. Party politics would continue to play a major role in county elections for Sheriff until 1910, when progressives rendered certain county offices nonpartisan. Nine years after this election, the sheriff's support for the Republican Party would pay big dividends.

Governor Henry T. Gage appointed Martin Aguirre as Warden for the San Quentin Penitentiary in 1899. The ex-sheriff packed his belongings and moved up to the Bay Area. Ironically, his new job would require him to oversee several state executions. This was something that he could never have expected when he was lobbying the legislature to change the law. Aguirre was a progressive warden, implementing recreational periods and shower baths. He also increased safety by drastically reducing the amount of contraband that entered the prison. Aguirre told his guards, "Gentlemen, that dope doesn't fly in here, and it doesn't crawl in, the prisoners can't go outside to get it, you can draw your own conclusions."[19] The guards got the point and the drug trafficking stopped. However, not everything went smoothly for the warden, as politics would turn a good thing ugly for him.

A Republican reform group called the Primary League of San Francisco teamed up with the *San Francisco Call* to accuse Governor Gage of corruption. Among other things, the charges included accusations that the governor had received free furniture made by San Quentin prison workers. Governor Gage countersued for libel, and Aguirre was called to testify. During the trial, Aguirre was accused of nepotism and mishandling prison funds. To add to his problems, a support group for prison convicts called the "California Prison Commission" accused the warden of torture and overuse of straight jackets to punish recalcitrant inmates. The *Call* continued to publish negative articles. The libel case was eventually dropped, but not before damaging Aguirre's reputation. By July, 1902, he was glad that his time at San Quentin was coming to an end.

Before he left the prison, over 1,300 inmates presented the warden with a scroll of their testimonials, part of which read:

> We the undersigned committee, all of whom have been many years within these walls and all under several and some under many administrations, do unsolicited, gladly and most earnestly testify that you have governed this Institution with an earnestness and fidelity but too rarely found in public officials.[20]

Aguirre finished his term as warden and went back to Los Angeles in 1903.

He was not long back in Los Angeles when the government of El Salvador contacted him. They had heard of his accomplishments at San Quentin and they offered him a position supervising the construction of a new prison. Aguirre stayed there for a short while and then consulted with the Cuban government on their jail system, offering suggestions on how to improve the custody environment. After fulfilling those contracts, he returned to the place in which he was most comfortable: the Los Angeles County Sheriff's office.

Over the next twenty years Aguirre served as a deputy for three sheriffs, including his boyhood friend William Hammel. He learned to work the county jail and picked up where James Thompson had left off. Aguirre also served as a bailiff in the courts and was appointed Senior Criminal Deputy by Sheriff William Traeger in the 1920s.

In his later years, the one-eyed ex-sheriff talked about his thoughts on life and "modern" law enforcement:

> These automobiles and telephones and radios—what have they accomplished? These deputies go out. They telephone in every five minutes. When we went out, no one even knew

when we were coming back. These fellows get twenty feet off a highway and they are lost.

Aguirre also had something to say about the horse versus the patrol car: "We didn't have flat tires, either, . . . we couldn't go 150 miles a day—but what have they accomplished with their autos (that we couldn't with horses)?"[21]

Martin Aguirre was a man who deserved much more credit than he ultimately received. He was a true hero in every sense of the word. The mere fact that a Latino man was elected in a time when Anglo political power was nearing its peak is an amazing accomplishment. On February 25, 1929, bachelor Aguirre died of cancer at age seventy-one. More than 200 honorary pallbearers attended his funeral.

Sheriff Edward D. Gibson, November 1891–December 1892

Edward D. Gibson was elected to office on November 4, 1890, to serve out the 1891-1892 term of office. His father, Fielding Gibson, was a prominent southern California rancher who came to Los Angeles around Cape Horn in 1853. Mr. Gibson settled with his wife, Betsy, in the area near what is now South Pasadena. The Gibsons had five children, the oldest of whom was Edward, born on March 21, 1853. Fielding Gibson kept busy tending the livestock, making brooms, and serving on the board of supervisors.

Edward grew up with a great interest in ships and sailing. He

In 1891, Sheriff Ed Gibson spent $825 a month to cover payroll expenses for his 11 employees. Today the Los Angeles County Sheriff's Department has close to 14,000 employees.

started an import-export business that operated out of Laguna Beach. He often went on voyages and, at one point, tried his hand at prospecting for gold in Alaska. Upon his return to Los Angeles, Edward married Alma Jaqua and she bore him two children.

Once Gibson took office, the County Board of Supervisors authorized him to spend $825 a month to cover his payroll expenses for eleven full-time employees. This included one Undersheriff, one traveling deputy, one civil process server, two court deputies, one jailer, three assistant jailers, one matron, and one bookkeeper.

After his term in office ended, Gibson took a job with the Internal Revenue Service. He retired to a quiet life in South Pasadena and passed away on March 19, 1935, from a heart attack. He was eighty-one years old.

Sheriff John C. Cline, January 1893–December 1894

John C. Cline was elected Los Angeles County's 20th sheriff. He was born in Ballarat, Australia, on May 2, 1860, to a Scottish mother and an American father. The family moved to Frederick, Maryland, where John's father found work as a farmer and fisherman. The restless Clines then decided to move west, stopping in Gary, Indiana, for two years before finally settling in Los Angeles in 1869. After John graduated from high school he attended business college and was offered a position working for the Southern Pacific Railroad.

Cline enthusiastically tackled the new job, starting as an apprentice surveyor. To enhance his career, he studied engineering and railroad construction in his spare time. Cline worked long hours under the hot New Mexico sun, but he enjoyed the freedom of working outdoors. He was such a diligent and conscientious laborer that, by the end of his first job, the surveying crew voted him as best "instrument man" of the entire group.

Back in Los Angeles, Mr. Hansen, the City Surveyor, was looking for a new staff member to fill a vacancy. Cline heard of the job opening and immediately applied. Hansen was impressed with the young man's qualifications and hired him as a junior surveyor. Cline lived up to his four-star reputation and, shortly after being hired, he was promoted to Chief Deputy City Surveyor. While surveying for the city, Cline became heavily involved in politics. At age twenty-three he decided to make a run for Township Constable, and he won the race from six opponents.

Soon thereafter, he thought of running for sheriff, but was dissuaded by friends who told him that he would have a difficult time running against Sheriff Kays. After hearing of the young man's ambitions, the Sheriff went to meet Cline in person. Like other employers before him, Kays was impressed by the young man, and he offered him a job as deputy. Cline worked in that capacity for six years, serving under Kays, Aguirre, and Gibson. In 1892, believing that he had enough experience and political support, he ran for the office of sheriff and won. Emerson wrote, "He was probably best known in his day as Sheriff of the County, as an officer in whom political astuteness was combined with business shrewdness and personal charm."[22]

1893 was a tough year to be elected to any government office. On May 5, the "Panic of 1893" hit and the bottom dropped out of the stock market. Wall Street stock prices tumbled, 500 banks closed their doors, and 15,000 businesses went bankrupt. Even the railroads were in trouble; the Northern Pacific, the Union Pacific, and the Santa Fe all went into receivership. Since the trains were not rolling, farm products, including southern California's citrus produce, could not be shipped. County employees were asked to take a 10% pay cut, and many others lost their jobs. Angelenos would suffer through the depression until the turn of the century.

Sheriff "Johnny" Cline, as everyone called him, did not seem to mind the hard times. He was a progressive sheriff and, despite the economy, the sheriff's office saw growth under his command. Cline was elected sheriff twice, with a twenty-year hiatus between terms. Not long after taking office the first time, he was allowed to increase his workforce to twelve deputies. He hired his brothers, William and Caspar, to help with the workload. It was during this time that Riverside County was separated from Los Angeles County, making Cline's job that much easier.

Alva Johnson and Kid Thompson: The Train Robbers

The sheriff's office saw action in the form of two daring train robberies in the San Fernando Valley. On December 23, 1893, Kid

A former Los Angeles City Surveyor, Sheriff Johnny Cline was forced to leave in disgrace during his second term of office. – LOS ANGELES COUNTY SHERIFF'S DEPARTMENT ARCHIVES

Thompson and Alvarado (Alva) Johnson robbed the Number 20 Southern Pacific Los Angeles Express Train four miles north of the Burbank Station. Using a black powder bomb, they blew a hole in the Wells Fargo Express boxcar door and got away with $150. Seven weeks later, on the night of February 15, the same train approached Roscoe station. A pair of desperadoes attempted to flag down the train using a torch, which they threw down on the tracks next to a railroad switch. Next, they fired a rifle shot into the locomotive cab. The engineer yelled, "Look out boys, they're shooting!" He decided to run past the bandits, by increasing the steam pressure and pushing the throttle wide open.[23]

Seeing that the engine was increasing its speed, the bandits pulled the track switch, putting the locomotive onto a railroad spur with a dead end. The engine swerved off the main line, slammed into a pile of railroad ties, and then crashed into a 6-foot ditch. One man was killed by gunfire and Fireman Arthur Masters was crushed underneath the train. Engineer David Thomas jumped clear of the train prior to impact, and escaped with light injuries.[24]

The robbers ran up to the train with a Winchester rifle and two six-guns. One of them shouted, "The son of a bitch! I'll show him whether he'll stop or not!"[25] This time, the desperadoes used dynamite to blow a hole in the express car. The pair took $100 in cash and $1,200 in Mexican silver coins. When the robbers heard about the man who was crushed in the accident, one of them exclaimed, "God damn the luck, If I'd known this would happen, I wouldn't have held up the train." As soon as the bandits had left, a brakeman ran to a nearby farm, where he borrowed a horse and rode into Burbank. From there, he telephoned Sheriff Cline's office in Los Angeles. U.S. Marshal George Gard, who had finished with Sontag and Evans eight months earlier, immediately took charge of the case.

The outlaws were tracked to the Lankershim Ranch in the Cahuenga Pass, where the trail was lost. Word was sent to Los Angeles that the robbers might be headed that way. Sheriff Cline posted five deputy sheriffs on the bridge at Arroyo Seco to watch inbound traffic. Just before dawn, an outgoing milk wagon approached the bridge coming from the city and headed toward the Cahuenga Pass. The deputies recognized the drivers as a Big Tujunga Canyon rancher named Alva Johnson and his helper named William (Kid) Thompson. The pair chatted with the deputies and asked them what was happening. They were told of the train robbery and warned to be on the lookout for bandits. The pair of smiling outlaws passed the roadblock and continued on their way.

Reward money for the capture of the robbers was piling up as well as the sensational journalism. The *San Francisco Examiner* commented, "It was the boldest train robbery that ever took place in Southern California, or, for that matter, in the State."[26] On February 23, Alva's brother John walked into Sheriff Cline's office. He told the Sheriff that he thought that Alva had committed the robbery along with George Smith, one of Alva's ranch hands. He said that he saw Alva and George with twenty-dollar gold pieces just like the ones that had been taken in the robbery. He also noticed Alva's wagon wheel tracks coming from the direction of the crime scene on the same day that the train was robbed. Although the evidence was weak, Sheriff Cline knew that it was the only lead that they had, so he notified Southern Pacific and Wells Fargo detectives.

The detectives found that the 36-year-old red-haired rancher was married and had two small children and two teenage stepdaughters. He had a good reputation in the community, and his only problem was a dispute over water rights with his brother John. People considered George Smith a harmless old man who worked on Alva's ranch in exchange for room and board. When the detectives looked into Kid Thompson's background, however, they found something more interesting. Thompson was a wild 22-year-old from Hill City, South Dakota, who liked to drink, gamble, and spend money on prostitutes. While rustling cattle in Maricopa County, Arizona, Thompson received a crease in his head from a bullet by Constable Shankland.[27] Southern Pacific Detective Will Smith and Wells Fargo Detective John Thacker had a hunch that Alva, Smith, and the Kid might be involved, so they began to dig a little deeper.[28]

During questioning, Alva became nervous and denied any wrongdoing. Kid Thompson suddenly left town on March 26, making the case a little stronger. Constable Lester Rogers made a decision to arrest Johnson and Smith with the little evidence that he had, in the hope that either man might talk while in custody. Alva had no such plan. He hired defense attorneys, and the judge soon dismissed the case due to lack of evidence.

Marshal Gard gathered weak evidence that three other men in the Tujunga Canyon area were possibly involved in the crimes. He decided to use an undercover detective named J.V. Brighton to help him gather evidence. Brighton was known as "The Ferret of the Sierra" because he had eighteen years of detective experience and was known to have tracked down many outlaws in his day, including Ike Clanton, who was famous for his part in the shootout at the O.K. Corral. With Brighton's assistance, Gard collected enough information to lead him to believe that John Comstock, Walter Thorne, and Pat Fitzsimmons were involved in the crimes.

All three men were indicted by the grand jury for train wrecking, and the trial began on June 6. On June 15, after the jury had heard testimony from 150 witnesses, they decided that all three men were not guilty. Jurors felt that Brighton had perjured himself and that there were enough witnesses to back up the suspects' testimony. Later investigation revealed that, in fact, all three men were innocent of any wrongdoing.

The frustrated detectives were back to square one. When Will Smith tracked down Kid Thompson in Arizona, they thought that they might get a break, but the Kid denied any knowledge of the crime. Once again, the detectives came up empty-handed. The detectives were now getting so desperate that they even tried using Alva's wife and sister as agents to coerce a confession. This tactic also ended in failure. But, as happens with many criminal cases, a breaking lead sometimes comes from the most unexpected source.

Southern Pacific's special officer William Breakenridge was working the Phoenix office when he received a visit from an old rancher named Baker. Baker brought with him a 34-year-old cigar maker named Charles Etzler. Etzler said that he had met Kid Thompson while hitching a free ride on the train from Bakersfield to Los Angeles. The Kid took a liking to Etzler and said that he wanted to include him in his next holdup.

Thompson took him to meet Alva Johnson, and the outlaws relayed their robbery story in great detail. They had an especially hearty laugh when describing how they had fooled the sheriff's deputies at the Arroyo Seco Bridge by placing a tarp over a chicken coop to make their buckboard look like a milk wagon. When they had finished their tale, Johnson took them both into town and gave Etzler $2.50 and a loaded gun. He told the vagabond, "For God's sake, get Thompson out of the country."[29]

Johnson promised Thompson that he would ship his money to Arizona, where he could pick it up later. A few weeks later, Etzler saw the Kid pick up his $600 in ill-gotten gains from the Wells Fargo Office in Tempe, Arizona. After spending all of his money in a wild celebration, the Kid asked Etzler to join him in another train robbery. Etzler panicked and eventually told his employer, Baker, all about Kid and the robberies. Baker wasted no time in getting Etzler to Breakenridge's office.

Breakenridge transported Etzler to Los Angeles, and Will Smith went out to track down Kid Thompson. After an all-night shootout with a Maricopa County Sheriff's posse, the Kid gave up. He had a .44 caliber pistol and sixty cents in his pocket. He was transported to Los Angeles, where he refused to talk. Alva was re-arrested and brought to jail. Realizing that he was facing the death penalty, Alva was persuaded to testify against the Kid in exchange for a life sentence. On May 8, the jury found Kid Thompson guilty of train wrecking. Judge B. N. Smith read the sentence as follows:

> That within ten days from this day you be by the sheriff of this county conveyed to the state's prison at San Quentin and

there delivered into the custody of the warden of said state's prison, and that you be, by him, upon a day and time to be hereafter fixed in the warrant of your execution, hanged by the neck until you are dead.[30]

But the Kid did not go easy. His attorneys filed two appeals to the Supreme Court, one of which overturned the conviction on a technicality. His second trial began in April 1897. During this trial, the Kid tried to get a pistol smuggled in to him by a worker inmate. The plot would have worked if it were not for a conscientious jailer who saw the handoff and jumped on the worker and stripped the gun from his grasp. The gun was fully loaded, and the worker had nine more rounds in his pocket. All of the conspirators were arrested and taken to jail. Thompson was found guilty in his second trial, but his sentence was reduced to life. The Kid was paroled in 1909 but he spent the rest of his life in and out of prison. He died in 1925, still on parole.

Alva Johnson attempted to escape from San Quentin in 1900. His partner was killed by a guard's shotgun blast, and Alva made it as far as the hill behind the prison, where guards caught up to him. He gave up; they arrested him and charged him with escape. He was paroled in 1907 and received a full pardon in 1910.

Cline's Career Ends in Disgrace

Train robberies aside, the county's overall violent crime rate was still dropping. There was already a longing on behalf of many Angelenos for the old frontier days. Sheriff Cline must have sympathized with these nostalgic citizens, for he helped them to organize a three-day cultural fiesta, complete with a parade of floats, a block-long Chinese dragon, and a mounted *Caballeros* group. The sheriff's caballeros posse consisted of highly-skilled equestrians, and was the forerunner to Sheriff Biscailuz's renowned Silver Mounted Posse.

When Sheriff Cline was not busy with his law enforcement duties or the parade committee, he was helping to organize William McKinley's presidential campaign. His active work within the Republican Party helped to secure many votes for McKinley in the West. His unwavering support would pay off after the election in the form of a four-year appointment as Collector of Customs for the District of Los Angeles. At the time, this powerful office included responsibility for the ports of Los Angeles, San Diego, San Pedro, and Santa Barbara. Upon Theodore Roosevelt's election, he was reappointed for another four years. He retired from public life for several years and then decided to make another run for sheriff in 1914.

Cline's second term of office would prove to be much rockier than his first. Sheriff Johnny still thought that things could be done the "old way," and it was hard for him to understand that twenty years was a world of difference in a rapidly growing county such as Los Angeles. He believed that he still had the power to instantly hire and fire whomever he chose; the county charter and the board of supervisors heartily disagreed. This infuriated the sheriff and ultimately led to many fights over budgeting, asset allocation, jurisdiction, and even deployment of deputies. Cline stated, "No weak-kneed County Charter is going to take rights from me!"[31] The *Los Angeles Times* complained:

> He has shown by his own statements that, unless he reforms, he is not the man to be sheriff of Los Angeles County in the year 1920, because he seems to regard his public office as one to be run as a private business. He is wrong. The "boss" method of building up a political machine by appointing deputy sheriffs and with them behind him defying the legally-constituted overseeing authorities of the county is out of date."[32]

The internal strife continued throughout his second term and well into his third term. It was during his third term that the board of supervisors ultimately accused Cline of twenty-one separate violations, including misappropriation of funds, misuse of county equipment, ordering speeding tickets destroyed, and appointing more "special deputies" (reserve deputies) than the law allowed. He even required employees to purchase their equipment at Cline and Cline, a company owned by his brother. Things really began to unravel for the sheriff when several of his own deputies began to speak out against him.

Although a few of the charges were politically motivated, some very serious allegations were most likely based in fact.[33] In 1921, after serving six consecutive years, the board of supervisors had had enough of Johnny Cline. On March 2, 1921, Judge Monroe found the sheriff guilty of seven of the twenty-one counts brought against him.[34] Cline left the office in disgrace. It was an unglamorous ending for a man who had enjoyed such a positive image prior to his final years in office.

Johnny Cline survived his wife, Margaret, who died in 1941. He suffered a stroke in 1953 and passed away on December 12, 1954 at the age of ninety-four.

Sheriff John Burr, January 1895–December 1898

On November 6, 1894, John Burr was elected to the office of Sheriff. He was the first sheriff to serve the legislature's newly enacted four-year term. Burr was a serious, hard-driving politician, more concerned with attaining the title of sheriff than actually serving the law enforcement needs of the community. Historian Dr. Frank Emerson wrote:

> His election to the office was more in the nature of a recognition for political services rendered than for any particular liking, ability and capacity for the position. His natural bent was entirely away from that of a law enforcement officer.[35]

Crittenden commented simply, "His name was placed on the ballot in return for political favors."[36]

John Burr was born in Scotland on November 13, 1854, where he was raised and attended public schools until age fifteen. He practiced horticulture for a few years and eventually found his way to the United States. Burr landed in San Francisco, where he worked at a variety of odd jobs until he met Senator Fulton. The senator offered young John a job working on his San Mateo estate as a gardener and landscaper. He did well in this occupation, and within a few years he had saved enough money to buy a 250-acre ranch in Tulare County near Visalia. He lived there for three years but, when he was told of the fertile farmland and warmer climate in the San Fernando Valley, he decided to investigate. After researching the Valley's farming potential, he decided to sell his land in Tulare and invest in a fruit orchard down south.

In 1881, Burr traveled back to Europe to marry his childhood sweetheart, Anna Philpot. The 27-year-old farmer brought his bride to the San Fernando Valley, where they settled. Burr's farm thrived, and he raised three children in the booming Los Angeles suburb: John, Charles, and William.

By the time Burr was ready to run for the office of sheriff, the county population was rapidly advancing toward 200,000 and the radio, the automobile, and cable cars were making their debuts. As the county grew, so did the politics of office. In a technical blunder, Burr failed to take the oath of office within ten days of his election. This caused his predecessor, Cline, to file a petition to the board of supervisors claiming that the office was vacant and that, therefore, the incumbent should remain as sheriff. Burr's attorneys asked the board to appoint him to office on the grounds that he won the election in a fair and straightforward manner. The board of supervisors agreed and appointed him as sheriff on January 8.

Excepting Deputy Celis' accidental death in 1883, it had been almost forty years since tragedy had struck the sheriff's office. Over the years, sheriffs and their deputies had survived many scrapes, and fate seemed always to be on their side. Unfortunately, this string of good luck would not hold out forever. It was on Burr's watch that, on December 27, 1896, Deputy George Lee

Sheriff John Burr was more of a politician than a law enforcement officer. During his term of office the population of Los Angeles County was approaching 200,000.
— LOS ANGELES COUNTY SHERIFF'S DEPARTMENT ARCHIVES

Wilson and Constable Albert Smith were detailed to search for an attempted murder suspect.[37]

They received information that their suspect, Jose Morales, was staying at his brother's house near Monrovia. At approximately 8:00 p.m., the officers knocked on the door of the Morales home. After receiving no reply, Wilson threatened to break the door down. Jose's brother, Jesus suddenly opened the door and let them in. Constable Smith was carrying a lantern in one hand and a gun in the other.[38] He used the lantern to search the house. Jesus had a lamp in his bedroom, where his girlfriend was lying in bed. Adjacent to Jesus' room, the officers saw another bedroom, where two other persons were lying in bed. When they shone their lantern on the bed, they saw a man pull the covers over his head.

The officers uncovered a man and a woman lying next to each other. After identifying the man as their suspect, they told Jose that he was under arrest and ordered him to get dressed. As Morales was dressing, he noticed a .45 caliber pistol in the deputy's coat pocket. Smith and Wilson searched the room and found a "murderous knife" under Morales' pillow. As Smith was securing the blade in his pocket, Jose asked permission to get his shoes from the next room.

Wilson agreed to let the outlaw retrieve his shoes but noticed a pair of shoes under the bed. Sensing a ruse, the deputy ordered Morales to come back. Morales returned and asked Wilson to hand him his shoes. When Wilson bent over to get the shoes, Morales grabbed the pistol from the deputy's coat pocket and ran for the door. Before he left the room, the bandit turned and fired one shot at the officers. The round smashed through the bottom of Smith's lantern, extinguishing the light, and then plunged deep into Wilson's right thigh.

Upon hearing the gunshot, Jesus assisted his brother by blowing out the lamp in his room, causing the entire house to be shrouded in darkness. Smith drew his pistol and fired a shot at Jose. The constable tackled Morales to the floor, where the two men struggled in darkness for at least a minute. Smith lost his hat and his pistol during the fight, but neither man could retrieve the gun because of the darkness. As soon as Morales was able to break free, he jumped out a window and escaped into the night.

Wilson stumbled out into the street, calling, "I am shot through and through."[39] Fifty neighbors gathered in the street, and some of them rushed Wilson to the hospital. Sheriff Burr responded from Los Angeles with deputies Clement and Aguirre and took Jesus Morales into custody. The doctors could not find the bullet in Wilson's thigh, so they took him home. In another attempt the doctors removed the bullet, but there was so much hemorrhaging that Wilson was unable to recover. He lapsed into a coma, and died on January 8, 1897.

Almost four years later, on September 20, 1900, Mexican law enforcement officials tracked Jose Morales to Ensenda, Mexico. In a brief shootout, the outlaw was struck in the face, causing a grievous injury. He continued to resist, but after an hour-long gun battle, the bandit was overtaken and brought to justice.[40] He was convicted of manslaughter and sentenced to ten years in prison.

There would not be another deputy killed in the line of duty for eleven years, and it would not be until the late 1950s that deputies were slain with much greater frequency.[41] This upward trend in murders of law enforcement officers was due in large part to the ever-increasing population surge that the county continues to experience.

At the same time that he was dealing with Wilson's murder, Burr was addressing another major problem. Approximately two weeks before Deputy Wilson was killed, a recently-released inmate named Charles Matthews, also known as "Alabama Charley," approached Sheriff Burr with some disturbing information.[42] Charley, who had just served ninety days for petty larceny, told the Sheriff that Deputy Charles Mahone had involved him in a plot to help an inmate to escape.[43]

The deputy was allegedly going to be paid $500 to break the notorious bank burglar J.J. McCarty out of jail. Charley handed over a key and a hand-drawn map of the jail to the sheriff. He said that Mahone gave these items to him. The items were to be provided to McCarty along with a rope to help the burglar escape via the roof. The sheriff began a discreet investigation, hoping to catch Mahone red-handed. In a statement to the *Los Angeles Times* he said:

I think there is not the least doubt that the plan would have been carried out successfully if we had not found out what was going on. While I do not wish to divulge the details, I have no hesitation in saying that the plan of escape was entirely feasible, and McCarty could have gotten out at the top or bottom with the assistance of one man. The scheme was a very clever one, but after we dropped onto it, the first man to have stuck his head out at the proposed place of exit would surely have been killed. We were prepared for him and had a nice surprise in store for the conspirators, but after all it is perhaps better that the matter turned out as it did.[44]

REWARD!

STATE OF CALIFORNIA,
EXECUTIVE DEPARTMENT.

WHEREAS, On the night of December 27, A. D. 1896, at Monrovia, County of Los Angeles, State of California, G. L. WILSON, of San Gabriel, a Deputy Sheriff of this County, was murdered by one JOSE MORALES;

Now, Therefore, I, JAMES H. BUDD, Governor of the State of California, by virtue of the authority in me vested by the Constitution and laws of this State, do hereby offer a reward of

$500

(Five Hundred Dollars) for the arrest and conviction of the said JOSE MORALES. Said reward to be paid only upon conviction.

IN WITNESS WHEREOF, I have hereunto set my hand and caused the Great Seal of the State to be hereunto affixed this, the 12th day of January, A. D. 1897.

[SEAL.]

JAMES H. BUDD,
Governor.

Attest:
L. H. BROWN, Secretary of State.

DESCRIPTION.

A Mexican, 28 to 30 years of age; height, five feet seven or eight inches; weight, about one hundred and seventy five pounds; hair black; stands up straight like an Indian; has mustache; shaggy beard; scar on inside of right hand at base of thumb; has wart on knuckle of first finger of left hand; has scar on right side of scalp, inflicted by a club; wears a No. 7 shoe; is very fond of playing cards, and is of a daring and fearless disposition.

In 1897, the search for Deputy George Lee Wilson's killer was in full swing as evidenced by this wanted poster. – JOHN BOESSENECKER COLLECTION

Jail inmate worker Clifton Mayne overheard a conversation about the investigation of Deputy Mahone. Feeling sorry for the deputy, he warned the jailer that Sheriff Burr had him under surveillance. Mahone went to his supervisor, Deputy Kennedy, who offered him the chance to resign in lieu of prosecution and public scandal. Mahone agreed and signed his resignation but, soon changed his mind. When he asked Burr for his job back, the sheriff refused, saying that once he had accepted Mahone's resignation the transaction was final.

Leaky internal investigations such as the Mahone jailbreak plot clearly demonstrated the need for a more professional method of handling internal wrongdoing. Along with law enforcement agencies around the country, the sheriff's office would eventually develop a formalized internal affairs bureau to meet this need.

While Burr was not a wicked man by any means, there were definitely two sides to his personality. On one occasion he was traveling by buggy through the town of Glendale when he came across a young girl who was crying. The girl explained that her mother had given her a nickel to buy whatever she wanted at the store. As she was walking along, she had dropped it somewhere along the way and began to search for it, in vain. The sheriff recognized the girl and knew her father. He pulled a nickel from his pocket and said, "Now don't cry anymore, and tell your father that Sheriff Burr gave you the nickel."[45]

This heartwarming story contrasts greatly with a quote from Historian Eunice Crittenden's work: "John Burr could not be considered a popular sheriff by even his best friends. He was a dour Scot and not a friendly man."[46] After serving his four-year term, Burr switched from County Sheriff to County Horticultural Commissioner. On November 6, 1909, the former sheriff was involved in a horrible automobile accident. A friend, Fred Boruff, was driving his Columbia touring car with three passengers, including Burr. Boruff accidentally drove into the middle of a long-distance car race. The dust and exhaust from one of the speeding racecars caused Boruff to swerve and strike a fire hydrant. Of the four men in the vehicle, three were seriously hurt. Burr suffered a fractured skull and the doctors gave him only live a few days to live.[47] The tough old sheriff surprised everyone, however, by making a miraculous recovery. After five weeks in the hospital, he was moved to his home in the San Fernando Valley. Four years later, John Burr passed away on September 20, 1913. He was fifty-eight years old.

Sheriff William A. Hammel, January 1899–December 1902

William Augustus Hammel brought the sheriff's office into a new century and, in doing so, closed the chapter on the first fifty years of service to the residents of Los Angeles County. His time in office brought an unprecedented level of stability to the small agency. Hammel was elected three times, with one interruption after his first term. During his twelve years of service the office made great strides forward, including hiring one of the first woman deputy sheriffs in America in 1912, and the introduction of the automobile into county service.

William Augustus Hammel was born on March 13, 1865, in Los Angeles to Dr. William and Mrs. Barbara Hammel. Dr. Hammel was a "forty-niner" who brought his family to San Francisco in search of a new life in the gold country. He was a member of the San Francisco vigilantes and an early Los Angeles settler. The well-respected doctor built one of the first brick houses in the city, on San Pedro Street between Second and Third. Young William grew up on these streets with his eleven brothers and sisters and his best friend, Martin Aguirre. He was educated in public schools and attended Santa Clara College, where he met "Mountain Charlie's" daughter, Catherine McKiernan. Thus began one of the greatest sheriff's love stories of all time.

A Sheriff's Love Story

Catherine's father had received his nickname because he lived in and hunted game in the mountains. His beautiful daughter fell in love with the dashing William Hammel. Realizing that he was in love, too, he asked her to marry him. Catherine agreed, and the two were engaged. Sadly, the romance was short lived because, like many young men, William had dreams he wanted to chase first. He left Catherine and went to Arizona to seek his fortune as a cowboy. It was out on those lonely trails, looking up at the stars, that William realized that he would never be happy without Catherine.

As the best cowboy poets do to this day, William began to write to his lost love, apologizing and explaining that he should have stayed with her. He waited patiently for a return letter, but it never came. William wrote other letters in hopes that Catherine would respond, but he had no such luck. The final blow was struck when William received word that his sweetheart had married another man. Heartbroken and tired of the lonely cowboy life, William returned to Los Angeles to try his hand at another line of work.

Without much trouble, Hammel found jobs working for a variety of government agencies, including a stint with the Los Angeles Police Department, service as county clerk, and several years as a Deputy Sheriff under Aguirre and Burr. At age twenty-seven, William put aside his boyhood dreams of spending his life with Catherine and, on June 22, 1892, married Mary Lillian Phillips, whose father was a well-known Los Angeles lawyer. The couple lived happily enough and had a young daughter named Phyllis. In 1898, Hammel was elected sheriff.

Tragedy struck his life when Mary died in 1907, leaving the sheriff a widower with a teenage daughter. Three years later, he took Phyllis to the State Teachers College in San Jose for enrollment. While he was there, he overheard talk that Catherine was living not far from the area. To his surprise, he also heard that she had never married and had been waiting her whole life for a young cowboy who had moved to Arizona! Hammel could not believe his ears. He immediately contacted her and discovered that she had never received his letters. The two made joyful amends and happily returned to Los Angeles together. They were married on Thanksgiving Day, 1910, and lived happily ever after.

Hammel Takes the Sheriff's Office into the 20th Century

William Hammel was well-connected in the county. His brother-in-law was former Sheriff Gard, who married his sister. His father's many business connections and his own prior work for the sheriff's office made him well-qualified. It was also due in no small part to his many Republican Party political contacts and reputation as an honest and hard-working man that Hammel won the November 8, 1898, election. The Los Angeles Times beamed, "Hammel, one of the most brightest and promising young gentlemen in the County of Los Angeles."[48]

While this book is a study of the department's history until the year 1900, it would be an injustice to Sheriff Hammel's legacy to ignore mention of his entire contribution to the office, if only at least in brief summary. What follows are a few highlights of his second and third terms of office, 1906 to 1914.

In late 1906, Hammel took back his office from Sheriff William White by winning the November election. Before he was sworn in, he called all of his deputies together for a meeting. It was an occasion that none of them would ever forget. Martin Aguirre stepped forward as a representative for the entire group and handed the Sheriff one of the most elaborate badges ever given to a California law enforcement officer. Looking into Hammel's watery eyes, and with great emotion, Aguirre said in a broken voice:

Mr. Hammel, your deputies desire to present you with this little token, hoping you will wear it as you have other stars, a credit to manhood and to the country. We hope you will wear it not only during your term of office, but indefinitely.[49]

Hammel accepted the badge. When he looked down at it, he noticed that it was strangely familiar.

The "little token" was a solid gold shield surrounded by a wreath fashioned of old gold. It was his old badge from his previous term but remodeled out of all semblance of itself. In place of a small stone that had been in it was a three and a half carat diamond. A great gold bear strode along the top of the wreath and above a shield of red, white and blue enamel a dove with spread wings crusted with 137 chip diamonds gazed with ruby eyes, sparkling redly at a gold bar bearing Hammel's name in black enamel.[50]

Sheriff-elect Hammel dried his eyes and cleared his throat. He looked up at his men and gave them his philosophy on police work. He told the deputies what he expected of them. He ordered that there be no drunkenness on duty and that, while men might take an occasional sip, nobody would be allowed to go overboard.

Keep sober. Just because you wear the star of a deputy sheriff, don't imagine that you are commissioned to soak up all the booze in sight. If you are insulted by a bully in the office, don't lick him there; it is bad for the reputation of the office. There are plenty of dark alleys.[51]

In 1912, Hammel made a great stride forward for women's rights by hiring Margaret Q. Adams. She was among the first women in the nation to claim the title of deputy sheriff.[52] Another big step forward was the county's purchase of the "locomobile." This early form of automobile was a brilliant red convertible that comfortably seated five. It had a 12-inch-diameter searchlight mounted on the hood, powered by a carbide tank that was mounted to the running board.

In 1913, the California State Legislature approved a special charter for Los Angeles County that allowed for a stronger, more centralized county government. The new charter also instituted the civil service system for county departments.[53]

When he was not busy maintaining his new vehicle, watching over the jails, or handling criminal cases, the sheriff enjoyed taking part in community events. One of Sheriff Hammel's favorite pastimes was participating in the annual Fiesta Parade as Grand Marshal. He always wore traditional Mexican regalia while riding his horse and waving to the crowd.

Sheriff Billy Hammel brought the sheriff's office into the 20th Century. He was responsible for many positive changes during his two terms of office. — Los Angeles County Sheriff's Department Archives

It was during times like this that he must have reminisced about the old days, before cars, electricity, and radios. He surely recalled the days when he was a scruffy kid, running in the hot dusty streets with Martin Aguirre and then jumping into the water hole to cool off. He surely remembered the time when the adults talked about Sheriff Rowland chasing after Tiburcio Vasquez and the outlaw's final capture at Greek George's cabin. Hammel knew what it was like to be the sheriff and catch the bad guy. He knew what it was like to ride the range as a cowboy, become sheriff, marry the girl of your dreams, and ride off into the sunset. Sheriff Hammel died on New Year's Day, 1932.

Chapter 6

1850-1900: ANALYZING MURDER STATISTICS AND REFLECTING ON RACIAL CONFLICT IN LOS ANGELES

Bringing About Law and Order

The fact that the LASD helped to bring law and order to the county can be partially demonstrated by citing crime statistics. After adjusting for population, author John Boessenecker calculated murders in 1851 Los Angeles to be 1,240 homicides per 100,000.[1] This standard is how the Federal Bureau of Investigation (FBI) measures the homicide rate. When compared to homicide statistics from 1900, one can easily see that a dramatic impact was made upon the crime rate.

Patrick Adams, Chief of the FBI's program support section, stated that Los Angeles County crime statistics gathered prior to 1960 are not useable for any comparative research. In 1960, the advent of the Universal Crime Reporting program remedied this problem; but this does nothing to aid with research prior to that time.[2] Therefore, in an effort to study crime rates antecedent to this period, records were reviewed from historical articles, news clippings, the LAPD, and experts in the field. These records were then interpreted as accurately as possible to determine the homicide rate at the time.

The Los Angeles Police Historical Society maintains archived annual crime reports dating back to 1897. The format of these early police crime reports listed the type of crime, how many persons were arrested, the number of cases dismissed, number of convictions, number of convictions for lesser offenses, number of persons held to answer, and number of cases pending.[3] While the information is useful, it does not paint a clear picture of the crime rate because it does not state how many crimes were actually committed.

University of California, Los Angeles, History Professor Eric Monkkonen has researched crime statistics in Los Angeles dating back to 1830. Professor Monkkonen's research indicates that in 1900 there were 15 homicides in the city and 14 in the county area.[4] When compared the to the county's population of 750,000[5], the resulting measurement is 3.9 per 100,000. These statistics clearly demonstrate a dramatic drop in the homicide rate from the 1850s forward.

Sometime around 1914, the LAPD started to record the total number of crimes committed. These data give a much clearer picture of the crime rate at that time. The 1920 *Annual Report Police Department* listed the crimes committed from the years 1915 to 1920. To confirm that the 1900 crime statistics were not an aberration, a study of the homicide rate from this time period is in order.

From 1915 to 1920, the average homicide rate in the City of Los Angeles was 42.2 per year.[6] Using an average yearly population of 512,304[7] for the same time period and coupling it with the FBI benchmark of homicides per 100,000, the crime rate was 8.2 homicides per 100,000. This is still a startling difference from the 1850 rate of 1,240 per 100,000. It also compares positively with the 1990s rate of 9 homicides per 100,000. It is interesting that the statistics reveal that from 1850 to 1900 the rates generally dropped. After 1900 however, the homicide rate began to increase again. This is most likely due to the overcrowding associated with rapid urban development.

The San Benito Historical Society makes an interesting comparison between the crimes committed by Joaquin Murrieta in the 1850s and those committed by Tiburcio Vasquez in the 1870s.

The decades that elapsed between this time [1850s] and the years 1873 and 1874, in which Vasquez committed his greatest depredations, had witnessed the complete organization of the counties of our state under the proper authority of law, police, judges, and jury. Hence it is that the exploits and escapes of Vasquez excel those of Murrieta, in being performed at far greater hazards, and against greater odds.[8]

While the organization of counties may not have been entirely "complete," there is no question that great strides forward were being made by California's criminal justice system.

Author Robert Blew listed some of reasons that crime in early Los Angeles was so rampant:

> Not only the drifters but the dwellers were also a source of potential trouble. Most were young, aggressive bachelors hoping to improve their fortunes. Many of the married men were without their wives and families. A portion of them did not plan to establish permanent ties here, but, rather, they planned to return to the eastern states. In addition, many of these men were Southerners, especially from Texas. Among this group, personal honor was not a trifle, and any slight or injury, real or imagined, required atonement. This touchy honor, combined with the "macho" of the native Californio, provided the spark to ignite many an explosive situation.[9]

Several combined factors actually aided law enforcement in bringing the horrific crime rate down to safer levels. The influx of women and children had a "civilizing" effect upon the mostly male population. As some of the wild cowboys, miners, and gamblers married, settled down, and had families of their own, the crime rate began to drop. As the city grew, so did the power of the residents to organize and fight crime. The demolition of the Calle de Los Negros in 1887 served to hasten the process of bringing order to the city.

Another critical factor that must not be overlooked was the invention of the telegraph and its critical role in law enforcement. Receiving pertinent information in an expeditious manner makes the difference between effecting an arrest or having a suspect slip through your hands. In 1870, Officer Joseph Dye telegraphed Santa

Looking up at Robber's Roost, a possible lookout spot for bandits awaiting their prey.
— AUTHOR'S COLLECTION

Barbara regarding a Chinese female suspect possibly residing in their jurisdiction. When Marshal Warren and his assistant arrived in Santa Barbara, the local constables had the woman in custody and were awaiting the marshal's arrival.

Sheriff Rowland was constantly updated via telegraph regarding the whereabouts of Tiburcio Vasquez. Upon the bandit's capture in 1874, the sheriff telegraphed the good news to Governor Booth. During an 1887 jailbreak, Sheriff Kays used the telephone and telegraph to notify other agencies that fifteen men had escaped from his jail. Due to his efforts, at least four of the inmates were later recaptured.[10] These examples clearly demonstrate that criminals could no longer commit crimes in Los Angeles County without fear of consequences.

After the lynching of Michel Lachenais in 1870, the public began to put more faith in the legal system. The turning point came when Sheriff James Burns demonstrated to the populace that he could send outlaws to state prison for many years, in some cases for life. The need for vigilante groups diminished. As stronger and

217

more secure county jails increased the public's confidence regarding the detention of criminals, lynch mobs began to dissipate. From the first adobe jail to the 1853 brick jail and then the New High Street jail, each facility offered increasing degrees of security, not only for the public, but for inmates as well. Although there were attempts, there is no record of anyone escaping from the 1853 brick jail. The escapes from the New High Street Jail were due largely to an error in procedure and not the actual construction of the jail. As is the case today, an adjustment in policy and procedures usually brings about the desired change, thus solving the problem.

The formation of the city marshal's office which later became the Los Angeles Police Department, along with expanding numbers of town constables in outlying areas, helped to deter and combat crime. As communication between officers increased, so did the efficiency at catching criminals. Sheriff Martin Aguirre could not have captured William Chormicle as easily as he did were it not for assis-

The infamous Calle de Los Negros as it looks today. The calle was destroyed many years ago and part of it is now Los Angeles Street. – AUTHOR'S COLLECTION

tance from Ventura County Sheriff Reilly. Teamwork among local agencies only furthered the drop in violent crime rates.

Adding to the formula for success was the influx of a more "civilized" population. The increase in law-abiding families made it difficult for outlaws to hide. It would be hard for an outlaw to conceal himself at a place like Vasquez Rocks when tourists come by the score to visit and climb all over the strange-looking monoliths. This fact, combined with effective communication tools such as the telegraph, created a synergistic effect that served to enhance the likelihood of apprehending criminals and to bring about a safer Los Angeles.

Dealing with Racial Conflict

From its inception, the Los Angeles County Sheriff's Department has had to deal with racial conflict and class divisions. Strong leadership from men such as George Burrill, Tomas Sanchez, James Burns, and Martin Aguirre set stellar examples for the rest of Los Angeles to follow. Burrill navigated Los Angeles through the stormy Lugo/Irving party incident in 1851, when Latino and Anglo tempers ran hot. Tomas Sanchez saved the day on numerous occasions, chasing down outlaws and apprehending criminals of both races while simultaneously keeping the peace between racists from many cultures. James Burns risked his life to stop the Chinese Massacre of 1871, and Martin Aguirre broke through overwhelming prejudicial and cultural barriers to become sheriff. The examples set by these men demonstrated to the populace that harmony, understanding, and peace could be achieved despite sentiments of cultural and racial intolerance.

When George Burrill arrived in Los Angeles, he did not bring with him an Anglo woman, but rather a Latino woman. In keeping with the "mixed marriage" traditions of the first Los Angeles settlers, many early sheriffs and frontiersmen practiced harmonious multicultural lifestyles among races. Sheriff Billy Rowland was half-Latino and half-Anglo. During times of strife, it was these leaders to whom the people looked for guidance and wisdom. Most of the time, the sheriffs and their deputies were able to live up to the peacekeeping oaths that they took when they pinned on the badge.

Appendix *A*

LOS ANGELES COUNTY SHERIFFS, 1850-1900

NAME	ELECTED	TERM OF OFFICE	DECEASED
George Thompson Burrill	Apr., 1850	Apr. 1, 1850 – Sep., 1851	Feb. 7, 1856
James R. Barton**	Sep., 1851	Sep. 3, 1851 – Aug., 1855	Jan. 23, 1857
David W. Alexander**	Sep., 1855	Sep., 1855 – Aug., 1856	Apr. 29, 1886
Charles E. Hale*	Aug., 1856	Aug. 1, 1856 – Nov. 3, 1856	Unknown
James R. Barton**!	Nov., 1856	Nov. 4, 1856 – Jan. 23, 1857	Jan. 23, 1857
Elijah Bettis*	Jan., 1857	Jan. 24, 1857 – Sep. 1, 1857	Unknown
William C. Getman!	Sep., 1857	Sep. 2, 1857 – Jan. 7, 1858	Jan. 7, 1858
James Thompson*	Jan., 1858	Jan. 8, 1858 – Aug., 1859	May 12, 1895
Tomas Sanchez	Sep., 1859	Sep. 1859 – Feb., 1868	June 24, 1882
James Burns	Sep., 1867	Mar. 1, 1868 – Feb., 1872	Jan. 5, 1921
William R. Rowland**	Sep., 1871	Mar. 1, 1872 – Feb., 1876	Feb. 2, 1926
David W. Alexander**	Sep., 1875	Mar. 1, 1876 – Feb., 1878	Apr. 29, 1886
Henry M. Mitchell	Sep., 1877	Mar. 1, 1878 – Feb., 1880	Dec. 7, 1890
William R. Rowland**	Sep., 1879	Mar. 1, 1880 – Dec. 31, 1882	Feb. 2, 1926
Alvin T. Currier	Nov., 1882	Jan. 1, 1883 – Dec. 31, 1884	Aug. 13, 1922
George E. Gard	Nov., 1884	Jan. 1, 1885 – Dec. 31, 1886	Mar. 10, 1904
James C. Kays	Nov., 1886	Jan. 1, 1887 – Dec. 31, 1888	Mar. 27, 1917
Martin G. Aguirre	Nov., 1888	Jan. 1, 1889 – Dec. 31, 1890	Feb. 25, 1929
Edward D. Gibson	Nov., 1890	Jan. 1, 1891 – Dec. 31, 1892	Mar. 19, 1935
John C. Cline**	Nov., 1892	Jan. 1, 1893 – Dec. 31, 1894	Dec. 12, 1954
John Burr	Nov., 1894	Jan. 1, 1895 – Dec. 31, 1898	Sep. 20, 1913
William A. Hammel**	Nov., 1898	Jan. 1, 1899 – Dec. 31, 1902	Jan. 1, 1932

*   Appointed by the Board of Supervisors to fill a vacant position
** Served as Sheriff in more than one term
!   Killed in the line of duty

Appendix B

LOS ANGELES COUNTY SHERIFF'S DEPARTMENT HISTORICAL LOCATIONS

Gravesites

The remains of Constables William Little and Charles Baker and Sheriffs James Barton and William Getman were transported from the old city cemetery (Campo Santos) to Rosedale Cemetery in 1914. Cemetery records show that Little's remains were removed from Rosedale in 1944. The graves of the other three men are still located at Angeles-Rosedale Cemetery, 1831 W. Washington Blvd., Los Angeles, CA 90007. Telephone: 323-734-3155.

Sheriff James Barton:	Section N, subsection A, Grave 1S
Sheriff William Getman:	Section N, subsection A, Grave 5S
Constable Charles Baker:	Section N, subsection A, Grave 2S

There is a small grass field, adjacent to the Spanish-American War Veterans graves in Section N subsection A. This small clearing is where all three lawmen are buried. Unfortunately, none of the graves are marked with headstones, so there is no way to tell the exact location of each lawman's grave.

Barton's Mound

Barton's Mound is the location where Sheriff Barton and his posse fought with Juan Flores and his Manillas gang. It is registered California State Historic Landmark #218. Unfortunately, the mound was destroyed when the Highway 133 overpass was constructed adjacent to the 405 Freeway.[1] The Orange County Board of Supervisors petitioned the State of California for the landmark on October 16, 1934. The State of California designated it as historical landmark #218 on June 20, 1935. Two photos of the mound remain in the state's archives.[2]

Flores Peak

Flores Peak is the cliff where Juan Flores, Jesus Espinoza, and Leonardo Lopez made their daring escape from Tomas Sanchez and his posse. The exact location can be found on the United States Geological Survey map entitled Santiago Peak at latitude 33 42 48, longitude 117 37 14. The peak is easily accessible from a trailhead at the Tucker Wildlife Sanctuary located on Modjeska Canyon Road.[3] One can view the peak after a short hike on the Harding Trail. The peak can be seen from the west side of the trail.

Upon viewing the peak, one can easily understand how Flores ran into this "dead end" trap. The west side of Flores Peak is long and gradually sloped, while the east side ends in an abrupt 300-foot cliff. Flores and his men probably thought that they could ride down the east side as easily as they had come up the west side. When they reached the top, however, they were shocked to see that they had ridden into a trap.

People who are being pursued often run to high ground in order to get a good look behind them. This allows them to see whether they are still being chased and, if so, how far away the hunters may be. This is most likely the reason that Flores went up the peak in the first place. The bandits climbing down the cliff with the lawmen hot on their trail must have been an incredible sight to behold.

Hangman's Tree

When General Pico learned that Flores and his two comrades had eluded their guards and escaped into the night, he became so angry that he vowed that his two prisoners, Francisco Ardillero and Juan Silvas, would never get the chance to escape: He took them to a nearby tree and hanged them forthwith! While there is no concrete evidence exactly where this lynching occurred, folklore suggests that it was somewhere near the intersection of Hangman's Tree Road and Santiago Canyon Road. The street address is 17151 Santiago Canyon Road (*Orange County Thomas Guide* page 802, D6).

There are many old sycamore and oak tree groves in this area. Meadows described the location as being "in the little valley on the right of the Santiago Canyon Road, about 2/10 of a mile before Irvine Lake is reached when going into the Santa Ana Mountains."[4] It is not too difficult to imagine that Pico may very well have meted out his frontier justice at or near this area. The area is also near a fresh water source (Santiago Creek), which would have made a suitable camping location for the weary lawmen.

Robber's Roost

Robber's Roost is shrouded in mystery and legend. Exact details about the origin of its name are elusive at best. Some sources say that it was the cave in which Flores was captured after his daring escape from Tomas Sanchez and his posse.[5] Meadows described the location as being "northeast from the road approaching Irvine Park (not to be confused with Irvine Regional Park), and far across the wide valley of Santiago Creek, a conspicuous nubbin of rock (square topped butte) stands clear against the horizon."[6]

The United States Geological Survey (USGS) lists a "Robber's Peak" as being located on the "Orange" map at latitude 33 49 40, longitude 117 45 24. Robber's Peak and Robber's Roost are most likely not the same place, and there is no accurate historical record of either location. The USGS Robber's Peak is on private property. Robber's Peak can be viewed from trails emanating from Santiago Oaks Regional Park. The park is located at 2145 North Windes Drive in Orange. The view from Robber's Peak is truly amazing. One can see in all directions for many miles, and it is possible that early out-laws used this hilltop as a hideout, a lookout, or both.

Casa Adobe de San Rafael

The Casa Adobe San Rafael is registered as California Historical Landmark #235. It was the home that Sheriff Tomas Sanchez and his family lived in. The house was said to be constructed in 1871. The adobe, along with its surrounding grounds, is owned and maintained by the city of Glendale. Visitors can tour the grounds during daylight hours, but the adobe, which is now a museum, can be viewed only in the wintertime from 1:00 p.m. to 3:00 p.m. on the first Sunday of each month and in the summertime from 1:00 p.m. to 3:00 p.m. every Sunday. The Casa Adobe San Rafael is located at 1330 Dorothy Drive in the City of Glendale, CA 91202, telephone (818) 956-2000.

Calle de Los Negros

The infamous Calle de Los Negros, scene of the Chinese Massacre and countless murders, was destroyed long ago; however, the area where it once stood is a street and can still be seen today: the 400 block of North Los Angeles Street. The alley ran south, starting at the southeast corner of the old pueblo plaza adjacent to the old fire station and then traveled a short distance to Arcadia Street, where it ended.

The Bella Union Hotel

Not only was the Bella Union Hotel the site of one of the bloodiest shootouts in the West, it also served as courtroom, sheriff's office, and polling place during the 1850s. The hotel is long since gone, but the place where it once stood is marked by a plaque denoting it as California Historical Landmark #656. The monument is located where the Los Angeles Mall stands today at 314 North Main Street, Los Angeles, CA 90012.

The Montgomery Saloon

The aristocratic gambling saloon that Sheriff Billy Getman once managed has long since been destroyed, but the location where it once stood can still be viewed. The Montgomery was located west of Main Street at Arcadia Street.

Los Angeles County Sheriff's Museum

The Los Angeles County Sheriff's Museum is located at 11515 South Colima Road in Whittier, California, 90604, telephone (562) 946-7081. The museum contains artifacts and special collections from the Department's 150 years of history. It is operated by the Sheriff's Relief Association; web address: www.sheriffsrelief.org.

Appendix *C*

THE EXPLODING GUN

At first thought, one might wonder how Juan Flores' gun exploded simply by getting smashed against the side of a cliff? The concept is especially perplexing for modern handgun users who may have little or no knowledge at all about cap and ball pistols. Over the years the handgun has developed many safety features that 1850s hand guns did not have.

When Juan Flores was in a running gun battle with Tomas Sanchez and his posse, he most likely had to reload in a hurry. Reloading cap and ball pistols is much more complex and time consuming than reloading handguns today. The actual process is somewhat similar to that used by riflemen in reloading black powder muskets in that the weapon is loaded from the front.

A Colt cap and ball pistol was loaded by charging the cylinders with black powder. Next, an over-powder wad was seated with the loading lever and then a lead ball was rammed home. When reloading in a hurry, the over-powder wad was omitted. The gas seal without the over-powder wad was not as reliable.[1] Also, it was customary to grease each cylinder to effectively seal the weapon, which protected it from moisture and prevented the powder from fouling. The grease also helped to prevent accidental discharge from external sources such as cooking fires, torches, and candles. Lastly, a percussion cap was placed on each of the six nipples located at the rear of each cylinder. The caps could be left off if the gun was not expected to be used in the near future, and often times a cap was not placed underneath the cylinder where the hammer lay, so as to prevent accidental discharge during transport.

Since Flores was in a rush, it is highly unlikely that he included the over-powder wad or took the time to wipe excess gunpowder residue from the front of each cylinder. It is also highly unlikely that he greased each cylinder to prevent "flash over" (also called "chain fire"). Flash over can occur when the gun is fired and sparks from the firing cylinder jump across or "flash over" from one chamber to the next. If there is exposed gunpowder in a neighboring chamber, that chamber can ignite and cause an explosion.

The Colt Navy pistol is designed to fire only the chamber that is lined up with the barrel. An explosion in any other cylinder is called "firing out of battery." Firing out of battery can cause several different things to happen, including the possibility that the gun may break apart.

Percussion caps on Colt Navy pistols are slightly exposed from the outside. When Flores was hastily climbing down the rocky cliff, one of these caps probably smacked against a rock, causing a chamber to fire out of battery. At this point, two or more things could have occurred. The bullet that was fired from the chamber could have struck Flores directly in the arm, or it may have ricocheted off a rock, causing debris to strike him. The undirected expanding hot gasses could also have seriously burned him. Even if the weapon was properly loaded, cleaned, greased, and primed, the very nature and design of the pistol could still have caused it to be accidentally discharged.

The worst-case scenario is that when the chamber fired, the expanding hot gasses ignited a neighboring chamber, causing "flash over." This could have enabled one or more chambers to ignite, causing the gun to explode. The resulting explosion could easily have injured Flores' arm and would explain why Sanchez's posse found a broken weapon at the bottom of the cliff. The above scenarios shed light on a fascinating gun battle that occurred on Flores Peak more than 145 years ago.

BIBLIOGRAPHY

Adams, J. (2001). *Judge Roy Bean: Law West of the Pecos.* Retrieved February 23, 2003, from http://members.fortunecity.com/tokenguy/tokentales/page49.htm

American Heritage Dictionary of the English Language. (1982). Boston: Houghton Mifflin.

Annual Report of J. M. Glass, Chief of Police, to the City Council of the City of Los Angeles, California. (1897). Los Angeles: McBride Press.

Annual Report Police Department, City of Los Angeles, California. (1920). Los Angeles: Author.

Armistead, G., C. (2003) "The Los Angeles Mounted Rifles" California State Military Museum Website

Barnum Museum. (2003). *Cast of Characters.* Retrieved March 31, 2003, from http://www.barnum-museum.org/orig/html/lind.htm

Barton, J. R. (1854). Original Letter from James Barton Probate Papers (the "letter" does not state to whom it is written but it is signed by Barton). Available in the Department of Archives and Special Collections, Charles Von der Ahe Library, Loyola Marymount University, Los Angeles.

Beers, G. (1960). *The California Outlaw: Tiburcio Vasquez.* Los Gatos, CA: The Talisman Press.

Beilharz, E. A. (1971). The Pueblo of Los Angeles is Founded. In J. Caughey & L. Caughey (Eds.), *Los Angeles: Biography of a city* (pp. 68-71). Los Angeles: University of California Press.

Bell, H. (1930). *On the Old West Coast: Being Further Reminiscences of a Ranger.* New York: Grosset and Dunlap

Bell, H. (1881/1999). *Reminiscences of a Ranger: Early Times in Southern California.* Oklahoma City: University of Oklahoma Press.

Black, E. B. (1975). *Rancho Cucamonga and Dona Merced.* Redlands CA: San Bernardino County Museum Association.

Blew, R. (1972, Spring). Vigilantism in Los Angeles. *Southern California Historical Quarterly*, 11-13.

Blodget, P. J. (1999). *Land of Golden Dreams: California in the Gold Rush Decade 1848-1858*. San Marino, CA: Huntington Library Press.

Boessenecker, J. (1988). *Badge and buckshot: Lawlessness in Old California*. Oklahoma City: University of Oklahoma Press.

Boessenecker, J. (1998). California Bandidos: Social Bandits or Sociopaths? *Southern California Quarterly, 80,* 419-434.

Boessenecker, J. (1998). *Lawman: The Life and Times of Harry Morse,* Oklahoma City: University of Oklahoma Press

Boessenecker, J. (1999). *Gold Dust and Gunsmoke*. New York: Wiley.

Burgess, R. O. (2003). *Colt Third Model Dragoon*. Retrieved April 18, 2003, from http://www.sweetwaterpress.net/sweet11.htm

BusinessWare. (2003). *Santiago Oaks Regional Park*. Retrieved April 18, 2003, from http://www.goodtime.net/ora/lcora031.htm

California Peace Officers Memorial. (2003). *In Remembrance*. Retrieved April 17, 2003, from http://www.camemorial.org/19th.htm.

Castaic murderers. (1890, March 11). *Los Angeles Times*. Retrieved May 22, 2003, from http://www.scvhistory.com/scvhistory/chormicle-times-031190.htm

Caughey, J. (1969). The Country Town of the Angels. In J. Caughey & L. Caughey (Eds.), *Los Angeles: Biography of a city* (pp. 73-78). Los Angeles: University of California Press.

Caughey, J., & Caughey, L. (Eds.). (1977). *Los Angeles: Biography of a City*. Los Angeles: University of California Press.

Central Missouri State University, Department of Criminal Justice. (2003). *Alphonse Bertillion*. Retrieved April 14, 2003, from http://www.cmsu.edu/cj/alphonse.htm

Citizens of the Monte. (1854, October 12). *Southern Californian*, n.p.

City of Los Angeles. Department of Recreation and Parks. (n.d.a). *Campo de Cahuenga*. Retrieved April 11, 2003, from http://www.laparks.org/ dos/historic/campo.htm

City of Los Angeles. Department of Recreation and Parks. (n.d.b). *Drum Barracks Civil War Museum*. Retrieved April 11, 2003, from http://www.laparks.org/ dos/museums/drum.htm

Cleland, R. G. (1959). *From wilderness to Empire*. New York: Knopf.

Cleland, R. G. (1969). *The Cattle on a Thousand Hills*. San Marino, CA: Huntington Library Press.

Crespi, J. (1769). First Travelers Through the Land. In J. Caughey & L. Caughey (Eds.), *Los Angeles: Biography of a city* (pp. 49-54). Los Angeles: University of California Press.

Crittenden, E. (1958). *Angels . . . More or Less*. Los Angeles: Morrison.

BIBLIOGRAPHY

Crittenden, E. (1958). Henry M. Mitchell, Sheriff 1878-80. *Star News, 20*(1), 3-5.

Dana, J. F. (1931). Ten Decades on a California Rancho: Random Memories of Stirring Events in the Golden State Under Three Flags. *Westways, 23*(11). Retrieved March 3, 2003, from http://www.historyinslocounty.com

De Neve, P. (1777). Recommending a Pueblo on the Porciuncula. In J. Caughey & L. Caughey (Eds.), *Los Angeles: Biography of a City* (pp. 63-66). Los Angeles: University of California Press.

Earp, W. (1998). *Wyatt Earp Speaks! My Side of the O.K. Corral Shootout.* Cambria Pines by the Sea, CA: Fern Canyon Press.

Edwards, H. L. January, The Tombstone Epitaph, 1993 vol. XX no. 9, p. 1) *True West Magazine* p. 48

Emerson, F. W. (1940). *History of the Los Angeles Sheriff's Department 1850-1940.* Pasadena, CA: Federal Writers Project.

Field, R. (1997). *Brassey's History of Uniforms: Mexican-American War 1846-48.* Herndon, England: Brassey's.

Gould, J., & Gould, B. (2000). *Gould's Penal Code Handbook of California* (2001 ed.). Longwood, FL: Gould.

Green, C. and Sanford, W. (1995). *Judge Roy Bean.* New Jersey: Enslow Publishers.

Guinn, J. M. (1915). Gold! Gold! Gold! from San Francisquito. In J. Caughey & L. Caughey (Eds.), *Los Angeles: Biography of a City* (pp. 107-108). Los Angeles: University of California Press.

Harris, T. (2002). *Judge Roy Bean's Passion for Dodgy Dealings.* Retrieved April 5, 2003, from http://www.theage.com.au/articles/2002/11/17/1037490050546.html

Hayes, B. (1929). *Pioneer Notes: From the Diaries of Judge Benjamin Hayes.* Los Angeles: Marjorie Tisdale Wolcott.

Hill, L. L. (1931). *La Reina: Los Angeles in Three Centuries.* Los Angeles: Security First National Bank of Los Angeles.

Hoffman, A. (1984, Fall). The Controversial Career of Martin Aguirre. *California History, 63,* 295-304.

Holliday, J. S. (1999). *Rush for riches: Gold Fever and the Making of California.* Oakland: Museum of California and the University of California Press.

Hoyle, M. F. (Compiler). (1976). *Crimes and Career of Tiburcio Vasquez.* Hollister, CA: San Benito County Historical Society.

Jackson, J. H. (1949). *Bad Company.* New York: Harcourt Brace.

Katz, B. (2003). *Law West of the Pecos: Judge Roy Bean.* Retrieved April 5, 2003, from http://www.desertusa.com/mag98/aug/papr/du_roybean.html

King, F.M. (1935). *Wranglin the Past.* Los Angeles: Privately Published by King, Haynes Corporation

Knight, S. (n.d.). *Los Angeles County Sheriff's Badge History.* Unpublished manuscript.

Levy, J., & Mace, H. (2002). *Elephant.* Retrieved April 11, 2003, from http:// www.goldrush.com/~joann/elephant.htm

Lloyd, E. (1967). *Law West of the Pecos.* San Antonio TX: The Naylor Company.

Longstreet, S. (1977). *All Star Cast: An Anecdotal History of Los Angeles.* New York: Crowell.

Lopez, R. (1971, Summer). The Legend of Tiburcio Vasquez. *Pacific Historian,* 20-31.

Los Angeles Almanac: General Population by City. (2003). Retrieved May 8, 2003, from http://www.losangelesalmanac.com/topics/population/ po26.htm

Los Angeles Star Newspaper, 1850-1871.

Los Angeles Times Newspaper, 1881 to present

Marti, Werner H. (1960). *Messenger of Destiny.* San Francisco: John Howell Books

Martin, W., & Dixon, M. (2000). *150 years: A Tradition of Service—A Turbulent Beginning.* Paducah, KY: Turner.

Meadows, D. (1963). Juan Flores and the Manillas. In E. Edwards (Ed.), *The Westerners Brand Book: Book Ten* (pp. 153-171). Los Angeles: The Los Angeles Westerners.

Nadeau, R. (1974). *The Real Joaquin Murieta, California's Gold Rush Bandit: Truth v. Myth.* Santa Barbara, CA: Crest.

Nadeau, R. (1977). *City Makers: The Story of Southern California's First Boom.* Corona del Mar, CA: Trans-Anglo Books.

Newmark, H. (1984). *Sixty Years in Southern California: 1853-1913* (4th ed.). Los Angeles: Dawson's Book Shop.

National Law Enforcement Officers Memorial Fund (NLEOMF). (2001). *Mentally Ill Pose Great Danger to Police.* Retrieved January 15, 2003, from http:// www.nleomf.com/fallenOfficers/LineofDuty/mentally.html

Palfrey, D. H. (1998). *The Spanish Conquest 1519-1521.* Retrieved April 11, 2003, from http://www.mexconnect.com/mex_/travel/dpalfrey/ dpconquest.html

Parrish, M. (2001). *For the People: Inside the Los Angeles County District Attorney's Office 1850-2000.* Santa Monica, CA: Angel City Press.

Pitt, L. (1966). *The Decline of the Californios.* Berkeley: University of California Press.

Pitt, L., & Pitt, D. (1997). *Los Angeles A to Z: An Encyclopedia of the City and County.* Berkeley: University of California Press, Berkeley.

Poole, J., & Ball, T. (2002). *El Pueblo: The Historic Heart of Los Angeles.* Los Angeles: Getty Conservation Institute and the J. Paul Getty Museum.

Poos, P. (1972). *The Era of Do It Yourself Justice: The First Twenty-One Years of the Los Angeles County Sheriff's Department.* Unpublished manuscript, California State Polytechnic College, Pomona.

Rambo, R. (1968). *Trailing the California Bandit Tiburcio Vasquez.* San Jose, CA: Rosicrucian Press.

Rangers. (1854, October 12). *Southern Californian*, n.p.

Reid, H. (1851). A Way of Life. In J. Caughey & L. Caughey (Eds.), *Los Angeles: Biography of a City* (pp. 8-14). Los Angeles: University of California Press.

Robinson, W.W. (1962). *People Versus Lugo: Story of a Famous Los Angeles Murder Case and its Aftermath.* Los Angeles: Dawson's Book Shop.

Romer, M. (1961, June). The Story of Martin Aguirre. *The Historical Society of Southern California, 43,* 125-126.

Rosa, J. G. (1993). *The Age of the Gunfighter.* New York: Smithmark.

Royster, L. (1864). Letter from Lawrence Royster to John E. Roller. Retrieved May 15, 2003, from http://new.vmi.edu/archives/manuscripts/0171013.html

San Diego Historical Society. (2002). *San Diego Biographies: Juan Rodriguez Carillo.* Retrieved April 11, 2003, from http://www.sandiegohistory.org/ bio/cabrillo/cabrillo.htm

San Gabriel Mission. (2003). *Our History.* Retrieved April 11, 2003, from http:// sangabrielmission.org/our_history.htm

Secrest, W. B. (1994). *Lawmen and Desperadoes: A compendium of Noted, Early California Peace Officers, Badmen and Outlaws.* Spokane, WA: Clark.

Secrest, W. B. (1995) *Dangerous Trails, Five Desperados of the Old West,* Barbed Wire Press, Stillwater OK

Secrest, W. B. (2000). *California Desperadoes.* Clovis, CA: Quill Driver Books/Word Dancer Press.

Secrest, W. B. (2001). *Perilous Trails, Dangerous Men: Early California Stagecoach Robbers and their Desperate Careers.* Clovis, CA: Quill Driver Books Word Dancer Press.

Sheriff's and Constables. (1907). Oakland, CA: W. S. Harlow.

Sherrard, R. (1996). *Centurions Shield: A History of the Los Angles Police Department, its Badges and Insignia.* Newport Beach, CA: RHS Enterprises.

Shot the Deputy Sheriff. (1996, December 28). *Los Angeles Herald*, n.p.

Shumate, A. *James F. Curtis: Vigilante.* San Francisco Corral of the Westerners, Eagle Rock CA, 1988 p. 27.

Sonnichsen, C.L. (1991). *Roy Bean: Law West of the Pecos.* Lincoln NB: First Bison Book Printing.

Stammerjohan, G. (n.d.). *History of Fort Tejon.* Retrieved February 20, 2003, from http://www.forttejon.org/history.html

Stanley, J. (1998). *L.A. Behind Bars 1847 to 1903: Establishing the County Jail System in Early California.* Unpublished manuscript.

Texas State Library. (2004). *Texas Declaration of Independence.* Retrieved January 26, 2004, from http://www.tsl.state.tx.us/treasures/republic/declare-01.html

Thompson & West (Albert J. Wilson). (1959). *History of Los Angeles County, California, with Illustrations Descriptive of its Scenery.* Berkeley, CA: Berkeley Press.

Thornton, B. (2003). *Searching for Joaquin: Myth Murieta and History in California.* San Francisco CA: Encounter Books.

United States Marshals Service. (2003). *United States Marshals Service.* Retrieved February 20, 2003, from http://www.usdoj.gov/marshals/

Vasquez Rocks, Origin of the Name: Historical Notes. (2003). Retrieved May 7, 2003, from http://aeve.com/digitaldesert/vasquezrocks/origin.html

Vaughn, B. (2003). *Blacks in Mexico: A Brief Overview.* Retrieved March 20, 2003, from http://www.mexconnect.com/mex_/feature/ethnic/bv/brief.htm

Warner, J. J. (1936). *An Historical Sketch of Los Angeles County California.* Los Angeles: O. W. Smith.

Watson, B. (1998). "Hang 'em First, Try 'em Later." *Smithsonian Magazine.* Retrieved April 5, 2003, from http://www.smithsonianmag.si.edu/smithsonian/issues98/jun98/bean.html

Weaver, J. D. (1973). *El Pueblo Grande: A Non fiction Book about Los Angeles.* Los Angeles: Ritchie.

Wilkman, J. (1999). *Tiburcio Vasquez.* Retrieved February, 20, 2003, from www. Socalhistories.org/biographies/vasquez

Willard, C. D. 1901, "The Herald's History of Los Angeles City" Los Angeles Kingsley Barnes and Neuner Publisher Los Angeles

Woods, D. B. (1851). *Sixteen Months at the Gold Diggings.* New York: Harper.

Woodward, A. (1959). Channel Island Artifacts. In J. Caughey & L. Caughey (Eds.), *Los Angeles: Biography of a City* (pp. 15-20). Los Angeles: University of California Press.

Woolsey, R. C. (1996). *Migrants West: Towards the Southern California Frontier.* Claremont, CA: Grizzly Bear.

Zorro. (n.d.). Retrieved March 26, 2003, from http://www.geocities.com/Hollywood/Theater/5119/Zorro2.html

ENDNOTES

Chapter 1

1. Earp, Wyatt, 1998, p. 178.
2. Pitt & Pitt, 1997, p. 504.
3. Ibid.
4. Woodward, 1959, p. 18.
5. Pitt & Pitt, p. 504.
6. Bell, 1999, pp. 35-36.
7. Weaver 1973 p. 26.
8. Caughey & Caughey, 1977, p. 50.
9. Longstreet, 1977, p. 10.
10. De Neve, 1777, p. 64.
11. Beilharz, 1971, p. 70, Los Angeles *Times* "City of Angels First Name Still Bedevils Historians" March 26, 2005.
12. Beilharz, 1971, pp. 70-71.
13. Vaughn, ¶ 5.
14. Caughey, 1969, p. 77.
15. Nadeau, 1977, pp. 18, 22, 38.
16. Laws for governing California; Pitt & Pitt, 1997, p. 11.
17. Emerson, 1940, pp. 20, 30.
18. Longstreet, 1977, p. 19.
19. Weaver, 1973, pp. 18-19.
20. Longstreet, 1977, p. 28.
21. Thornton, 2003, p. 53.
22. Pitt & Pitt, 1997, p. 155.
23. Marvin Dixon, retired LASD, personal communication, January 17, 2003.
24. Levy & Mace, 2002, ¶ 2.

25. Guinn, 1915, p. 107.
26. Ibid, p. 108.
27. Blodget, 1999, p. 30.
28. Woods, 1851, p. 103.
29. Holliday, 1999, p. 174.
30. Pitt, 1966, p. 49.
31. Bell, 1999, p. viii.
32. Ibid, p. 13.
33. Ibid, p. 13.
34. As cited in Holliday, 1999, p. 170.
35. Weaver 1973 (p. 26.
36. Holliday, 1999, p. 26.
37. As cited in Weaver, 1973, p. 26.
38. Longstreet 1977 pp. 37-38.
39. Newmark, 1984, p. 31.
40. Ibid, p. 56.
41. Warner, 1936, p. 90.
42. Cleland, 1969, p. 95.
43. Newmark, 1984, p. 51.
44. Ibid, p. 53, Burns, James, May 1, 1900, memoirs Huntington Library.
45. Newmark, 1984, p. 51.
46. Los Angeles *Daily Star* "The Hunt Ended" May 15, 1874.
47. United States Marshals Service, ¶ 1, 2.
48. Stammerjohon, n.d., ¶ 1.
49. Willard, 1901, p. 284.
50. Edward Godfrey, LASD, personal communication, February 18, 2003.
51. Los Angeles *Times*, "Alleged Extortion" July 30, 1899, p. D1.
52. Gould & Gould, 2000.
53. Joseph Rosa 1993, p. 24.
54. Cleland, 1969, p. 97.
55. Rosa, 1993, p. 160.

Chapter 2

1. Emerson, 1940, p. 83.
2. Crittenden, 1958, p. 17.
3. Emerson, 1940, p. 88.
4. http://www.eastlosangeles.net/streetnames.html.
5. Stanley, 1998, pp. 5-7.
6. As cited in Crittenden, 1958, p. 41.
7. Cleland, 1969, p. 93.
8. Crittenden, 1958, p. 52.

9. Barnum Museum, 2003, ¶ 8.
10. Boessenecker, 1999, p. 58.
11. Parrish, 2001, p. 24.
12. Boessenecker, 1999, p. 59.
13. Ibid, p. 60.
14. Ibid.
15. As cited in Boessenecker 1999, p. 60.
16. Los Angeles *Star* "Irving Party," May 31, 1851.
17. Thompson & West, 1959, p. 80.
18. Robinson, 1962, p. 25.
19. Newmark, 1984, p. 190.
20. Robinson, 1962, p. 31.
21. Ibid, pp. 35-36.
22. Thompson & West, 1959, pp. 80-81.
23. Parrish, 2001, p. 25.
24. As cited in Secrest, 1994, p. 177.
25. As cited in Bell, 1999, pp. 100-101.
26. *Southern Californian* "Rangers," October 12, 1854, n.p.
27. As cited in Secrest, 1994, p. 180.
28. Los Angeles *Star* "Obituary," January 19, 1856, p. 2.
29. California Peace Officers Memorial, 2003.
30. Boessenecker, 1999, p. 63.
31. Hayes, 1929, p. 79.
32. Ibid, p. 75.
33. Warner, p. 80.
34. Newmark, 1984, pp. 206-207.
35. Woolsey 1996, p. 76.
36. As cited in Boessenecker, 1999, p. 64.
37. Parrish, 2001, p. 25.
38. As cited in Boessenecker, 1998, p. 426.
39. Los Angeles *Star* "Lower California Affairs," May 12, 1860.
40. Thompson and West 1959, p. 127.
41. Boessenecker, 1999, p. 74.
42. As cited in Nadeau, 1974, p. 30.
43. Boessenecker, 1999, p. 84.
44. Crittenden, 1958, p. 79.
45. Los Angeles *Star* "Assassination of Gen. Bean," November 13, 1852;
    Nadeau, 1974, p. 24.
46. Crittenden, 1958, pp. 77-78.
47. Nadeau, 1974, p. 86.
48. As cited in Sonnichsen, 1991, p. 31.

49. Bell, 1999, p. 83.
50. Sonnichsen 1991, p. 39.
51. Watson, 1998, ¶ 1, Lloyd, 1967, p. 63.
52. Bell, 1930, p. 230.
53. Katz, 2003, ¶ 9.
54. Ibid, ¶ 10, Sonnichsen, 1991, p. 119.
55. Harris, 2002, ¶ 2.
56. Adams, 2001, ¶ 3) (Lloyd, 1967p. 63.
57. Bell, 1999, p. 404.
58. Barton, 1854, p. 1.
59. Los Angeles *Star* "Citizens of the Monte," October 12, 1854.
60. Bell, 1930, p. 73.
61. As cited in Boessenecker, 1999, p. 65.
62. *Southern Californian* January 11, 1855.
63. Warner, 1936, p. 71.
64. Ibid, p. 71.
65. Woolsey, 1996, p. 77.
66. Newmark, 1984, p. 140.
67. *Southern Californian* January 18, 1855.
68. Emerson, 1940, p. 98.
69. Ibid., p. 98.
70. Secrest, 1995, p. 41-45.
71. Los Angeles *Star* "Shooting Affray," April 19, 1856, p. 2.
72. Ibid.
73. Los Angeles *Star* "A Man Killed," July 26, 1856.
74. Ibid.
75. Ibid.
76. Boessenecker, 1999, p. 67.
77. Los Angeles *Star* "A Fatal Affray," March 10, 1855, p. 2.
78. Newmark, 1984, p. 77.
79. Bell, 1881, 1999 p. 401.
80. As cited in Meadows, 1963, pp. 156-157.
81. Los Angeles *Star* "The Late Murder of Sheriff Barton," January 31, 1857.
82. Jackson, 1949, p. 270.
83. Boessenecker, 1999, p. 119.
84. Los Angeles *Star* "The Late Murder of Sheriff Barton," January 31, 1857.
85. Los Angeles Daily *Star*, May 15, 1874.
86. Los Angeles *Star* "Horse Stealing," July 25, 1857, p. 2.
87. Los Angeles *Star* "Statement Concerning Chino," February 14, 1857.

88. Los Angeles *Star* "The Pursuit of the Robbers," February 7, 1857.
89. Ibid.
90. Boessenecker, 1999, p. 124.
91. Los Angeles *Star* "The Pursuit of the Robbers," February 7, 1857.
92. Los Angeles *Star* "Mr. Thompson's Party," February 7, 1857, p. 2.
93. Los Angeles *Star* "Expedition to Santa Barbara," February 14, 1857, p. 2.
94. Los Angeles *Star* "The Affair at the Mission," February 7, 1857, p. 2.
95. Ibid.
96. Ibid.
97. Newmark, 1984, p. 209.
98. Boessenecker, 1999, p. 128.
99. Los Angeles *Star* "Public Meeting," February 21, 1857, p. 2.
100. Ibid.
101. Pitt, 1966, p. 171.
102. Crittenden, 1958, p. 182.
103. Los Angeles *Star*, December 12, 1857.
104. Judy Gauntt, City of Irvine Historian, personal communication, March 10, 2003.
105. Newmark, 1984, p. 221.
106. Crittenden, 1958, p. 239.
107. Ibid., p. 188.
108. Los Angeles *Star* "Inquest," October 3, 1857, p. 2.
109. Crittenden, 1958, p. 188.
110. Los Angeles *Star* "Execution of Thomas King and Luciano Tapia" February 20, 1858.
111. Los Angeles *Star* "Execution of James P. Johnson," October 10, 1857, p. 2.
112. Ibid.
113. Los Angeles *Star* "Murder of Sheriff Getman!!!," January 9, 1858, p. 1.
114. National Law Enforcement Officers Memorial Foundation, 2003, ¶ 4.
115. Bell, 1999, p. 14.
116. Crittenden, 1958, p. 197.
117. Boessenecker, 1999, p. 130.
118. Warner, 1936, p. 96.
119. Boessenecker, 1999, p. 131.
120. Los Angeles *Star*, "The Recent Execution" December 4, 1858.

Chapter 3

1. Bell, 1930, p. 75.
2. Bell, 1999, p. 80.
3. Emerson, 1940, p.115.

4. Cleland, 1959, p. 157.

5. Crittenden, 1958, pp. 227-228.

6. Ibid., p. 250.

7. Ibid., p. 252.

8. Secrest, W., 1995, p. 128.

9. Crittenden, 1958, pp. 270-271.

10. Newmark, 60 years p. 1916 2nd ed p. 324.

11. Thompson & West, 1959, p. 84.

12. Los Angeles *Star* "Murder of Mr. Edward Newman," January 9, 1864, p. 2.

13. Los Angeles *Star*, "Horrible Tragedy" January 11, 1855.

14. Crittenden, 1958, pp. 265, 280.

15. Black, E., 1975, p. 136.

16. Crittenden, 1958, p. 281.

17. King, 1935 Wranglin the Past, p. 18.

18. Black, E., 1975, p. 135.

19. Crittenden, 1958, p. 292.

20. Ibid.

21. Ibid., p. 289.

22. Warner, 1936, p. 5.

23. Burns, James F. May 1, 1900 memoirs Huntington Library.

24. Crittenden, 1958, p. 305.

25. Ibid., p. 301.

26. Los Angeles *Star*, "Criminal Statistics" January 13, 1871.

27. Nadeau, 1977, p. 42.

28. Ibid., p. 43.

29. Ibid., p. 44.

30. Los Angeles *Star*, "Shooting Affray" November 1, 1870, p. 2.

31. Los Angeles *Star*, "Coroners Inquest" November 2, 1870, p. 2.

32. Los Angeles *Times*, "Filled With Lead" May 15, 1891, p. 3.

33. Newmark, 1984, p. 418.

34. As cited in Secrest, 2000, p. 166.

35. Secrest, 2001, p. 81.

36. Parrish, 2001, p. 27.

37. Nadeau, 1977, p. 45.

38. Ibid., p. 46.

39. As cited in Emerson, 1940, pp. 127-129.

40. Thompson & West, 1959, p. 85.

41. Los Angeles *Star*, "Ye Heathen Chinee" July 19, 1871, p. 2.

42. Parrish, 2001, p. 110.

43. Los Angeles *Star* "Yo Hing Interviewed" October 30, 1871, p. 2.

44. Burns, J.F. May 1, 1900, memoirs, Huntington Library.
45. Crittenden, 1958, p. 349.
46. Bell, 1930, pp. 170-172.
47. Nadeau, 1977, p. 47.
48. Thompson and West, 1959, p. 85.
49. Nadeau, 1977, p. 48.
50. Ibid., pp. 48-49, Los Angeles *Star*, October 28, 1871.
51. Los Angeles *Star* "Development of Highly Interesting Particulars" October, 28, 1871.
52. Emerson, p. 137.
53. Los Angeles *Star* "The Night of Horrors" October 26, 1871, p. 2.
54. Nadeau, 1977, p. 52.
55. Crittenden, 1958, p. 360, Burns, James F. May 1, 1900 memoirs Huntington.

Chapter 4

1. Los Angeles *Times*, "Rowland Rites at Cathedral" February 6, 1926, p. A-5.
2. Nadeau, 1977, p. 95.
3. Secrest, 2001, p. 215.
4. Lopez, 1971, p. 22.
5. Boessenecker, 1998, p. 420; Lopez, 1971, p. 23.
6. Thompson & West, 1959, p. 85.
7. Secrest, 2001, p. 216.
8. As cited in Secrest, 2001, p. 217.
9. As cited in Secrest, 2000, p. 134.
10. Boessenecker, 1998, Lawman, p. 196.
11. Secrest, 2001, p. 219.
12. As cited in Secrest, 2001, p. 53.
13. San Francisco *Chronicle*, May 16, 1874.
14. Boessenecker, 1998, Lawman, p. 207.
15. Beers, 1960, p. 263
16. Los Angeles *Daily Star*, "The Hunt Ended" May 15, 1874 p. 2.
17. Beers, 1960 p. 265.
18. Ibid., p. 70.
19. Crittenden, 1958, p. 391.
20. Los Angeles *Star*, May 12, 1874.
21. As cited in Crittenden, 1958, p. 392.
22. As cited in Secrest, 2000, p. 155.
23. Ibid., p. 224.
24. Ibid., p. 54.

25. Ibid., p. 56.
26. As cited in Crittenden, 1958, p. 395.
27. Sherrard, 1996, p. 42.
28. Los Angeles Police Historical Society pamphlet, December 19, 2003; L.A. *Star* "The Hunt Ended" May 15, 1874.
29. Secrest, 2001, p. 198.
30. As cited in Secrest, 2002, p. 201.
31. Ibid., p. 202.
32. Newmark, 1984, p. 500.
33. Mary Kludy, librarian, Virginia Military Institute, personal communication, March 12, 2003.
34. Royster, 1864, p. 1.
35. Emerson, 1940 p. 158 and Crittenden, 1958 p. 422
36. Thompson & West, 1959, p. 87.
37. Crittenden, 1958, p. 437.
38. (as cited in Crittenden, 1958a, p. 439)
39. Los Angeles County Court Records, Huntington Library 1871.
40. Los Angeles *Times*, "Adolph Celis Killed" April 19, 1883, p. 0_4.
41. Hoffman, p. 296; Los Angeles *Times*, February 26, 1929, p. A-1.
42. As cited in Stanley, 1998, p. 37.
43. As cited in Stanley, 1998, p. 38.
44. Stanley, 1998, p. 39.
45. Secrest, 2000, pp. 192-193.
46. As cited in Secrest, 2000, pp. 200-201.
47. Secrest, 2000, p. 205.
48. As cited in Secrest, 2000, pp. 206-207.
49. Ibid., p. 209.

Chapter 5

1. Stanley, 1998, p. 41.
2. Archibald Henderson, LASD, personal communication, May 1, 2003.
3. Crittenden, 1958, p. 478.
4. Loyola University: History Overview, April, 2005.
5. Los Angeles *Times*, "Aguirre Last Old Sheriff" February 26, 1929, p. A-1.
6. Romer, 1961, p. 128.
7. Los Angeles *Times*, February 26, 1929, p. A-1.
8. Ibid.
9. Hoffman, 1984, p. 298.
10. Los Angeles *Times*, "Lucky Martin," January 30, 1886, p. 3.
11. Emerson, 1940, p. 178.

12. As cited in Hoffman, 1984, p. 298.
13. Los Angeles *Times*, Sheriff Aguirre Shot" May 3, 1889, p. 4.
14. As cited in Hoffman, 1984, p. 299.
15. Los Angeles *Times*, "Attempted Rape" May 14, 1891, p. 3.
16. Los Angeles *Times*, "Aguirre Last Old Sheriff" February 26, 1929, p. A-1.
17. Romer, 1961, p. 134.
18. Los Angeles *Times*, "Castaic Murderers," March 11, 1890.
19. Los Angeles *Times*, "Aguirre Last Old Sheriff" February 26, 1929, p. A-1.
20. As cited in Emerson, 1940, p. 181.
21. As cited in Hoffman, 1988, p. 304.
22. Emerson, 1940, p. 191.
23. Boessenecker, 1987, p. 181.
24. Edwards, 1988 or 1993? p. 48.
25. Boessenecker, 1988, p. 181.
26. As cited in Boessenecker, 1988, p. 183.
27. Edwards,1993, p. 48.
28. Boessenecker, 1988, p. 184.
29. As cited in Boessenecker, 1988, p. 183.
30. Ibid., p. 194.
31. As cited in Emerson, 1940, p. 192.
32. Los Angeles *Times*, January 26, 1920 p. II1.
33. Martin & Dixon, 2000, p. 46.
34. Los Angeles *Times* March 3, 1921 p. II 1.
35. Emerson, 1940, p. 203.
36. Crittenden, 1958, p. 519.
37. Los Angeles *Times*, "Officer Shot," December 28, 1896.
38. Los Angeles *Herald*, "Shot the Deputy Sheriff," December 28, 1896.
39. Los Angeles *Times* "Officer Shot," December 28, 1896.
40. Los Angeles *Times* May 29, 1901.
41. California Peace Officers Memorial, 2003.
42. Los Angeles *Times* "Jail Breakers' Plot," January 8, 1897, p. 4.
43. Los Angeles *Times* "Jail Break Foiled," January 7, 1897, p. 1.
44. Los Angeles *Times* "Jail Breakers' Plot," January 8, 1897, p. 4.
45. Emerson, 1940, p. 204.
46. Crittenden, 1958, p. 526..
47. Los Angeles *Times*, "Car Skids Crashes" November 7, 1909 and November 18, 1909.
48. Los Angeles *Times*, September 14, 1898, p.8.
49. As cited in Crittenden, 1958, p. 540.

50. Crittenden, 1958, p. 540.
51. Los Angeles *Times,* "Pin Badge on Sheriff Elect," December 20, 1906, p. II3.
52. Emerson, 1940, p. 208.
53. Ibid., p. 211.

Chapter 6

1. Bell, 1999, p. viii.
2. Patrick J. Adams, personal communication, May 1, 2003.
3. *Annual Report of J. M. Glass,* 1897, p. 6.
4. Eric Monkkonen, personal communication, May 19, 2003.
5. Crittenden, 1958, p. 527.
6. *Annual Report Police Department,* 1920, p. 8.
7. *Los Angeles Almanac,* 2003, ¶ 1.
8. Hoyle, 1976, Preface.
9. Blew, 1972, p. 12.
10. Stanley, 1998, p. 42.

Appendix B

1. Judy Gauntt, personal communication, March 10, 2003.
2. California State Historical Landmark #218, State Archives.
3. *Orange County Thomas Guide* page 832, G-7.
4. Meadows, 1963, p. 170.
5. Ibid., p. 169.
6. Ibid.

Appendix C

1. Burgess, 2003, ¶ 2.

INDEX

SIX
GUN
SOUND

The Early History
of the Los Angeles
County Sheriff's Department

BY SVEN CRONGEYER

Craven Street Books
Fresno, CA

SIX GUN SOUND

By
Sven Crongeyer
Cover by James Goold

© 2006 Linden Publishing

135798642
ISBN: 1-933502-00-2
ISBN: 978-1-933502-00-7
Printed in USA

Crongeyer, Sven, 1965-
    The early history of the Los Angeles County Sheriff's Department, 1850-1900 / by Sven Crongeyer.
        p. cm.
    Includes bibliographical references and index.
    ISBN-13: 978-1-933502-00-7 (pbk. : alk. paper)
    ISBN-10: 1-933502-00-2 (pbk. : alk. paper)
1. Los Angeles County (Calif.). Sheriff's Dept.—History.
2. Police—California—Los Angeles County—History.
3. Law enforcement—California.
HV8145.C2C76 2006
363.28'2097949309034–dc22   2006000730

A Craven Street Book
Linden Publishing Inc.
2006 S. Mary, Fresno CA
www.lindenpub.com
800-345-4447